Irish Women's History

Editors

ALAN HAYES
DIANE URQUHART

IRISH ACADEMIC PRESS
DUBLIN • PORTLAND, OR

First published in 2004 by
IRISH ACADEMIC PRESS
44 Northumberland Road,
Dublin 4, Ireland

and in the United States of America by
IRISH ACADEMIC PRESS
c/o ISBS, 920 NE 58th Avenue, Suite 300,
Portland, OR 97213-3786

Website: www.iap.ie

British Library Cataloguing in Publication Data

Irish women's history
1. Women – Ireland – History 2. Women – Ireland – Social
Conditions
I. Urquhart, Diane II. Hayes, Alan
305.4'09415

ISBN 0-7165-2702-2 (cloth)
ISBN 0-7165-2716-2 (paper)

Library of Congress Cataloging-in-Publication Data

A catalog record of this book is
available from the Library of Congress.

Typeset in 11/12.5 Ehrhardt by Vitaset, Paddock Wood, Kent
Printed by
Colourbooks Ltd., Dublin

Contents

Acknowledgements

Diane Urquhart and Alan Hayes would like to thank colleagues at the Queen's University of Belfast, the University of Liverpool and the National University of Ireland, Galway; in particular Marie-Therese Flanagan and Mary O'Dowd in Belfast; and Mary Clancy, Brendan Flynn, Gearóid MacNiocaill, Dáibhí Ó Cróinín and Mary O'Leary in Galway. Thanks also to Kieran Hoare, Archivist, NUI, Galway for helpful proofreading and critical suggestions.

Special thanks are due to all the contributors whose patience and constant support motivated us during the course of this work and to Margaret MacCurtain for her kind foreword and her inspiration. Our thanks also to our anonymous reader and to Linda Longmore, Rachel Milotte and Jonathan Manley at Irish Academic Press.

Foreword

MARGARET MacCURTAIN

It is a personal opinion but for me writing a foreword marks a special occasion. The publication of *Irish Women's History* is such an occasion. Just over twenty years ago *Women in Irish Society: The Historical Dimension*, first heard in a series of Thomas Davis lectures delivered over Radio Éireann, was courageously published by Catherine Rose of Arlen House. She was the third publisher I approached and I had been assured that this was a Thomas Davis series that would not convert into a book, as it would evoke little interest. The book, published towards the end of 1978, was rapidly reprinted in 1979 and was snapped up by Greenwood Press in the United States. It became an indispensable tool for working journalists and researchers until the specialised studies in women's history began to appear in the 1980s.

Alan Hayes and Diane Urquhart, in compiling a new diverse range of essays, have drawn on new research and new methods of writing women's history over the last twenty years. Though the historical background is the broad framework of this wide-ranging collection, the topics reflect the editorial freedom which Hayes and Urquhart can exercise at this point in time. Themes such as family, religion, the techniques of using the testimony of oral history in recalling the recent past, emigration, infanticide and mental illness can now be explored in a manner which would have been peripheral to the mainstream of Irish history in the 1970s.

In their introduction the editors hope that *Irish Women's History* will be as stimulating as the Thomas Davis series of twenty years ago. Emphatically I can assure them that they have brought together a collection which opens up new horizons in women's history and shows that the discipline is a strong indigenous tree whose roots and branches spread in directions unclear to those who pioneered women's history in Ireland two decades ago.

Introduction

ALAN HAYES and DIANE URQUHART

This collection, *Irish Women's History*, presents new research on a diverse range of aspects of the lives of women in both the north and south of Ireland and of Irish women living in Britain. Our decision to compile this book arose from our own experiences of researching and working in women's history in our respective institutions and witnessing the immense growth and interest in the field, both in academic and popular contexts. The timing of this new collection coincides with the twenty-fifth anniversary of the pioneering Arlen House publication, *Women in Irish Society: The Historical Dimension* edited by Margaret MacCurtain and Donnchadh Ó Corrain. Indeed, several parallels can be drawn between these two works. Both address a myriad of themes and aspects of Irish women's lives, cover a wide chronology and contain work written by female and male historians. However, *Irish Women's History* is also indicative of the impact of MacCurtain and Ó Corrain's groundbreaking work which prompted new questions and presented major challenges to Irish academia. It also generated an immense interest in the history of women in Ireland amongst a more popular readership.

The papers included in *Irish Women's History* also highlight the diversity of methodologies which are being used by historians in an attempt to recreate women's past lives. These include personal testimony, the assessment of primary sources such as diaries, letters, memoirs, institutional and organisational records, as well as new analyses of secondary material. Several of our contributors also discuss the shortcomings of using these materials as an accurate source for women's history and suggest that some material presents women in a manner which may not be wholly representative of their lived realities.

The contributors to this collection were reached through a wide call for papers circulated on a number of international women's history and women's studies email discussion lists. We had no strict criteria on academic status, age or gender in our selection process, but solely the quality of the work presented. We requested that papers would be written in as accessible a manner as possible, in order to be useful to academic scholars and to appeal to a more general readership. This resulted in contributions from established and emerging scholars in the field of Irish women's history from four countries – Ireland, Britain, the United States and Australia.

While this work covers the medieval to the modern period, strong themes have emerged such as the pivotal importance of the family, work, religion, politics and social mores. However, we have resisted the temptation to compartmentalise women's lives into neat categories as each of these papers demonstrate the composite intersection of these themes. Lisa M. Bitel, for example, assesses the relationship between religion and power in a new examination of representations of St Brigit in early medieval Ireland. This work effectively counters imagery of Brigit as a weak and ultra feminine saint, as well as the more extreme claims which have been made for her persona. Instead Bitel presents St Brigit as a complex figure, a woman who acted as a mother and nurturer to other ecclesiastics and parishioners, cultivating traditionally feminine qualities and not challenging male colleagues or authoritarian figures. Thus gender is instrumental in understanding how St Brigit validated her authority and used religious influence to extend her political jurisdiction to lasting effect throughout the ecclesiastical settlements and lay communities of medieval Ireland. Dianne Hall, in her analysis of female religious living in community during the late medieval period, also demonstrates how religion and power were intertwined. Using fragmentary sources, Hall has revealed how women religious were able to extend their influence into the wider lay community, even whilst living under the strictures of enclosure. Whilst religious observance was an integral part of daily life and could prove to be extremely restrictive for women in enclosed orders, Hall demonstrates how female religious, their lay supporters and their detractors could negotiate spaces where they could live and support one another, with a significant degree of freedom.

However, women's daily routines could be seriously disrupted by external events. The world wars of 1914–18 and 1939–45 are seen as major dislocations in Europe's past which brought long-term changes in their wake. But to date there has been little examination of the wartime experiences and work of women in either the north or the south of Ireland. Mary Muldowney's study of women workers in Belfast and Dublin during the Second World War addresses this issue. This study, based on oral testimonies of women who were in paid employment during the war, reveals the diversity of women's wartime experiences. This diversity was caused by regional variations and by the neutrality of the south in comparison to the patriotic fervour which characterised much of the north of the country. Perhaps what emerges most clearly is the fact that at a time of emergency and national crisis women's position could be, however fleetingly, transformed into a public role of some significance. Moreover, the value of women's oral testimony as a historical source is also clearly apparent. Oral history also provides the basis for Sharon Lambert's work on Irish women emigrants in Lancashire from the 1920s onwards. It emerges that the economic pull of emigration did not mark an end to family ties and responsibilities. Indeed, for many women a desire to help their family financially was a core reason for emigrating. But from the testimonies of women who left Ireland during the early years of the Irish Free State it also seems that the moral strictures of the newly established state were another push factor for leaving the country. The taboo of sex and women's lack of sexual knowledge, coupled with little or no available contraception, could lead to pregnancy. Thus from Lambert's study it appears that a desire to protect their family's name and reputation from the shame of illegitimacy led some women to flee from Ireland. But for other women in a similar predicament, emigration was simply not an option.

From Louise Ryan's analysis of several newspapers in the 1920s it is clear that infanticide was a frequent, if not a daily, occurrence in Irish society. What is just as striking as the regularity of infanticide is the apparent reluctance of juries to convict women who were accused of these crimes. Ryan suggests that this may be a result of high infant mortality and the low value which was attached to illegitimate infant life. It is also possible that juries were influenced by their knowledge of the restrictions and social mores placed on unmarried working-class women. Such women had limited choices when faced with pregnancy. Indeed, for many of these women, it seems that infanticide was the only option to avoid being dismissed from employment, socially ostracised or even institutionalised. However, some women could not escape institutionalisation. Áine McCarthy's assessment of Enniscorthy Lunatic Asylum in the early twentieth century demonstrates that women who broke social conventions and refused to conform could be committed. Furthermore, women suffering from depression or experiencing problems associated with childbirth, miscarriage, menstrual irregularities and other physical ailments could also be institutionalised. The struggle endured by these women who were incorrectly judged as 'mad', as they tried to cope with familial misfortune, constraining codes of behaviour and economic insecurity brings to light hidden aspects of the restrictions which were often placed on women.

Not all institutions were as restrictive in their assessment of women who were vulnerable or in need of assistance. Gráinne M. Blair's work on the Salvation Army in the late nineteenth century uncovers the non-judgmental care system which was established by this organisation. This gave many Irish women support, shelter and assistance during troubled times. From this perspective the Salvation Army emerges as a progressive association whose ethos was markedly different from many of its contemporaries. Female salvationists played a pivotal role in this work and in the augmentation of the army throughout the British Isles. But this geographical expansion of the army aroused allegations of proselytising. In Ireland these fears were manifested in serious opposition to the army's work and, on occasion, this opposition erupted into violence.

Moira Egan's analysis of the nursing experiences of Irish Sisters of Mercy during the Crimean War not only adds to our knowledge of the work of women religious, but also of the impact which accusations of proselytising had on their work. These fears did not prompt violence, as was apparent in the resistance to the Salvation Army's arrival and development in Ireland, but nonetheless, proselytising was a contentious issue for Irish women nursing in the Crimea. Fears that the Sisters of Mercy would attempt to convert hospitalised soldiers significantly affected their relations with Florence Nightingale and the British government. This ultimately led to restrictions being placed on the work of the sisters. In addition to this religious issue, Egan also assesses the impact of ethnicity, questioning why the Irish Sisters of Mercy were seen as a potential religious threat, whilst lay nurses, lady volunteers and even women religious from English convents were not subjected to the same scrutiny.

The relationship between religion and family life was similarly complex. The family was central to the development of Methodism in eighteenth-century Ireland. Rosemary Raughter's work uncovers the impact of Methodist conversion on individual women and on their kin network. Indeed it seems that it was common for a woman to convert not only her spouse, but also her children. In addition to this women also opened their homes for use as meeting houses and centres for the Methodist faith. This often facilitated the conversion of other women from outside the confines of the immediate familial circle. But for some women, conversion to Methodism was akin to an act of independence which led them to reject the traditional path for eighteenth-century women – that of marriage and motherhood. Religion could also affect a particular facet of family life – mothering and child feeding practices. This is examined by Caitríona Clear in her article on the decline of breast-feeding in twentieth-century Ireland. Clear has used oral and anthropological evidence to trace this often covert aspect of women's lives. Whilst for health reasons breast-feeding was often the ideal for both mother and child and was strongly recommended by both the Catholic Church and the medical profession, this practice declined. This was partly a result of negative societal pressure. In addition, Clear suggests that breast-feeding could have an isolating effect on women. It is also possible that breast-feeding was a way for women to exercise some control in a particular area of their lives – their reproductive rights. Thus in choosing bottle over breast many women consciously rejected religious and medical orthodoxy.

In the nineteenth and early twentieth century the family could provide aristocratic women with an opportunity to enter the socio–political elite and thus exert a measure of political influence. Diane Urquhart traces the significance of the political patronage which was exercised by three female generations of the Londonderry family amongst Tory and Unionist leaders such as Benjamin Disraeli, Edward Carson, Andrew Bonar Law and Ramsay MacDonald. This study reveals how birth and marriage into a politically prominent family allowed women of ambition and ability to use personal acquaintance, correspondence and social entertaining as political tools. However, the political role of aristocratic women like Ladies Frances Anne, Theresa and Edith Londonderry was not static. From the late nineteenth century upper-class women became more politically active in a public capacity: addressing political meetings, canvassing and leading the political auxiliary organisations which were established in an attempt to educate a mass electorate in the aftermath of a series of reform acts. A similar mix of favourable birth, personal drive and ability enabled Isabella Tod to take a central role in late nineteenth-century politics. Already acknowledged as one of the leading Irish feminists of the nineteenth century, Noel Armour's assessment of Tod's place within the Liberal Unionist movement adds another dimension to our understanding of her life. Tod was a self-educated woman of independent means with an exceptional commitment to the Unionist cause. This allowed her to become the only female member of the executive of the Ulster Liberal Unionist Association. She also pioneered the establishment of the Ulster Women's Liberal Unionist Association, an auxiliary organisation which provided an important model for later women's Unionist organisations.

Delia Larkin was another exceptional woman whose feminism, like Isabella Tod's, was intertwined with other contemporary political and social concerns. Alison Buckley's article on Larkin and the early years of the Irish Women Workers' Union (IWWU) not only assesses the feminism of Larkin and of the IWWU, but also highlights the breadth of concerns sheltering beneath the collective title of trade unionism. Indeed from her study it emerges that in the early twentieth century issues such as equal pay, women's working conditions, alcohol abuse and the belief that a woman's first duty was to her home and family all formed important components of trade unionism.

We round off this collection with an afterword assessing the development of women's history in recent years and calling for its integration and acceptance into the mainstream.

As editors, it is our hope that this book will be as stimulating as

MacCurtain and Ó Corrain's collection; asking new questions of old sources, uncovering and assessing new archival material, redressing the gender imbalance in some areas of historical inquiry and adding to the ever-growing body of knowledge on women in Ireland's past. Thus we believe that *Irish Women's History* will prove to be a valuable addition towards a comprehensive history of women in Ireland and further highlight the fact that women's history is one of the most, if not the most, exciting areas of historical inquiry.

1

'Hail Brigit!': Gender, Authority and Worship in Early Ireland

LISA M. BITEL

I

An Irish poem of about 800 begins:

'Slán seiss a Brigit co mbúaid', 'Hail', or more literally:

> Sit safely victorious Brigit
> Upon Liffey-side to the ebbing sea!
> You are the princess with banded hosts
> That rules great Catháir's family …

And it ends:

> O Brigit whose land I behold
> On which each [king] in turn has moved around
> Your fame has outshone the fame of the king
> It's you that are over them all.

This stirring lyric refers to the decline of secular kingdoms in Leinster, the south-eastern province of Ireland where St Brigit supposedly built her famous monastery of Kildare in the fifth century. The old pagan rulers are now buried under the green of the great royal fort at the hill of Ailenn, near Kildare. Their halls have disappeared along with the songs of their swords and their bards and, as the poet puts it, 'the jingling of chains on the wrists of men under blades of bloody five-edged spears'.[1]

By contrast, the poet declares, the reign of Brigit continues peacefully at her lively community of Kildare. By 800, Kildare was a well-populated settlement with developed suburbs, a sizeable and well-appointed church, houses of religious women as well as monks, priests, scholars and a bishop or two. It demanded the allegiance, rents and dues of other religious communities from southern Leinster to central Mide to the north and Connacht to the north-west. The leading political dynasts of the region, the Uí Dúnlainge, who regularly held the over-kingship of Leinster, patronised and staffed the settlement with their sisters and spare kinsmen. Hence, the poem was not merely a pious pronouncement about the superiority of spiritual over secular powers – it was a statement of political fact. Kildare and its Uí Dúnlainge officers really did rule. St Brigit, the fifth-century saint, was at once Kildare's founding spirit, basis of authority and principal symbol, sitting safely on the banks of the River Liffey.

Victorious Brigit, who was a saint of semi-servile descent turned holy queen in a land of macho kings, has been taken for a minor historical aberration. But, in fact, she is the crux of a potentially significant historical contradiction. As several historians and celticists have shown, all women in early medieval Ireland, including saints, were legally disenfranchised. No queens ruled on their own or in their own names. At best, Irish gender ideologies were generally ambivalent toward women and, at worst, rigorously misogynist.[2] Yet, as historians have also exhaustively demonstrated, Brigit's hagiographers in this and other texts of the period claimed primacy for her over all religious women and men, ecclesiastical establishments and lay Christians of Leinster – or even, they hinted, of all Ireland.[3] Brigit worked wonders, dealt with kings and warriors, took on parish duties and communicated with God on behalf of her devotees.

Nonetheless, the saint remained a socially conservative figure, observing gender protocols and accepting limitations not felt by male colleagues. She moved modestly through her *vitae* as a mother and nurturer to other ecclesiastics and parishioners, cultivating traditionally feminine qualities and never competing outright with male colleagues. In all the Brigidine documents, then, early medieval writers and their audiences were reading an explicitly unassuming female saint as the symbol of supreme ecclesiastical power and political rule. Just to complicate things, mysterious rumours abounded in early Irish literature – both in religious and secular genres – that Brigit had once been a goddess of fire, healing and the arts, complete with cult sites and everburning flame.[4]

Modern scholarly interpretation of Brigit has ranged from the devoutly Catholic ('Mary of the Gael') to the downright goofy (she was an ex-goddess lesbian living in a monogamous relationship with St Darlugdach).[5] Whether or not they have celebrated Brigit's femininity, scholars usually ignore it as incidental to her religious and political authority. They assume that her influence existed *despite* her sex and gender traits and that her propagandists toiled to overcome the fact that she was a woman.

In fact, Brigit's *vitae* and other accounts of the saint employ a consciously and intensely gendered vocabulary purposely designed to establish her authority at several levels. In many ways, Brigit was indeed a formulaic saint, but her miracles and personality were very different from those of male saints in contemporary texts. She was also unlike other female saints. She was no royal Radegund (a sixth-century Merovingian saint) claiming authority and power derived from men's rule on the basis of her noble birth. Nor was she a violated or murdered female saint, like those of late antiquity. Neither was she a male imitator like other female saints in the Irish hagiographic canon. Moreover, she was not, like St Íte, a cross old hag who defied gender through age, picking on monastic novices and practising sarcasm on her colleagues.

So how did Brigit's female followers, clerics, political allies, competitors and secular clients of the seventh and early eighth centuries interpret her powers and authority? How did they use gender characteristics and roles to understand her? Answers to these questions help illustrate the importance of gender concepts in ecclesiastical organisation and politics, as well as shedding light on the nature of spiritual authority in early medieval Ireland. This essay aims, in particular, to show how each of Brigit's earliest three *vitae* relied on the saint's gender attributes to substantiate her political powers, establish the prominence of her *paruchia* and validate her authority throughout the ecclesiastical settlements and lay communities of Ireland. These are the so-called *Vita II*, written by Cogitosus of Kildare after 650; *Vita I*, which is actually slightly later, composed in the midlands at the end of the seventh century and an Irish life, now called *Bethu Brigte*, which derived from a seventh-century Latin examplar which was probably also the source of *Vita II*.

II

In many ways, Brigit was one of the boys. Irish hagiographers employed stories of their heroes to map out the networks of local churches (paruchiae) and secular patrons that owed allegiance and dues to the saint's main settlement. Brigit's earliest three *vitae* unanimously insist upon the dominance of her church at Kildare among the churches of Leinster and southern Mide. Historians and celticists are still working out the relation between these *vitae* and the history of Kildare's competition with Armagh, St Patrick's main church to the north, in Ulster. As McCone has skilfully shown, both Kildare and Armagh seem to have made bids in the seventh century to become head church of all Ireland. Kildare possessed the backing of aggressive Leinster kings. However, the clerics of Armagh cleverly secured an alliance with the mighty Uí Néill, who moved from Connacht down into central

Ireland in the sixth and seventh centuries, taking clients and hostages as they went.[6]

The seventh-century *vitae* of both Patrick and Brigit tell a history of ritualistic encounters between the saints and hostilities between Leinster kings and the triumphant Uí Néill. Eighth-century passages in Armagh's *Liber Ardmacha* show how Armagh and Kildare worked out a solution to the tension felt by religious communities in contested territory. At stake was the whole question of primacy in Ireland:

> Between holy Patrick and Brigit, pillars of the Irish, there existed so great a friendship of charity that they were of one heart and one mind. Christ worked many miracles through him and her. The holy man, then, said to the Christian virgin: 'O my Brigit, your paruchia will be deemed to be in your province in your dominion but in the eastern and western part it will be in my domination'.[7]

In other words, according to this Armagh source, Brigit's foundations outside Leinster became allies of Armagh – Brigit kept control of all the churches in Leinster. Once the northerners took over Mide, Brigit's churches in this area lost the political backing of Leinstermen. They necessarily became clients of Uí Néill allies while negotiating paruchial obligations to either Patrick or, less likely, the patroness of Leinster, Brigit.[8]

Brigit's three early *vitae* tell the Kildare version of these political changes. The gendered vocabulary of these *vitae* extends and enhances the hagiographers' aspirations for Brigit and Kildare and counters the claims of Armagh and Patrick. Brigit's traditionally feminine actions and character may seem to modern readers to undermine the political influence that hagiographers attributed to her and her settlement elsewhere in the very same *vitae*. Within her story, the saint's personal power – according to the very male-exclusive medieval definition of political power – was limited. Her hagiographers were likewise restricted in how they could reveal her influence and stake her claim to ecclesiastical dominance in the face of the more obvious authority of Patrick, who not only had the Uí Néill on his side, but who was also male and a bishop. Brigit, despite her sometimes superior abilities, seems surprisingly obsequious in her interactions with male colleagues in all three early lives, particularly with bishops and especially with Patrick. Even Cogitosus' *vita*, written safely and loyally at mid-seventh century Kildare, admitted a slight qualification of the woman saint's influence. He declared Brigit's settlement to be:

> the head of *almost all* [my emphasis] the Irish Churches with supremacy over all the monasteries of the Irish and its paruchia extends over the whole land of Ireland, reaching from sea to sea.[9]

Yet Cogitosus allows that the community did not rule all Irish churches, as Patrician *vitae* and the *Liber Ardmacha* claimed for Armagh, but 'almost all' the settlements from sea to sea, though he did argue that Brigit's abbess was 'she whom all the abbesses of the Irish revere'.[10]

How could a savvy hagiographer place his subject in such an ambiguous situation while simultaneously claiming pre-eminence for his saint? Even if he had no previous female hagiographical models to work with, why did he not adapt the saint's persona to fit Kildare's political ambitions? He might have called her a descendant of an Uí Néill mother, say, as St Áed mac Bricc supposedly came of mixed northern and southern ancestry; or he might have shown her politicking more flagrantly from her cloister, like the later St Samthann did, not to mention plenty of Merovingian and Anglo-Saxon queen-saints. In fact, Brigit's hagiographers were actually laying exorbitant claims for her and for Kildare by exploiting the very gender characteristics that normally deprived a woman of franchise and power. They were not claiming male-based or male-derived authority for the saint. Instead, their emphasis on the saint's traditional gender traits, laid out in her actions and attributes, was part of an elaborate argument for the political dominance of Kildare. Although Brigit's three early *vitae* differed in what they exacted for Brigit, all three used the same gendered hagiographic symbols to do so. Hence, gender was no limit to either the saint or her propagandists but, on the contrary, a marvellously flexible weapon in the struggle for saintly pre-eminence.

The first *vita*, Cogitosus' life, begins with Brigit's parentage – Dubthach, a Leinster nobleman of the Fothairt and Broicsech. Later *vitae*, although not that of Cogitosus, reveal that Broicsech was a slave girl from Connacht and that Brigit was sold to a druid from Munster and his wife. She eventually returned after childhood to her father in Leinster before taking a religious vow. Cogitosus almost immediately turns from Brigit's birth to her veiling by the Leinster bishop Mac Caille. The author moves on to a few domestic miracles – she gives away butter and bacon, which miraculously reappear; turns water into ale; spares a nun birth-pangs and hangs her cloak on a sun beam.[11]

In general, according to Cogitosus, Brigit specialises in hospitality and healing, curing blind, dumb and leprous clients. But she also performs a few unusual miracles. For instance, she preaches to nine *díkergaig*, marauding headhunters who live in the wild; her preaching has little effect, but she does cast an illusion which makes them believe that they commit murder, while in reality preventing the crime.[12] In another episode she undermines a king's judgement upon a man who killed his pet fox by substituting another fox which later disappears.[13] In a third story, she saves her own local *túath* (tribal kingdom) a lot of labour. They were ordered to divert the course of a river by digging it a new direction, then to construct a road for their overlord on the newly-dry ground. Brigit miraculously moved the river.[14] Each of these miracles depicts the holy woman countering traditional male authority – warrior bands, royal judgement and labour dues of lordship. Yet such gestures constitute only a small portion of the *vita*. They are far outnumbered by smaller, more commonplace wonders.

The woman Brigit is a modest character throughout Cogitosus' life. In fact, she is dull as bricks. When she encounters the *díberga*, Brigit is 'reverent and affable' and preaches with 'mellifluous eloquence' rather than employing any of the piss and vinegar for which other Irish saints are so famous. Patrick, in a similar situation in contemporary *vitae*, strikes misbehaving warriors with paralysis or even death.[15] When someone denies Patrick a gift, he inflicts the miser and his horse with death. In contrast, Brigit reacts to the worst catastrophes by praying ceaselessly. This demonstrates her extraordinary faith (as well as that of her hagiographer) that things will turn out well. It is, in fact, one of her two ideally feminine traits. She never gets angry, and she also never says no (except when asked to marry). When an 'unpleasant leper' approaches her and demands her best cow and best calf, she hands them both over and, what is more, sends them in her own chariot so as not to fatigue the leper with herding.[16] Her generosity, along with her docility, serenity and all her graces, were exactly those praised by Irish gnomic literature and canons of the period – a good woman was sensible, prudent, modest, well-spoken, delicate, mild, honest, wise, pure and smart. A bad woman was promiscuous, stole and lied, chattered and argued.[17] In fact all the feminine typecasting has a purpose. According to Cogitosis her virtues win Brigit rewards:

> Famous therefore for such great miracles, full of humility of heart, purity of mind, restraint of character and spiritual grace, she merited to acquire such great authority in divine worship and a prestige renowned above all the virgins of her time.[18]

The author writes that the saint's authority, worship and prestige – and hence those of her church – came directly from her feminine virtues of humility, purity and restraint, not to mention her feminine miracles of feeding, supplying, nurturing and healing. In the same passage Cogitosus mentions 'una ex adhaerentibus sibi extrinsecus femina', (one of [Brigit's] female followers from outside) who came to the saint seeking a cure for her dumb twelve-year-old daughter; once healed, the child chose to remain a virgin in Brigit's community. In this passage, we begin to glimpse the hagiographer's plan. Cogitosus craftily combines his presentation of the source of Brigit's power – her restrained feminine virtues – with a reference to the basis of her constituency, female recruits. Brigit was, as Cogitosus points out, 'she whom all the abbesses revere', as well as, presumably, the other religious men and women under the direction of abbesses. What a bold manoeuvre by this Kildare cleric – he substantiates a claim to Brigit's political power over churches, bishops, priests, religious women and lay clients by an appeal to the very traits which normally made a woman less than powerful in a warrior society. Cogitosus illustrates this lesson throughout the *vita* with stories detailing Brigit's ignoble birth, submissive behaviour and quietly subversive miracles.

Cogitosus was ambitious. No other texts claim a coast-to-coast paruchia for St Brigit. Yet the real substance of the hagiographer's claim lies not in the seeming attempt at primacy, but in his twofold aims for Kildare: that it should govern the churches of Brigit's territory, Leinster and the midlands; and that, more importantly, it should rule communities of women through-out Ireland. Since many ecclesiastical communities in early Ireland included women in various stages of religious commitment, this was actually a much grander demand than it at first seems. It was much more outrageous than calling outright for an island-wide paruchia. Paruchiae were not necessarily territorial, but usually locally-based clientage networks of ecclesiastical settlements. Some, like those of Armagh and Iona, focused on a particular region and included outlying houses in regions across the island. But Cogitosus was demanding, on Brigit's behalf, allegiance from every settle-ment in Ireland which included a woman. This meant that anywhere a woman settled as a religious professional she owed first obedience to Kildare, rather than to her local superior or any other patron community that tried to include her settlement in its network. Every little family church with a woman in it, every major monastery with a separate women's house, every local shrine with a female attendant was supposedly loyal first to Kildare. And the source of Brigit's claim lay not in the Uí Dúnlainge, not in her own Fothairt ancestry, not in royal parentage, not in manly miracles and maledictions, not in legal rights of any sort and not even in any missionary claim to have founded the houses she dominated. It lay in her *auctoritas* as an unassuming female. Cogitosus expressed his claims squarely in gender terms. No male saint ever provided such a blatantly sexist argument for such a grand ecclesiastical ambition.

The two slightly later *vitae* and related documents assume that, while most of Brigit's professional followers were women, churches under Kildare's control included many mixed-sex settlements. In a list, believed to be from the eighth century, of some eighty communities subject to Kildare, judging by the names of dwellers, many, if not most, were of mixed sex. For instance, there was 'Finán and his two sisters at Tech Airthir' and 'Berchan mac Nemnaill, and Brig and Coip and Lassar, three daughters of Nemnaill, and

Broccán and Cronan, two sons of Mac Lochin, at Cell Lathrach os thuile'.[19] Kildare itself provides the most famous example of a Brigidine mixed community. Cogitosus describes Brigit's cathedral, which was sub-divided for sub-communities of nuns and widows on one side and monks, priests and bishops on the other.[20] The monastic annals from the seventh century onwards confirm that Kildare consisted of a coalition of subgroups, probably with separate ecclesiastical functions, including women, monks, priests, bishops, scholars and all sorts of visitors, ruled in Brigit's name by a junta of abbess, abbot and one or more bishops.[21] This continued to be the case until at least the twelfth century, when the monastery may have disappeared, or possibly until the sixteenth-century dissolution, when the nuns finally left.[22]

Both Cogitosus and later sources are at pains to demonstrate that the saint's lay clients and devotees came from both sexes. All of her hagiographers were very careful to portray Brigit as tending, as any mother, to both men and women – healing, supplying food and preaching to both sexes. When she works a wonder for a man, the episode is often paired with a miracle performed to benefit a woman.[23] Hence, although Brigit's authority and miracles are typically feminine and although her ecclesiastical followers theoretically included more women than men (at least outside Leinster), her worship was double-gendered. Writers and audiences read Brigit as a female symbol on some levels, but as nonetheless a stalwart intercessor for both men and women.

After Cogitosus' initial effort in the mid-seventh century, Brigit's hagiographers extended and revised her claims to dominance based on gender. Scholars have argued that the two other early *vitae* of the saint focus mainly on Brigit's authority in northern Leinster and the midlands of Mide, in an attempt to maintain her paruchia to the north against Armagh's encroachments.[24] As with any of her colleagues, male or female, her travels to foreign territory signify her church's influence elsewhere. However, Brigit's relationships with male and female colleagues beyond Kildare, as well as with lay clients, also indicate different, more explicitly gendered hagiographical politics. Unlike Cogitosus' life, *Vita I* and *Bethu Brigte* both place Brigit and Kildare in a traditional relationship of subservience to bishop Patrick and his church at Armagh. Yet, by conceding Patrick's nominal authority, hence that of Armagh, in the contested territory of the midlands, Brigit substantiates her own gender-based authority over religious women everywhere. Even when she bows to the authority of Patrick or his male cronies, Brigit's passive sanctity outshines theirs. Just as Cogitosus uses Brigit's feminine virtues and miracles to illustrate her authority, *Vita I* and *Bethu Brigte* show the saint at once conceding the gendered nature of the ecclesiastical hierarchy while proving her own personal *virtus* superior (power and sanctity).

Thus, the hagiographical corollary runs, Kildare's claims to authority transcend the institutional organisation of Irish churches.

Once Cogitosus had created the rhetoric of Brigit's highly gendered authority, later hagiographers readily employed it. For instance, in these later texts, Brigit becomes the companion of Patrick's friends, bishops Mel and Melchu of Tethbae in Mide (Uí Néill territory). She takes the veil, according to *Vita I*, not from Mac Caille of Leinster (as in Cogitosus) but from these two bishops; hence her vocation gains the imprimatur of Patrick, despite the fact that Mel bungles the ceremony. The bishops also turn up later in the *vita*, to insist that Brigit seek a doctor for her terrible headaches. En route, the saint falls out of the chariot and bumps her head – 'her head was gashed by a stone and blood gushed out', writes the author – but even this incident reveals her superiority when contact with her blood heals a couple of mute women.[25] In other words, the bishops tell her what to do, but cannot control the holy consequences. Mel and Melchu also invite Brigit to go north with them to meet Patrick at a clerical assembly at Tailtiu – not coincidentally, an old Mide inaugural site symbolic of non-Leinster kingship.

At the assembly, Brigit's abilities become obvious when she performs a miracle in the midst of all the bishops, abbots and male saints. The incident is dramatic. A nun accuses another Patrician bishop, Brón, of impregnating her. He claims innocence. No male lawyer can prove innocence or guilt.[26] So the council demands that Brigit – not Patrick – make a judgement in the case. Brigit initially defers to Patrick who asks his 'beloved daughter' to make the call. She signs the cross on the woman's mouth, which swells up along with her whole head and then blesses the baby's tongue. The child pipes 'My father is not Bishop Brón but a certain fellow ... a most despicable type, base and depraved'.[27] Brigit's initial courtesy to Patrick showed that she herself acknowledged his official authority amongst the clergy. However, the story further suggests that she could wield equal, if not superior, spiritual power. She only lacked appropriate venues in which to exercise it.

The complicated gendered balance of power informs her other interactions with Patrick. In another visit to Patrick, Brigit makes a pointed comment on his authority by falling asleep during his sermon. She begs forgiveness on account of a prophetic dream she has while sleeping. She saw, she explains, four ploughmen sowing fast-ripening seeds and streams of new milk in the furrows, followed by four dark ploughmen who uprooted the crop and water in the furrows. Fortunately, Patrick's priestly duties included oneiromancy – he interprets the dream for her:

> Maiden the vision you have seen is a true and wonderful one. We are the good ploughmen who cleave human hearts with ploughs and sow the word of God and his milk of elementary teaching.[28]

Although Patrick must articulate the dream's meaning, his message is that he and Brigit equally share the missionary work of Ireland's salvation. Besides a statement in support of Kildare's prestige, the episode is also an early instance of feminine mystical experience trumping male adherence to formal ritual. She, after all, gets the truth in a dream directly from God while he is preaching.[29]

Brigit's time with Patrick on his own turf not only brings her into contact with the male saint, but also allows her to perform miracles and demonstrate her holiness in politically contested territory. While visiting the north, she predicts the place of Patrick's burial and is entrusted with the duty of weaving his shroud which is, needless to say, the customary duty of a wife or kinswoman. Brigit gains reflected glory by clothing her comrade for his final rest. But the story also reminds its audience that she will outlast Patrick, continuing with her pious work long after he is gone.[30] She also intervenes in Uí Néill politics although she backs a less successful dynasty than Patrick's Armagh.[31] This is not to say that Brigit bows out of Leinster politics in the later *vitae*. For example, in *Vita I* she returns home to grant the king of the Leinstermen long life and success in every battle (although he rejects her promise of successors and salvation). He wins thirty battles against his enemies and nine campaigns in Britain; she even leads the charge, in phantom form, staff in hand and a fiery column shooting from her head. What is more, even after he dies his blessed body prevents an invasion by Brigit's less intimate friends, the Uí Néill.[32] Despite Leinster-Mide conflicts and the submissive tone of her *vitae*, Brigit continued to be recognised as both a political force and a patroness of the Leinster kings. Not coincidentally, the *Fragmentary Annals* report that in 722, when the Leinstermen went to battle against the northerners, 'Brigit was seen [in a vision] over the Laigin'.[33]

However, the most compelling difference between *Vita I* and Cogitosus' *vita* of Brigit derives not from straight politics, but from the fact that *Vita I* places the saint in the company of women. Everywhere Brigit goes, her nuns follow. When she takes the veil, eight women accompany her. When she travels outside Leinster she takes an ever-increasing retinue of female followers. Her hospitality miracles take place explicitly in the presence of her sisters. Her disciple Darlugdach even insists on dying with the saint, although Brigit makes her wait a year.[34] Whenever Brigit outshines Patrick and his allies the event is witnessed by Brigit's sisters and followers. What is more, Brigit interacts with more lay women in *Vita I* and *Bethu Brigte*. And the miracles are, as in Cogitosus' version and *Vita I*, womanly wonders performed explicitly in the presence of women. Brigit replenishes butter jars, provides an abundance of beer, gives food or animals to disagreeable lepers and heals women and children. Women, who had limited property rights under Irish laws, make prominent appearances as donors in these *vitae*; one gives cows and calves, another gives a fabulous necklace, nuns give dues of produce and other nuns yield their religious settlements to her direction.[35]

There is no question that the two other *vitae* present Brigit as even more of a woman's woman than Cogitosus does. Their vocabulary is more obviously gendered than his. But the ultimate result is the same – all three *vitae* make claims for Brigit, not despite her gender, but on account of it. Her official role is as a leader of women and she defers publicly to her proper superiors, such as Patrick. Nonetheless, her spiritual powers are even more profound than his, for she can judge more wisely in some matters, especially matters of gender relations like paternity suits. Wherever she goes in Ireland – even when in Patrick's own territory, or in the watchful company of Patrick's henchmen – she is the ultimate authority among women.

This may be why Brigit became an accidental bishop. Her hagiographers were not imaginative enough to invent a newly feminized vocabulary for her unique spiritual authority; they could not think beyond the traditional ecclesiastical hierarchy and institutional organisation of their own day (nor should we expect them to have done so). So the author of *Bethu Brigte* played with gender and ritual by making the saint an exceptional, womanly kind of bishop. At Brigit's veiling, bishop Mel becomes intoxicated by her sanctity and accidentally reads the rite for consecrating a bishop over Brigit. The bishop covers himself by explaining, 'This virgin alone in Ireland … will hold the episcopal ordination'.[36] God clearly approves of Mel's accident, though, because a column of fire shoots from Brigit's head. No woman could be a bishop in medieval Christendom, yet Brigit, a woman, was a bishop. No plainer indication of the complex gendered vocabulary of these *vitae* exists than this curious episode. Brigit exercises her public political authority only in the presence of clerics such as Patrick and Mel; she becomes a bishop, but only by accident and with divine assent; she rules a kind of paruchia, but a strangely gender-segregated one.

One more episode from *Bethu Brigte* further illuminates the paradox. When Brigit leaves the assembly where she judges the alleged episcopal philanderer, Brón, she retires to a layman's house. She cannot enter, though, for she divines that her host is a heathen and she will not eat there. The man wants to convert, but she cannot baptise him. She has to call on Patrick for a priest, whereupon the male saint announces: 'You should not go about without a priest. Your charioteer should always be a priest.' And, as the hagiographer admits, 'that was observed by Brigit's abbesses to recent times'.[37] She is limited by her very sex from conducting rituals that a lowly parish priest might perform. Nonetheless, the woman bishop and her abbatial successors solve the gender problem by hiring drivers who can double as priests. Perhaps the incidents functioned as literary acknowledgements of Armagh's superiority over Kildare and that of male bishops over religious women generally. More likely, though, the stories reinforced the primary lessons of Brigit's *vitae*: she is saintly, thus powerful, because she is a woman; the religious hierarchy must accommodate her wherever she ventures and whatever she wishes to do. The view from the midlands and north Leinster at the turn of the seventh century, in these two *vitae*, is no concession to gendered ecclesiastical politics based on the model suggested by Cogitosus. Let Patrick have Mide, the hagiographers conceded, let him rule the official ecclesiastical hierarchy. Brigit had a normal paruchia in Leinster, dominance over religious women everywhere and lay followers 'on the outside' through-out Ireland, purely on account of her very female sanctity.

References to Brigit elsewhere and later in the canon of early Irish texts only reinforce the singularity of the saint and her immense powers while always emphasising her femininity and her affinity for female followers. Brigit could help everyone as a mother and 'fostermother of the Irish' – not as a wonder-maker in heroic style, but as an intercessor with the men of the family, healer of skinned knees and tarnished souls, nurturer and fixer of dinners.[38] Christian literature compared her to the mother of God, while other texts, also authored by clerical literati, linked her vaguely with previous Brigits and Brigs and even goddesses. The ninth-century *Glossary* of bishop and king, Cormac mac Cuilennáin defines the word (although not the specific saint) Brigit as:

> poetess, daughter of the Dagdae [Good God]. This is Brigit the female seer or woman of insight, i.e. the goddess whom poets used to worship, and her cult was very great and very splendid. It is for this reason that they call her the woman of leechcraft and Brigit the woman of smith-craft, i.e. goddesses, i.e. three daughters of the Dagdae are they. By their names the goddess Brigit was called by all the Irish.[39]

Brig also turns up as a healer in the mythological histories and a pre-Christian wise-woman and judge in the legal texts.[40] St Brigit's feast day, 1 February, was the ancient seasonal holiday of Imbolc, when the flocks moved up into the hills. Her pre-Christian reputation even won her the notice of Gerald of Wales, that bad-tempered chronicler of the Anglo-Norman invasions of Ireland – he reported that the nuns of Kildare kept an eternal fire, tended every twenty nights by the saint herself; the fire was surrounded by a hedge which no man could cross and survive.[41]

Early twentieth-century scholars (and some more recently) have attributed the Brigits/Brigs of these texts and Gerald's wild reports to a persistent pagan tradition that infiltrated written texts of the Christian period.[42] The Christian writers of the early middle ages were too clever to repeat mindlessly goddess legends about such a prominent saint as Brigit of Kildare, or any other saint, for that matter. They used goddess references purposely to reinforce Brigit's very femininity.[43] Goddesses and otherworldly women symbolised, above all other concepts, the pagan past. They represented everything un-Christian, disorderly and amoral about pre-Patrician times. Likewise, pagan decadence became synonymous, in many Irish texts, with women and femininity. It was a two-way trope.[44] Brigit was, above all, a woman, although a hyper-Christian woman. Nonetheless, it made sense to early medieval writers to signify her sometimes as a goddess-figure. By doing so, they consciously invoked for her nameless powers that belonged exclusively to women and had existed centuries before Patrick came to Ireland.

III

Being female was the source of Brigit's, and hence of Kildare's, prestige amongst other saints and their communities. Any rumours that she had a past as a goddess only reaffirmed the fiercely feminine basis of her authority and her solidarity with other females. So did her identification with the Blessed Virgin. Ultimately, then, the politics of Cogitosus and other early *vitae* of Brigit aimed in two directions. The hagiographers desperately wanted to substantiate Kildare's claims to settlements in Patrician territory in Mide and elsewhere. But, at the same time, they must have known that this was a losing battle. No woman could ever be the pre-eminent saint of Ireland, which was legally a man's island. Saints were no more genderless than the rest of the Irish. What is more, as Kildare clerics quickly learned, no Leinster church could ever dominate an Uí Néill-backed organisation. In such a situation, Brigit's hagiographers needed to devise an effective strategy to propagandise her powers, the authority of her abbesses and bishops and the precedence of Kildare. Hence, the second, more fruitful tactic of these hagiographers and others who wrote of Brigit's phenomenal sanctity was to emphasise the female nature of her power, her character and her network of clients. She was no male wannabe and no transgendered thaumaturge. As a woman, she could intercede with God on anyone's behalf. She was abbess of abbesses, wherever they might be in Ireland; she created a community with her virgins, in Kildare or wherever she moved, whether in Uí Néill territory, in Leinster or further afield. Likewise, the hagiographers were claiming that Brigit's successors as abbess at Kildare could demand allegiance from religious women everywhere. And when it came to miracles for the locals, Brigit could perform for men and women alike – although women were her speciality, both as recipients of miraculous aid and as thankful donors.

Brigit's was a unique authority – a woman-bishop for women. Ultimately, it was a claim that Kildare had trouble enforcing. Throughout the medieval period communities dedicated to Brigit remained in existence all over Ireland, but whether they paid dues and rents to Kildare rather than the local house of another saint, male or female, is a real question. Perhaps their loyalty was as feminine (in the early Irish definition) as the powers of Brigit – which is to say, fickle and insubstantial – rather than a solid commitment of resources and social and political support. But we know that people, especially women, continued to venerate Brigit for her womanly ways. Many still do.

Necessary Collaborations: Religious Women and Lay Communities in Medieval Ireland, c. 1200–1540

DIANNE HALL

I

Women in later medieval Ireland, as in medieval Europe generally, pursued many different avenues to their own and their families' spiritual salvation in an age where religious observance, if not religious conviction, was an integral part of daily life. Prominent lay women donated goods and property to their favoured church and monasteries, sometimes retiring from active secular life to live out their widowhood within the walls of a monastic house. Others attached themselves to monasteries and churches and lived as recluses, attaining reputations for great piety and charity. There was also the path of serving God through work in hospitals set up for the spiritual and physical care of the sick, poor and elderly. Living in community with other women, under a specified rule of observance and recognised by ecclesiastic authorities and the surrounding lay communities, was the most easily recognised way for women to pursue a life within the church. In Ireland there was a long tradition dating back to the first Christian settlements of profound piety amongst women and a proud legacy of women living together as nuns.[1] Most of the early history of these convents are lost in obscurity – nuns and their supporters only emerge with any degree of clarity in the period after the Anglo-Norman conquest, when record keeping became more organised. Even then the records for the nunneries within the areas controlled by the Gaelic Irish have not been well preserved and although some conclusions can be made about them, it is necessary to be aware that conditions may have been substantially different for Gaelic Irish religious women than for women living within the areas controlled by the descendants of the Anglo-Normans. Religious women living in medieval Ireland and the institutions which were established by and for them have often been mentioned in passing in histories of the Catholic Church in Ireland, though there has been little attempt to date to pull together the disparate threads of the surviving evidence to try to present any coherent picture of their lives or the institutions in which they lived.[2]

Records about nuns in later medieval Ireland are sparse and difficult both to access and interpret, as nuns have suffered from not being considered as important or as wealthy as their male religious counterparts in both original records and in the preservation of evidence pertaining to their lives as religious women. This is not the only problem when studying the sources for the history of medieval religious women in Ireland. Potential sources for women's history have also suffered from the general neglect and the disasters which have befallen all the sources for the history of medieval Ireland. No devotional material survives which can be said to have been written by or for medieval religious women in Ireland in the period under study, and very few of the routine business documents which the convents of medieval France and England left in such abundance have survived the ravages of time and history. At the centre of any investigation into religious life for women in medieval Ireland are thus a group of enigmatic figures, silent, eyes bowed, hands folded, their stance and dress marking them inviolate, quiet vessels through which prayers were to be channelled. The voices of the women who dedicated their lives to the church in medieval Irish communities remain largely silent in the surviving records, often only emerging into the historical record when they needed to interact with lay communities and institutions. To some extent it is only at such junctions between their collective silence and the outside secular world that evidence for their lives can be found. The spiritual centre of women's religious life is hidden from view. It is, however, possible to analyse the structures surrounding this centre and the boundaries within which women in medieval Ireland lived their lives dedicated to God. Thus, although the voices of the women themselves remain silent, to some extent the restrictions and opportunities with which they lived become visible.

Medieval monastic perceptions of space were created by the use of boundaries, which may be both real and ideal in nature. Hence, as Gilchrist has argued, whilst the boundary of a medieval monastic precinct demarcated legal ownership of land, it also symbolised the divide between secular and religious domains.[3] These boundaries were thus both physical and ideological, established and maintained by the necessary collaboration between religious women and the lay communities which founded and supported them. Physical boundaries in this sense are the buildings in which the women lived and the lands from which they received the necessary income to sustain their communities. Ideas woven around these physical boundaries by such elements as the collective community recognition of the ownership of the physical spaces and the crossing or dividing points between religious and lay space formed ideological boundaries in which religious women lived. One important idea which affected the divide between lay and religious space and physical presence was the concept of enclosure for religious women or restricted access by outsiders to the women and restrictions on the women's access to the outside world. This essay will concentrate on the ways that nuns were segregated from the outside world by rules of enclosure, and how these rules operated in medieval Ireland, as a means of interrogating the boundaries between lay communities and religious women.

II

One of the clearest differences between male and female monastic houses in the later medieval period was the application of the principles of enclosure. Since the earliest versions of the Christian monastic rules, men and women who devoted themselves to God were expected to separate from their families and communities and live separately, safely enclosed within walls – real or symbolic – in order to maintain purity of thought and deed and direct their energies to the work of God. These principles were described in later monastic rules as 'enclosure'. Although men and women were both expected to live under these rules, in reality they were applied much more strictly to women. During the twelfth century there was a European-wide movement to reform monastic orders so that monks and nuns would live away from the pressures and temptations of the lay world. There were a number of reforming orders established in continental Europe. One of them was established at the abbey of Arrouaise in France, where monks and nuns under the reforming leadership of Abbot Gervase followed a version of the rule known as Augustinian. St Malachy of Down, in his travels across Europe, visited this abbey and was so impressed by the reformed rule that he took it back to Ireland and most of the male and female monastic houses which were established or reformed under his influence in the mid-twelfth century were thus known as Arroasian. The adoption by nunneries of this version of the rule meant that, officially at least, the movement of nuns was restricted outside the immediate boundaries of their convent walls.[4] Since the circumstances of the foundation of most of the nunneries in Ireland are not well documented, it is not always possible to be certain that they were established under the principles of strict enclosure and ancient houses, such as St Brigid's at Kildare, were probably not founded on these principles. However, it is likely that the convents which were reformed or established from the twelfth century were under rules of enclosure. Certainly the priory of the Holy

Trinity at Lismullin in Co. Meath was founded with the express mention of enclosure in the documentation of its foundation.[5]

The most significant attempt to enforce enclosure on nuns throughout medieval Europe was the bull *Periculoso* promulgated by Pope Boniface VIII in 1298.[6] This document declared that all nuns, no matter which rule they followed, or in which part of Europe they lived, were required to submit to strict segregation from all contact with the outside world behind closed doors on pain of excommunication. They were no longer to permit the laity to enter their cloisters and were not permitted to leave except in certain restricted circumstances.[7] The transparent reason for this emphasis on increased enclosure was no doubt the protection of the nuns and the surrounding lay population from the stain of sexual sin. The wording of *Periculoso* leaves little doubt that this is what was intended and the commentators and episcopal visitation records where the bull was enforced reinforce this explicitly:

> Desiring to provide for the perilous and detestable state of certain nuns, who, having slacked the reins of decency and having shamelessly cast aside the modesty of their order and of their sex … to the grave offense of Him to Whom they have, of their own will, vowed their innocence, to the opprobrium of religion and to the scandal of very many persons.[8]

There is certainly evidence from all over medieval Europe of nuns being discovered bearing children while supposedly enclosed within the safe and chaste boundaries of their convents. Although, as Johnson has pointed out in her study of monks and nuns in medieval France, the rates of sexual sin for monks were probably greater, nuns were more easily caught because of the visibility of pregnancy.[9] Whether the nuns themselves were active participants in these sins, and so might be supposed to be chafing under the burden of enclosure, or were unwilling victims of violence who might have looked in vain for the purported safety of their convent walls to protect them, is not always clear in the records. It is probable that there were many instances of both occurring throughout the medieval period all over Europe.[10]

III

The extent of the enforcement of *Periculoso* in Ireland is not fully recoverable from the Irish sources, nor are the reactions of religious women to its rulings. It would appear though that women were expected to comply with the bull. In the early fifteenth century the Archbishop of Armagh, in a general attempt to reduce abuses in the church, listed the constitutions of *Periculoso* as a means of enforcing enclosure on nuns in the diocese.[11] The most explicit mention of its enforcement came in 1427 when John Swayne, Archbishop of Armagh, was in visitation of the priory of the Holy Trinity at Lismullin, Co. Meath and ordered that the nuns were to observe the constitution of *Periculoso*. The gates and other places of the convent were ordered shut and a copy of the bull appended to the order. There are two other undated entries which order Lismullin to comply with enclosure in the register, probably dated 1425 and later in 1427.[12] There are no explicit indications of whether the nuns obeyed his various commands, and the repetition of the order over such a short space of time indicates that enclosure was not being viewed with great respect by the nuns of Lismullin, nor was it being enforced despite the exhortations of the archbishop.

There is also evidence that there were errant nuns discovered in sexual sin in Ireland. In 1368, for example, the Archbishop of Armagh gave dispensation to Sir Roger Ogean of Down who had carnal knowledge with Matilda Stokys, a professed nun of the nunnery of Down.[13] There are no other details of how the relationship between Matilda and Sir Roger developed, although it is possible that he was a priest or clerk who had a legitimate reason for being within the conventual precinct. Another explicit mention of the rule of enclosure, and the sins which were perceived to occur when it was breached, came in the sixteenth century at the abbey of Kilculliheen, in what is now Waterford. In 1532, Elicia Butler was charged before the court of Milo Baron, Bishop of Ossory, that she had, amongst other offences, so depleted the resources of her convent that the nuns were forced to seek shelter elsewhere, 'against the observed rule'.[14] She was also accused of fornication and bearing a child.[15] In the minds of these ecclesiastical authorities, leaving the security of the cloister and sexual sin seem to have been inextricably connected.

Within the confines of the convent walls there were of course also many legitimate reasons why the women had contact with men. The nuns needed male supporters, especially priests and employees, and although the actual numbers of inhabitants of convents in Ireland is not always known, what evidence there is suggests that there were usually male inhabitants, as well as female, in most convents. When the Augustinian houses were reformed in the twelfth century under Malachy, it is most probable that many of the women's houses which were established were linked with adjacent men's houses, usually sharing the church. This has been most consistently traced for the nunnery of St Mary's at Clonard in Co. Meath and its dependencies. The nuns of Clonard seem to have continued their association with the canons of nearby men's houses until, at least, the early fourteenth century, because between 1282 and 1296, the names of three canons of nearby houses in Meath are recorded as being the representatives sent to conduct the nuns' business with the crown at the election of new abbesses.[16] Before about 1300 the prioresses of Lismullin were using canons described as being from their own house to represent them in the courts. For example, Brother Richard, canon of Lismullin, represented Roesia, prioress in 1269;[17] Ada when she was prioress was represented by 'a canon of the same house' in 1281.[18] Henry, a brother of Lismullin, is mentioned as representing the house's interests some time previous to 1301.[19] There is no evidence that Lismullin operated as a linked house in the same way that Clonard did, but the repeated appearance in court records of attorneys described as being brothers or canons from Lismullin does indicate that religious men were attached specifically to the priory to attend to the business, and probably the spiritual needs, of the nuns. After this time, the nuns seem to have employed professional lay lawyers in the courts, which is probably more suggestive of an increase in the number of professional lawyers than of a reduction in men working and living at the priory of Lismullin. For example, the usual inhabitants of the convent of Lismullin in 1367 included priests, clerks, bailiffs and stewards.[20]

IV

It was not for nefarious purposes that the nuns were usually called upon to leave their conventual walls or to invite lay people within, but for the management of estates and general business. Estate management and negotiations with lay and ecclesiastic authorities for the continued prosperity of convent property necessitated movement outside the boundaries of the convent walls, at least by the abbess.[21] Although abbesses were required by *Periculoso* to appoint attorneys and proctors to engage in their official business, it appears in later commentaries on the bull, that abbesses may have been permitted to go in person to do homage for land, even though it was preferred that proctors perform these duties on their behalf.[22] It is likely that such deviations from the letter of the rules of enclosure were tolerated, because it was impractical to do otherwise. In Ireland there are several recorded instances when the nuns themselves were engaged in pursuing the important business of managing their incomes and estates. Often a pressing time for a convent – where they held their lands from the king – was when the death or resignation of the abbess or prioress occurred and income from the monastic estates was transferred to crown revenue until the election of a new abbess or prioress. The recovery of the incomes necessitated swearing an oath of allegiance to the king and a formal handing over of the rights of the estates from the king's official, usually the escheator or his deputy in Ireland. There is a glimpse of what was required on these occasions when Gormlaith, described as the daughter of Okerra, was elected abbess of Clonard, Co.

Meath, after the resignation of Abbess Derboghyll in 1296. It was recorded in the records of the justiciary court that certain nuns of the house brought the necessary letters under their convent seal to the Justiciar in November and the election of Gormlaith was confirmed by the Bishop of Meath in the second week of Lent 1297, when the abbess came and did fealty. The writ for delivery of the incomes or temporalities was delayed, however, until the abbess gave the necessary letters which showed that this action would not be prejudicial to the crown; the record noted that she had given the letters and they were placed in treasury.[23] Although it is possible that all of this business was attended to by proctors it is as likely that the prioress, nuns and the new abbess all travelled to the courts of the justiciary and the bishop as required.

It is quite clear what is meant in the record of the action taken by the abbess of Kilcreevanty against the Archbishop of Tuam in 1308, when she is described as being present 'in her own person' and the archbishop is represented by his attorney Maurice Houne.[24] This may mark a time when it was becoming more unusual for religious women to represent themselves and travel outside of their convent walls. For example, in 1347, Margaret, prioress of Lismullin, is described in one court case as being represented by her attorney because she 'is not permitted by the rule of her order' to appear personally.[25] On the eve of the dissolution of the monasteries there was a vacancy in the office of prioress of Termonfeckin and the Archbishop of Armagh was engaged in finding a successor.[26] In the memorandum of this event, preserved in the registers of archbishops of Armagh, Maria Cusacke, a sister of Odder, is described as appearing in person before the archbishop at his court in Termonfeckin. The archbishop then required the abbess of Odder to appear in person and support her claim to the right to appoint the prioress of Termonfeckin, which she did. Later in the same year Margaret Silke, abbess of Odder, again appeared 'in person' before the archbishop to ask that Margaret Hubbard of the convent of St Mary del Hogges outside Dublin be admitted as prioress of Termonfeckin.[27] Besides the fascinating information about the networks between the nunneries, this also demonstrates that the nuns were required to appear personally. Moreover, the specificity with which the registers emphasise the personal presence of the nuns suggests that this may have been an unusual occurrence.

V

The visiting of relatives and friends was less well tolerated by ecclesiastical authorities. There is ample evidence that the nuns of various communities throughout England and the Continent strenuously resisted the rules of enclosure which shut them off from their friends and relatives outside the convent walls. This again suggests that the boundaries within which the nuns lived were less impermeable than authorities envisioned. The attendance at family functions, such as weddings, appears to have been particularly frowned upon, perhaps because of the levity of parties and the perceived opportunities for sin.[28] However, such family connections were important not only for the personal well-being of the nuns themselves, but also for the maintenance of friendly relations with the lay communities and families who were the advocates and supporters of the convents. Without such support, convents often found themselves in real danger of disaster. It appears that lay communities in the often violent societies of medieval Ireland could only afford and tolerate the existence of non-combatants, such as nuns, if they were an integrated and valued asset to the community. It is likely that the presence of abbesses at family functions or public events, such as weddings, was valued by the lay families who supported the convents. In 1501 in one of the protracted inquires into the matrimonial state of the father of Piers Butler, claimant to the earldom of Ormond, the evidence of the Abbess of Kilculliheen was listed as first witness, obviously a position of importance in the record. She was possibly a member of the Butler family, who were prominent supporters of the abbey, and she gave evidence that she had been present at the wedding between James Butler and Sabh Kavanagh, some thirty years before.[29] Nuns were also expected to continue to maintain their knowledge of relationships with lay families. In about 1455, another abbess, named as Benmon ingen Omellan and described as abbess of St Brigid's, was called to give evidence in the case where Felim McDomphnayll and Isabella ingen Neill were seeking dispensation to marry even though they were regarded as too closely related by the rules governing medieval marriages. Benmon gave evidence of the family tree of the Uí Néill which proved that the couple were related too closely for these strict rules. Her evidence was important and her knowledge of the family relationships speaks of being either a member of the family herself (in which case her name may have been mistranscribed) or having intimate knowledge of several generations of the family either through her own connections or that of her family's association with the ruling dynasty.[30] Either way, her evidence suggests that she was not so rigidly enclosed that she was unable to keep in contact with this prominent lay family. This may be a feature of the conditions of women in Gaelic Irish convents, but unfortunately it is not possible to do more than speculate.

The ideological boundaries of enclosures were intended to strengthen the physical boundaries which separated the nunneries from their surrounding communities. However, these ideological barriers were not practical within the close knit and interdependent communities of medieval Ireland of which the nunneries were a part. Nuns expected and were expected to maintain their relationships with the communities which surrounded them, both for managing their estates to maintain an income, and also to maintain their houses' interests in the fragile and constantly changing fabric of community relationships.

VI

The most visible manifestations of support given to religious women by outsiders were usually the lands and incomes with which they were endowed at foundation and after. Generally it was at foundation that the boundaries of the conventual estate were established in a form which, though subject to change over time, usually remained the core of the convent's estates and incomes. The greater the wealth of the convent at foundation, the greater its chances of surviving the ravages of time, shifting political allegiances, pestilence and the desertion of tenants. Foundation charters also give a good indication of the intentions of the original donors as well as their identity, rank and relationships to each other and to the personnel of the new convent. Records relating to foundation have not survived for many of the convents in medieval Ireland; some were founded long before the increased use of charters to document land grants in the twelfth century, and the charters of others have been lost. There is, however, quite good evidence relating to the foundation of some convents.[31] The nuns desiring to form themselves into a recognised monastic institution in the city of Cork in the last years of the thirteenth century had apparently gathered around a recluse, Agnes de Hareford. This indicates a rather informal arrangement which was common in the later medieval period when women wishing to live a religious life would become inspired by one charismatic person, often a recluse or anchorite, and would then form themselves into a community. At some point they often either sought official recognition or were pushed into doing so by church officials who believed that women in particular needed the security and the discipline of one of the recognised monastic rules and the official guidance of a bishop or neighbouring abbot. The official notices of Agnes de Hareford's proposed foundation of the convent of St John the Baptist were obviously the end result of a period of negotiation with the local land holders for donations of land and income to support the new convent. It is probable that the nuns had already been living together in community for some time before 1297 when the first inquiry was ordered into the grants of land for the convent in preparation for the necessary license from the crown. In this inquiry and the next in 1301, which mentions a slightly different list of donors, the nuns were to be granted land and incomes of churches mainly from the important Barry family of Cork. It is not possible to discern whether Agnes and her nuns successfully applied to the Barry family for donations or the driving force behind the foundation was the Barry family. Either way, the women were established in their convent with grants of land and income. In return for the donations the nuns would have been expected to provide services for the donors and also for the surrounding communities. Some of these services are acknowledged in the crown license to donate land, where the need for the convent is stressed, because:

> in the four neighbouring counties and five adjacent bishoprics there is no house for women religious save the said house of St John [and] it would be much to the convenience and utility of the country if the house should be founded for nuns, for there is no other house of nuns where knights and other free men in those parts may have their daughters brought up or maintained.[32]

This indicates that a nunnery was a valued asset to these 'knights and free men' in the education of their daughters and also as a place where those women with a vocation, or who could not find a husband, could be suitably housed. The evidence for convents in Ireland being involved in the education of children who were not bound for the cloister is mostly late but is worth noting nevertheless. Grace Dieu, a wealthy convent in Co. Dublin, was included in a list of six monasteries whose survival was requested from Thomas Cromwell at the dissolution on the grounds that these houses had value for the education of men, women and children within the English colony.[33] Killone, the Augustinian convent in Co. Clare under the patronage of the Uí Bhriain, may have combined charitable deeds with education as it was given a backhanded recommendation for its previous services after its dissolution:

> Whereas the abbey of Kyloyn in time past when it was possessed by a nun or an abbess was kept up indifferent well as a parish church and the revenues therof [sic] (which was great) converted for the most part to whoredom, gluttony and other kinds of excess and dissolute living, yet some relief was had there for the poor, feeding and clothing the needy, naked, hungry and impotent ...[34]

These sorts of community services were common to nunneries in most parts of Europe and, though the evidence is sketchy, there is no real reason to suppose that the convents in Ireland did not also use some of their endowments to provide charitable relief for the surrounding communities.

Although it is certain that the Priory of the Holy Trinity at Lismullin, Co. Meath, received donations from surrounding lay communities throughout its history, the foundation charters speak only of donations from ecclesiastical sources. By 1242 the site itself in the barony of Skreen, Co. Meath had been given to Avicia de la Corner by her brother, Richard, Bishop of Meath and she then donated it to the newly established priory of the Holy Trinity at Lismullin. Richard de la Corner also donated other lands in Counties Meath and Dublin, which formed the nucleus of the priory's holdings. The mechanism by which Richard acquired some of these lands was complex and involved considerable negotiation with other monastic houses. The collaboration of Richard de la Corner and his widowed sister, Avicia, in founding the convent of Lismullin shows the essential ingredients of co-operation needed to establish adequately the material base on which a convent of women could live. Family networks were vital to Avicia and Richard in their foundation and appear to have worked along lines which were common in other lay women and men's donations to prominent monasteries in twelfth and thirteenth-century Anglo-Norman Ireland. It is possible that Richard de la Corner was particularly keen to increase his episcopal control over the land in Skreen, the tithes and rectories of which had been granted some time previously by Adam de Feypo to St Mary's Abbey in Dublin. Although Richard tried to restore his bishopric's claim on the spiritualities of Skreen, he was ultimately unsuccessful.[35] In the case of the new priory of Lismullin it appears that compensation of some sort was arranged for lost tithes and revenues to the Abbey of St Mary's when Lismullin was established. A papal indult was obtained which exempted the nuns of Lismullin from:

> setting aside any portion of the offerings made to their church when the founders have shown to the diocesan a fair exchange for the mother church, which the abbot and convent of St Mary's Dublin hold to their uses.[36]

Such negotiations over land and tithes were necessary to find a place within the ecclesiastic framework for the new priory, which was established so much later than most of the other Anglo-Norman religious houses.

Although it is clear that the nuns of Lismullin employed bailiffs, stewards and attorneys to manage their estates and to represent them in court, it is most probable that supervision from the prioress of the extensive land-holdings with which the convent had been founded was necessary and expected. The prioress of Lismullin and the abbesses and prioresses of other convents in Ireland, were all, as far as can be determined, from wealthy families of the aristocracy or the gentry of the surrounding communities. Women of this class in England and Ireland were expected to be adept at managing estates either regularly or in the absence of their husbands and fathers.[37] Like other medieval land holders, the nuns and their employees had to keep a watchful eye on their investments and donations to ensure that their interests were maintained. The physical boundaries of estate property set up by the pious donations of the laity were liable to be broken if the nuns were not vigilant in defending their rights. In 1300, Brother Walter Truet and Richard de Hale, representing Avicia de Howth, prioress of Lismullin, brought a case against Richard de Kerdyf and John Herre over the non-payment of forty shillings rent in land in Balymacdrought. In the calendared version of the jurors' report, it appears that the rent had been donated to Lismullin by one William de Lanne in the time of the previous prioress, Auda. However, William quarrelled with the prioress when she refused to provide hospitality to a hunter of William's and so he refused to honour his commitment to continue to have the rent paid. Although a settlement was reached through the mediation of a friend or kinswoman of Auda's for a while, the rent was not paid for two years before Auda's death. William de Lanne was killed on the same day as his heir, another William, and the younger William's heirs were in the wardship of various local lords, during which time it appears that rent was not paid. Finally the heir of the younger William, Thomas de Lanne, recovered his right to the land and sold it to the defendant, Richard de Kerdyf. Avicia de Howth lost this case because she had not been in possession of the rent when she took over the position of prioress and eight years had elapsed since the rent had been paid.[38]

Here the original donation was based on the personal preference of the elder William de Lanne in supporting the convent, and when his interest waned, although efforts to maintain his obligations were made by the nuns and their supporters, the donation was rescinded. The deaths of everyone involved in the original transaction meant that there were no longer the personal ties and connections which had encouraged and sustained the donation. This episode clearly illustrates the dilemmas which faced the nuns in maintaining their vital connections with the local communities. Donations to particular religious institutions were often based on the personal ties which were built up between nuns and local community members, and so were vulnerable to ruptures in those relationships by death or discord. Although the record does not completely elucidate the source of the dis-agreement between Auda and William, it appears that the refusal to grant hospitality to William's hunter and dogs was integral to his decision to withhold the rent. Whether this refusal of hospitality stemmed from a desire by Auda not to break enclosure and admit a lay man within the boundaries of the convent is not clear. Indeed, it is possible the hunter sought hospitality on one of the estates of Lismullin and not within the convent walls. However, the refusal of Auda to give hospitality to the hunter indicates that, in the view of William, the delicate balance of support and obligation was broken and he did not need to continue his part of the agreement.

The web of lay familial support which was used so extensively by convents, both for the survival of the house and to further the interests of individual nuns, is demonstrated most dramatically by some of the events of the dissolution of the monasteries in 1540. There has long been a tradition that the convent of Grace Dieu, north of Dublin, survived in a depleted form after the dissolution with the active help of local Catholic families.[39] This evidence is not totally conclusive as there are other possibilities as to how this tradition started. It may have been simply through a misinterpretation of the records which continued to record lands of dissolved monasteries as being formerly owned by monastics until at least the early seventeenth century. However, a small group of women, perhaps only the prioress and one or two others, living together on one of their old estates under the protection of the new owners, was not an unusual way for ex-nuns to live out their days in England.[40] In this way the nuns of Grace Dieu may have successfully escaped detection because they were not official members of the convent. Either way the support of the local families, who may have been the families of origin or related in some way to the surviving nuns, was obviously essential.

The last prioress of Lismullin, Mary Cusack, received such a large pension – £16 per annum – when Lismullin was dissolved that historians have suggested that she may have been complicit in arranging matters so that her brother, Sir Thomas Cusack, one of the suppression commissioners, received favourable access to the property.[41] Certainly the pension was the largest paid to any Irish religious woman at the dissolution and Sir Thomas, later Lord Chancellor of Ireland, acquired the property of the priory of Lismullin and established his principal seat there.[42] Mary was probably quite young when she was made prioress, as she was still alive in 1570.[43] She seemed to have had trouble getting her brother to pay the pension from the designated estates, however, because in 1567 he acknowledged that he owed her over £32, and just before his death in 1570, he owed her £72, some of which may have been a loan.[44]

Concern for the enforcement of enclosure of nuns within the safety of their convent walls was a concept which recurs with suspicious regularity in the records of ecclesiastical authorities in medieval Europe. The nuns were expected to become as if dead to the outside world, immune from the concerns of their families, the lay communities in which they had previously lived and those lay communities which surrounded their convents. No doubt in many individual cases this is what the women themselves wanted in order to pursue lives of devotion and piety. But in medieval Ireland, there is considerable evidence that many religious women expected and were expected to maintain an interest in the world outside the boundaries of the convent walls. In fact, the boundaries between lay and religious communities were permeable to an extent which obviously distressed reformers. This is not to suggest that this permeability was necessarily indicative of moral laxity, but rather that the nuns, and especially their often hard-headed prioresses and abbesses, were aware of the importance of maintaining good relations with the communities which surrounded them, to ensure a flow of material and political support in return for the services which the nuns could offer. These services were the prayers and devotions of the women, of which unfortunately little evidence survives, and also their participation in the rudimentary social services which all monastic houses were expected to offer to the local communities. In some ways then the crossing points on the boundaries between lay and religious women's communities were as important as the boundaries themselves. Although in order to foster a sense of corporate and spiritual identity the nuns were differentiated from the laity by their dress, mode of life and adherence to specified rules, and lived within the boundaries formed by their physical separation, they were also expected to participate as required in the lay world, principally as land owners and family members. It is most likely that this was not usually seen as a contradiction, except to those churchmen intent on reform based on the letter of the rules rather than on practicalities. With the distance of time, we can see the contradictions more clearly, but we must not also be blind to the evidence of the individual contexts, which indicate that religious women in medieval Ireland were usually adept at managing their affairs and relationships with their supporters in many different circumstances. Most were successful in maintaining the boundaries around their convents sufficiently to ensure that there was space for women to live quietly, devoted to prayer, in communities which endured for hundreds of years.

'Mothers in Israel':
Women, Family and Community in Early Irish Methodism

ROSEMARY RAUGHTER

I

For John Wesley, as for many of the Protestant reformers who preceded him, the holy household was the essential basis for the safeguarding of piety and order within society.[1] Within it, the husband, as natural head of the family, had responsibility for the moral and spiritual welfare of all those in his charge: firstly for his wife, then for his children and servants, for, as Wesley reminded him, 'everyone under your roof that has a soul to be saved is under your care'.[2] Only by the strict observance of religion within the household and, implicitly, by the proper ordering of all its members, could harmony and holiness prevail. Therefore, Wesley advised:

> Let you, your yoke-fellow, your children, and your servants, be all on the Lord's side; sweetly drawing together in one yoke, walking in all his commandments and ordinances, till every one of you shall receive his own reward, according to his own labour![3]

Yet, as Wesley was well aware, the ideal of the godly and harmonious household was not always attainable. The experience of conversion and the intense commitment which Methodism demanded of its adherents could also have a seriously divisive effect, upsetting the structures of authority within the family and setting the believer at odds with kin and community. For women, whose lives were contained much more completely than men's within the limits of such relationships, the correlation between family, community and faith was surely stronger and the implications of any disruption correspondingly more traumatic. Yet it has also been suggested that women may have been attracted to Methodism precisely because it provided some possibility of escape from the obligations and expectations imposed on them by family and society.[4] This essay discusses women's attachment to Methodism during the first stage of its development in Ireland (1747–1800) and the impact which this attachment could have on existing ties of kin and community. It will examine the use which women made of such links in the furtherance of their faith and the effect which a newly-assumed and strongly-held religious conviction could have on relations between the individual and those with whom she came into closest contact. Finally, it will consider the view that in some cases conversion could represent an act of independence, an opportunity to defer or even to reject the options of marriage and motherhood in favour of the alternative offered by membership of the Methodist 'household of faith'.

In 1747 Ireland became one of the main areas of early Methodist missionary endeavour when John Wesley made the first of his twenty-one visits to the country. He was followed a few weeks later by his brother, Charles, who on 11 October recorded the conversion of a widow, Mrs M, 'a true mourner in Zion, till the Lord on Wednesday put the new song in her mouth. She set us all on fire with the warmth of her first love'.[5] As one of Methodism's first Irish converts, Mrs M typified the energetically positive reaction on the part of women, in Ireland and elsewhere, to its call to repentance, rebirth and evangelism. Methodism has been described as 'a woman's faith', and the specific nature of its appeal to women has been the subject of much speculation by historians.[6] It has been suggested that the more emotionally-charged and 'hysterical' aspects of some separatist Protestant sects were especially congenial to women.[7] However, the latitude which early Methodism permitted to the individual believer may provide a more tangible reason for its success. Lacking its own clergy and places of worship, the movement relied on the initiative, zeal and generosity of its adherents, both male and female. This dependence was reflected in its organisational structures, within which the laity enjoyed a greater influence than was allowed by any of the mainstream Christian denominations. The content of Wesley's message holds a further clue to the movement's advance. As Hufton has pointed out, Methodism equipped women with a realistic recipe for survival in an imperfect world.[8] The moral values which it promoted – such as industry, cleanliness, thrift and self-control – were qualities which, while far from heroic, nevertheless enhanced a girl's chances of making an advantageous marriage and enabled her, as a wife and mother, to advance both the moral and material welfare of her family. In addition, of course, women were influenced by the same factors which drew men to Methodism, among which have been cited Wesley's claims of 'special providences', providing assurance of protection in a hostile environment, and the shifting social, economic and political patterns of the period, in the face of which Methodism offered a sense of certainty and solidarity, as well as the assurance of ultimate victory.[9]

While the reasons for women's attraction may have been complex, the importance of their contribution to the development of Methodism is clear. Female support has been noted in virtually all studies on the topic as an important, and arguably a vital, element in the movement's growth. It has been stated that women were certainly in a majority, and 'perhaps a substantial majority' in early Methodism, and this contention is supported by surviving membership figures for societies in both Britain and America.[10] In relation to the Irish movement, research has confirmed the very significant part played by women in its expansion and consolidation during the second half of the eighteenth century.[11]

Contemporaries themselves quickly became aware of the appeal which the new revivalism held for women. For hostile observers, who accused itinerant preachers of taking advantage of the suggestibility and susceptibilities of 'silly women', the strong female support base was a cause of suspicion and tended to bring the movement into disrepute.[12] For those sympathetic to the movement, on the other hand, it was evidence of divine approval and a reason for thanksgiving. When Mrs Agnes Smyth, herself a recent convert, reported in about 1776 on the progress of the movement in her own area of Co. Down, she specifically noted the dynamic response given to it by members of her own sex. She wrote:

> I can give you but a small notion … How the Word of the Lord runs and is glorified. All around, young and old, flock to the standard of Jesus, as the doves to their windows. I think the class in this town [Strangford] consists of thirty six, almost all alive to God; and particularly some girls, who seem resolved to take the kingdom of heaven by violence.[13]

Conviction of such intensity found expression not only in praise for individual salvation but also in the imperative to bring others to an awareness of the overwhelming urgency and importance of 'the Word', the call to repentance and to reliance on God's grace, which was at the heart of the Methodist message. The initial focus of most women's missionary zeal was their own family and household and here mothers undoubtedly enjoyed a certain advantage, given their educative role and the authority which they were generally accorded on matters of religion and morality within the home. Many married women, having been converted, sought to persuade their children, their husbands and other family members to follow their example and in doing so acted as the spearhead of further Methodist advance. Thus, among many similar instances recorded by Crookshank, one woman was joined in the society by seven and another by nine daughters.[14] In Coleraine,

Mrs Clarke, impressed by a visiting Methodist preacher, induced her husband and her son, Adam, to attend and Mrs Henrietta Gayer of Lisburn, having become interested in the movement, brought her thirteen-year-old daughter with her to a meeting, where both were converted.[15] Shortly afterwards, her husband, who had previously had a 'strong feeling' against the society, was also won over and the Gayer household subsequently became a centre of Methodism in the area.[16]

Mr Gayer was not alone in his prejudice. Men of all social classes are frequently described as being initially hostile to the Methodist movement and taking action against their wives' and female relatives' participation in it. When Agnes Smyth, for example, wished to attend a service, her husband, a clergyman, 'did not wish it and her father forbade it, at the peril of forfeiting his favour'. Her sister-in-law, who converted during a visit to London, also encountered opposition from her husband and from friends.[17] Many of those who objected to Methodism emphasised its identification with the lower orders of society, despite the fact that Wesley's message was directed less towards the poor in Ireland than in England.[18] Agnes Smyth herself 'resented the association with a despised people' and feared that 'I shall be for ever called a "Swaddler"' if she attended one of their meetings.[19] Middle-class men certainly regarded Methodism as drawing their womenfolk into inappropriate company and surroundings. When Mary Smyth expressed her determination to hear a particular preacher:

> it was urged that he was a Methodist – an enthusiast – one whom it was improper for her to hear; and that to procure admittance to a place so crowded was utterly impracticable.[20]

Another woman's wish to hear John Wesley preach was opposed by her husband, who 'was unwilling that she should be identified with a sect which he considered disreputable'.[21]

The willingness of women to defy such directives is indicative of the extent to which religious feeling could justify independent action. In this one sphere of life, women could claim a degree of autonomy – indeed, for those convinced of the righteousness of their cause, there was no option but to do so, even at the risk of breaching family unity. In fact, in many of the recorded case histories, an initially suspicious or antagonistic husband was finally won over to Methodism by his wife's urgings and example.[22] However, while the moral authority conventionally allotted to the wife and mother was undoubtedly of use in securing conversions, young and unmarried women could also bring considerable influence to bear within the family circle. Thus, when the twenty-two-year-old Mary Teare was converted, her mother was initially alarmed that her 'connection with the poor and despised Methodists should prove injurious to her character ... and reputation'. In time, however, both Mrs Teare and her husband joined the society.[23] At Enniskillen, the entire Armstrong family was converted to Methodism by the influence of one of the daughters, and at Florencecourt a Miss Shanklin, a spinster living with her sister and brother-in-law:

> Exercised a considerable influence in her family circle. The preacher was invited to their house, where he and his successors ever after had a hospitable welcome, the family received much spiritual good: and their sober industrious habits secured the esteem of their neighbours.[24]

This household, like many of those already mentioned in which women took a prominent role, became a focus for Methodism in the neighbourhood. These domestic centres were a vital element in the expansion and consolidation of the Methodist movement both locally and nationally, providing lodging and hospitality for itinerant preachers and a meeting-place for the local congregation. Godly women, therefore, having created a secure base for Methodism within their own household, extended their influence into the community, in effect fulfilling a quasi-maternal role within the local congregation, or 'household of faith'. Thus, Alice Johnson, having been the first person to bring a Methodist preacher to Derryanvil, was popularly known in the neighbourhood as 'Mother Ailse'.[25] Others who earned the title of 'mothers of Methodism' or 'mothers in Israel' included Mrs Margaret McGee, one of the earliest members of the society in Limavady and Mrs Alice Dawes, a widow, who prepared a room in her house at Belturbet for the use of itinerant preachers and became 'the principal support of Methodism in the area'.[26] The routine, but vital, role performed by such women in their local congregations is summarised by Crookshank in his account of the work of Mrs Frizzell of Dungannon:

> In her own limited and humble sphere, [she] engaged in work for her Master. She met a class for many years … Her wisdom and piety drew many around her for spiritual counsel … She was also especially endeared to the young, whom, as the lambs of the flock, she carried to God in earnest, believing prayer; and many of them grew up to maturity, filled important positions in the Church and gratefully embalmed her memory in their hearts.[27]

As described by Crookshank, writing at a time when institutionalisation had long since had the effect of reimposing male domination within the church, the female contribution was primarily one of service and of inspiration within the family and community. However, the weak organisational structures of early Methodism, together with the exigencies of a missionary movement, also allowed women to assume a more active and interventionist role in the management of their local congregation. Mrs Eliza Bennis, for instance, took a leading part in the affairs of the society both in her native Limerick and in Waterford, where her energy and assertiveness combined with her zeal to make her a formidable proponent of Methodism. She frequently travelled between the two centres, established classes and bands, corresponded with Wesley and with other ministers and represented the feelings of the local faithful to the Methodist leadership. For example, her request to the Methodist Conference in 1769 on the allocation of a particular minister to Limerick is noted as 'the earliest instance on record of the voice of the people being heard in connection with a preaching appointment'.[28] Like other notable women activists, Bennis justified her 'presumptuous' behaviour by citing her ardour for the faith, and Wesley for his part clearly relied on her judgement and abilities.[29] He entrusted her with the settlement of internal disputes, accepted her advice on matters of organisation and discipline and approved her numerous interventions in the affairs of local congregations. He encouraged her:

> Be not idle ... neither give way to voluntary humility. You were not sent to Waterford for nothing; but to 'strengthen the things that remain'.[30]

The same argument, that female and male believers were acting not of their own will, but as the instruments of a higher providence, was advanced to justify women's preaching. This was the most dramatic means by which female influence was extended beyond the home and into the local and, ultimately, the wider community. Thus Alice Cambridge, following her own conversion, began her missionary career among her friends and neighbours by private urging and encouragement and by inviting them to the preaching house. Later she established meetings at a number of other centres, attracting criticism from 'Christian friends', including a number of male preachers, who declared 'her public addresses ... to be irregularities ... according to their notions of Christian discipline'.[31] Again, it was Wesley, with his over-riding concern for the salvation of souls, who sanctioned this departure from established patterns of female behaviour. Consulted by Cambridge, he advised her to exercise discretion and to 'avoid the first appearance of pride and magnifying yourself', but defended her right to preach. Conscience, he told her, 'will not permit you to be silent when God commands you to speak'.[32]

II

The sense of purpose and commitment which Methodism demanded of its followers, while it was not always so radically or publicly expressed, must have been a potent factor in the creed's attraction for older, unmarried and widowed women who played such a prominent role in its establishment. Mrs

Theodosia Blachford, for instance, saw her widowhood as an opportunity to turn her mind to religion and indeed to follow her own inclinations with respect to spiritual matters. She wrote:

> When death separated me from my poor husband ... my hopes were animated that I would now indeed devote myself to God ... In this state of mind I fell in with the Methodists.[33]

Mrs Blachford channelled her zeal and energy into a variety of philanthropic initiatives, among them a House of Refuge for unemployed and homeless young women which she established in Dublin in 1802. Her cousin, Lady Sophia Ward, who was involved in various benevolent, reforming and missionary causes both in Ireland and in England, was another of a growing number of women who found in good works, undertaken in co-operation with like-minded members of their own sex, a means of exercising their religious and moral concerns, and a role beyond the confines of family and community.[34]

While the majority of women members, reflecting the character of Irish Methodism in general, belonged to the middle ranks of urban or rural society, a small but influential minority came from aristocratic and gentry backgrounds. Both Blachford and Ward belonged to this category, as did Henrietta Gayer and Mary and Agnes Smyth.[35] Such women were in a position to offer financial as well as moral support and could serve as powerful agents for the promotion of Methodism within their local area and beyond. Henrietta Gayer, for instance, funded the building of a chapel at Lisburn, which in turn allowed for a significant growth in Methodist numbers in the town and neighbourhood.[36] John Wesley, during his final visit to Ireland in 1789, preached at Rosanna, the home of Mrs Sarah Tighe, Mrs Blachford's sister-in-law, to 'about one hundred of the most influential persons in the neighbourhood'.[37]

These aristocratic adherents could perform a further vital service by winning friends for the movement at the higher levels of society: as Crookshank remarked of Mary Smyth and her husband, 'occupying a high social position ... and ... being the centre of a large and influential circle of friends, they diffused through it a powerful influence for good'.[38] Mrs Blachford, described by Wesley as 'one of our jewels', also proved herself a powerful exponent of Methodism within her own circle, which included families such as the Tighes, the Hamiltons, the Jocelyns, the Howards and the Wingfields.[39] Few of these friends committed themselves formally to the society but, as an influential group within the Church of Ireland, they gave impetus to the evangelical movement of the next century. Another woman whose conversion had both immediate and long-term benefits was Mrs Knox, the wife of a leading member of Derry Corporation and a stalwart of

Methodism in the city for many years. Her services to the society were perpetuated by her son, Alexander Knox, who, though not himself a member, was sympathetic to the movement, defending it in print against its critics and, as private secretary to the chief secretary, securing protection for the itinerant Methodist preachers at the time of the 1798 rebellion.[40]

Within the community, however, women's influence appears to have been most effective among members of their own sex. Although this can be most clearly traced at the upper end of society, it seems to have prevailed at every level and, indeed, across class barriers. Thus, Henrietta Gayer was invited by baker's wife, Jane Cumberland, to attend a service at her house and later persuaded her niece, Agnes Smyth, to accompany her to another of Mrs Cumberland's meetings.[41] Agnes Smyth, in her turn, was credited with having a decisive influence upon several of her own acquaintances, including Mrs Blachford, Lady Mary Fitzgerald and Lady Sophia Ward. Beyond these contacts with members of her own class, Smyth took a particular interest in the female members of her local congregation and, with her husband, encouraged the blind Margaret Davidson to embark on her preaching career.[42]

Within Methodism, the sex segregation of band meetings facilitated close links between the 'sisterhood' of believers and many women in their personal accounts of conversion and of their religious lives emphasise the importance of such groups, both in the recruitment of new members and in providing mutual support and fellowship. Thus, the young Alice Cambridge was introduced to Methodism by some women friends who were already members of the society in Bandon. Her *Memoir* records the part which they played in her conversion and the value which she placed on their companionship and support:

> I was meeting in band with Miss Strickett, my cousin Mary Norris, and I think Mrs Magee ... It was on a Saturday evening, on the gallery in the old preaching house in Bandon ... Mrs Strickett was telling her experience of the gracious dealings of God towards her, and while she was thus delightfully speaking good of His name, He lifted upon me the light of his countenance; my mourning was turned into joy; I felt a change, which until that glad moment I had been a stranger to, and I rejoiced with joy unspeakable and full of glory. My dear friends rejoiced with me, and my loved Mrs Strickett sang the following verses coming down from the gallery where we met, and where my God had so peculiarly blessed me ...[43]

Shared experience and a sense of solidarity based on a common religious conviction could, and in many cases clearly did, serve to cement marital, familial and communal bonds. Thus, couples such as Jane and Hans Cumberland, Henrietta and Edward Gayer and Dorothea and John Johnson worked together over many years for the advancement of their shared faith. When the latter was appointed to take charge of the Methodist community at Lisburn in 1784, his new wife, Dorothea, took an equal part in his mission, having special responsibility for the female members of the congregation. John Wesley, visiting Lisburn in the following year, noted that the liveliness of the local society was 'owing chiefly to the good providence of God in bringing sister Johnson here'.[44]

Dorothea's personal commitment, as expressed in her journal and correspondence, was more than strong enough to counter any difficulties which she might have to face in a novel and challenging situation. Moreover, the Johnsons were a mature couple, free of the responsibility and expense of a young family.[45] Other preachers' wives, however, had to contend with considerable hardship, including the prolonged absence of their husbands on circuit,[46] inadequate lodgings and poverty, with many congregations being unable or unwilling to offer their married ministers sufficient financial support.[47] In such cases, wives might be required to supplement the family income. Thus, Mrs Bennis reported in 1771 from Limerick that Brother Hern's wife:

> finding the affairs of the Society much embarrassed, refused the usual subsistence and supported herself and children by working at her trade while here, though she had a young child at the breast.[48]

Conversion itself could in some cases also demand sacrifice. Thus, for instance, when Agnes Smyth's husband was deprived of his curacy at Ballyculter, Co. Down because of his Methodistical views, his wife gladly supported him and when the couple lost their house and had to move into a small thatched cabin, 'she entered heartily into the duties of her new position, rising early and late, taking little rest, and denying herself all but the mere necessaries of life'.[49]

The adoption of a new creed, therefore, could have the effect of adding a new and meaningful tie to those which already existed between the individual, her partner and family. In other cases, however, conversion proved to be a deeply disruptive influence, entailing the severing of links with the believer's former life, creating a sense of exclusivity and apartness based on supposed moral superiority, precipitating dissension and even violence. Reacting sharply to what they regarded as a flouting of approved authority, families and communities responded with varying degrees of force to the individual's assertion of spiritual autonomy and to the threat which it apparently posed to the integrity of the unit as a whole. Thus, when Anne

Devlin joined the society, her Catholic family at first brought in the local priest to reason with her and when argument proved unsuccessful, tried to force her into marriage. This prompted Devlin to leave home.[50] The reaction of Protestant families and communities to the defection of members was on occasion no less draconian. At Clara, a magistrate who objected to his wife and daughter attending Methodist services, hired men to attack and beat up the preacher, drove his wife out of the house and sent his daughter to Dublin in the custody of her aunts.[51] Catherine Stuart of Co. Monaghan, a member of the Seceding Church of Scotland, underwent a series of trials following her conversion at the age of fifteen. Her mother punished her severely, prevented her from going to the Methodist meetings and confined her to the house. When she married eight years later, her husband attempted to prevent her attending services and became violent when she continued to do so. On one occasion he followed her to a prayer meeting and:

> As she came out of the house, seized her, dragged her to a river at some distance, and, with imprecations too terrible to record, declared he would drown her if she did not swear never more to meet with the Methodists.[52]

Evidence of the attraction which Methodism held for young people is apparent in these frequent references to the harassment of converts by parents and guardians. A particularly dramatic example of such persecution concerned some of the younger members of the Henderson family of Co. Fermanagh, whose parents, on learning of their conversion, locked them in their rooms, deprived them of food and beat them 'severely'. The Hendersons also gave vent to their feelings against those whom they perceived as undermining their parental authority by inciting an attack on members of the local Methodist congregation.[53]

This is one instance where a family dispute escalated into mob violence. In such cases women did not escape involvement. Indeed, there are some indications that female believers may have been singled out for ill-treatment during such incidents. Thus, during a severe outbreak of persecution in Cork in 1749–50, a number of women were assaulted and a mob attacked the house of a clothier, William Jewell and beat his wife. During the same disturbances, one woman was 'struck ... on the head, and stunned', and another 'was not only called the grossest names, but literally almost murdered'.[54] At Enniskillen some years later a young man:

> Became the ringleader of the persecutors of the Methodists, and cruelly maltreated all who came within his reach, not sparing even his aged mother, whom he dragged out of one of the meetings, beating all who dared to interfere with his brutality.

On another occasion, the same individual broke into a prayer meeting, 'struck many with a loaded whip, and severely beat Nancy Armstrong ... leaving the poor girl on the floor apparently dead'.[55]

A number of factors may have contributed to intensify animosity towards female believers. Firstly, as already noted, women were frequently the agents by which Methodism arrived and took root in a locality. As a result, women tended to attract blame for subsequent conversions. Thus, Nancy Armstrong's attacker 'accused her of making his sister a Methodist'.[56] Even for those who nursed no personal grievance against the Methodist movement, mob action could provide an opportunity for sexual assault on women.[57] Attacks on female believers could also serve as a potent form of psychological humiliation directed not only at the victim herself, but at her male relatives or colleagues, who had shown themselves to be incapable of protecting her. Moreover, the novelty of many Methodist practices of religion and the privacy of the class and band meetings, tended to promote suspicions of nefarious and even lewd behaviour. Given such beliefs, female believers could be regarded as analogous to the 'fallen' woman and subject to the same community sanctions. Finally, the perception that Methodism was subversive of family and communal life has been noted as a major factor in mob attacks on its preachers and adherents.[58] The freedom which it apparently allowed to its women members certainly contributed to that belief, while in cases of conflict between parents and children, the rebellion – albeit on spiritual grounds – of young women may have been regarded as more radical and more culpable than that of their brothers, who were traditionally allowed a certain latitude in adolescence and early manhood.

However, despite the tendency of many Methodist victims to obey the biblical injunction to 'turn the other cheek' and to depend for redress and deliverance on the workings of divine providence, spiritually militant women could also be assertive in their own defence. Thus, when a hostile mob attacked a preacher in Bandon, the congregation, consisting of 'chiefly old women', resisted and drove it off.[59] In other cases, the social standing of a female supporter combined with her sex to intimidate opponents. When riots broke out at an open-air meeting in Dublin and an attacker attempted to pull the preacher down from the chair on which he was standing, it 'was held fast by Mrs Moore and a young lady, probably Miss Acton, whom the rascal dare not touch, or he would have had the whole crowd on him'.[60] As a member of a prominent Co. Wicklow gentry family, Miss Acton could undoubtedly command greater deference than her more humbly-born sisters. Her background and the wealth which she devoted to religious and charitable causes made her a particularly prized recruit to the movement. This incident is a reminder that the value of such converts lay not just in the financial benefits or status which they might bestow, but also in the protection which their presence provided to preachers and congregations threatened with violent attack.

III

If conversion could have the effect of arousing antagonism against the believer, it could also, however, imply a rejection on the part of the individual herself of her place within the family and community and of the conventional female destiny of marriage, motherhood and domesticity. In some cases this was entirely overt and indeed could be justified both by Wesley's view (which was implicitly denied by the great majority of Methodists) that the single life was preferable for believers and by the discouragement by the leadership of marriage between members of the faithful and 'unawakened persons'.[61] Thus, Alice Cambridge, following her conversion, broke off her engagement to a young man, 'having no other fault to find that I recollect, but that his mind did not bend heavenward; that indeed was enough'.[62] Dorothea King, a widow, refused an offer of marriage on similar grounds. She wrote:

> This day ... Have I been delivered from a strong temptation, to marry a person, for no other reason, but that *he* and the enemy persuaded me if I did *not*, it would prove *his* death; but God interposed, and sent a friend whose reasoning broke the snare, that might have proved my ruin.[63]

In the event, Dorothea's rejection of marriage was not permanent as some years later, she found in her second husband, John Johnson, a partner whose religious commitment matched her own and in whose work of ministry and evangelism she could fully participate. Nevertheless, her journal makes clear the absolute primacy of the spiritual over any earthly union. She recorded in the New Year of 1790:

> Since last I wrote ... All is sunshine from him that makes my day. The first of this year, I renewed my covenant with many others in the preaching house ... Once more I gave myself unreservedly to him, in marriage covenant, humbly depending on his Almighty arm for assistance to fulfil my solemn vow.[64]

Alice Cambridge, on the other hand, remained single and indeed it is difficult to see how marriage and family life could have fitted into the strenuous schedule of travel and preaching which she maintained over many years.[65] For those who were already married at the time of their conversion, Method-ism, with its emphasis on spiritual equality and on the priority of the individual's relations with her saviour inevitably entailed a reassessment of the value of earthly ties and affections. For some believers this apparently posed an actual barrier to salvation. Thus, Eliza Bennis, describing her progress towards a final commitment to her faith, wrote that:

> I saw that I did not love God with all my heart; my husband and children were idols set up in, and kept the place that God should have; neither could I by any means tear them thence, though I laboured hard to do it.[66]

Following prayer and reflection, however:

> The Lord did remove all my burden, and enlarged my heart, and admitted me to a closer communion with him than ever I had before. Then I said, I will now ask to have my idols taken out of my heart; but whilst I sought them, they were gone! taken away in a moment! and their place so filled with God, that there was no room for any thing beside.[67]

While it is unlikely that many women took such rhetoric to its logical conclusion, by deserting husband and children for their faith, it may well be the case, as Malmgreen has suggested, that for some at least 'religious commitment ... represented an act of independence, part of a prelude, or postlude, to marriage and family responsibilities'.[68] The prominent part played in the movement by widows and older women has already been noted, but it is clear that Methodism also held a strong appeal for adolescents and young adults, both male and female. Religious awakening therefore coincided with the period which for girls was chiefly marked by the formation of new emotional bonds, by the necessity to make decisions about marriage, by the death of a parent or parents and the breakup of the family home. Alice Cambridge, for instance, joined the society at nineteen, shortly after the death of her mother, to whom she had been deeply attached,[69] and Dorothea King's conversion at the age of twenty-five followed another emotional ordeal, in her case, the breakdown of her first marriage.[70]

For young women such as these, confused, hurt or disillusioned, religious commitment offered not simply a means of distancing themselves from family disputes and obligations but also an alternative community of faith, providing refuge and fellowship as well as a means of being active and useful. Anne Devlin, driven from home by the disapproval of her family, was eventually rescued by some members of the Methodist community, who 'received her as a sister and thus afforded her a holy and happy home'.[71] Similarly, Margaret Davidson, having left her unsympathetic family, was welcomed by a local congregation, before finding a permanent home with the Smyths.

Alice Cambridge, at the end of her preaching career, was taken in and cared for by some Methodist friends. Thus, the 'family' of Methodism could offer material as well as spiritual comfort to the believer who lacked – or chose to reject – the protection of the biological family.

Women, therefore, used their membership of the family of Methodism in order to extend the space available to them. Following their own conversion, they took upon themselves the duty of carrying the movement's message to all those with whom they came into contact. In doing so, they assumed a leadership role, not only within the household of which they were a part, but also in the local congregation and beyond, notably through public preaching and involvement in church administration. While this new allegiance had the potential to confirm and strengthen existing ties, it could also undermine them, leaving the believer bereft of the support structures traditionally provided by family and community. In such cases, however, the 'household of faith' offered a refuge and an alternative sphere of action.

However, the opportunities which Methodism offered to its female adherents were less radical than they appeared at the time to some enemies of the movement. Women, while they asserted their independence of belief and of action, did so in a spirit of service rather than of rebellion and were only permitted to do this in the interests of a pioneering missionary movement. With the institutionalisation of Methodism, these manifestations of autonomy, however limited, disappeared.[72] With them too, went any possibility that the revival was inimical to family life, or to the maintenance of the traditional balance of power between the sexes. Indeed, the 'household of faith' itself was from the beginning a patriarchal institution, mirroring the family in the allocation of roles to its male and female members. Wesley was the stern but loving father and women played a vital, respected but essentially supportive role. It was, however, a role which the women involved fully accepted. For the 'mothers in Israel' of early Methodism, the new Jerusalem was a purely spiritual entity and the temporary equality which they had enjoyed within the movement was not to be regarded as a criticism of their condition within the social or political arena. At the same time, the female response to Wesley's initial message suggests a profound dissatisfaction with existing structures in both religion and society and demonstrates a capacity on the part of women to grasp whatever opportunities were available to them in an ostensibly unfavourable environment.

Peeresses, Patronage and Power:
The Politics of Ladies Frances Anne, Theresa
and Edith Londonderry, 1800–1959[1]

DIANE URQUHART

I

In the nineteenth and early twentieth centuries aristocratic women's position in society essentially revolved around men. Marriage into a politically prominent family could facilitate a woman's entry into the political elite. Moreover, women who ventured into politics, which was arguably the most male defined of social landscapes, were largely dependent on their husband's position to give them access to power. However, once access to the political elite was attained, an individual woman's influence was effectively controlled by the strength of her own personal ambition and by her own abilities. This favourable combination of opportunity, ambition and ability was common to three female generations of the Londonderry family in the period 1800–1959, namely Frances Anne (1800–65), Theresa (1859–1919) and Edith (1878–1959). The Londonderrys are recognised by contemporaries and historians alike as one of the leading Tory families of the nineteenth and early twentieth centuries, being regularly listed amongst the fifteen wealthiest families in Britain and Ireland, with an estimated annual income of over £100,000 in the 1880s.[2] The Londonderry's landed holdings, which amounted to well over 50,000 acres in counties Durham, Down, Antrim and Donegal, were backed by extensive and profitable coalmining interests in Durham. As a result of these landed holdings, the family controlled several parliamentary seats in the early 1800s.[3] The family's immense wealth, therefore, was backed by a measure of political influence.

With this political and financial standing Frances Anne, Theresa and Edith Londonderry were well placed to exercise considerable influence. This influence was exercised in high society, where friends were cultivated for political means, where women were recognised as semi-official leaders and politics was discussed freely amongst politicians, their wives and their confidants. It was this social interaction which gave aristocratic women the opportunity to meet, entertain, correspond with and subsequently influence the politically powerful.[4] But how was this situation altered by the onslaught of democracy and the changing economic and political fortunes of the aristocracy? This study of the political activities of three female generations of the Londonderry family gives some indication of the changes which occurred.

II

Frances Anne, who was to become the third Marchioness of Londonderry, was the only child of Catherine Anne, Countess of Antrim and Sir Henry Vane Tempest, a Tory MP with extensive land and coalmining interests in Co. Durham. Frances Anne's upbringing was far from conventional. Of her parents she said 'they encouraged each others['] follies and rushed into every species of extravagance … Never was any child so harshly treated as I was by Father, Mother and Governess'.[5] Although some element of exaggeration was undoubtedly present in Frances Anne's recollections of her early life, few of her childhood memories were happy. The death of her father in 1813, when she was aged thirteen, made her one of the richest heiresses of the early nineteenth century. This was a position which she was all too well aware of, to cite her own words: 'I was mistress of all around me … an immense Heiress'.[6] Following her father's death, disputes between Frances Anne's joint guardians, her mother and her aunt, soon ensued. These disagreements were fuelled by Frances Anne's open rebellion to her mother and eventually resulted in her being made a ward of the Chancery Court.[7] At the age of fifteen, Frances Anne moved out of her mother's house and into rented accommodation in London with an allowance of £5,000 per year and a respectable widow and servants to care for her. This was an unorthodox move for any young woman in the early nineteenth century, but it was especially unusual for an upper-class heiress whose relations were anxious to protect the family's name and fortune.

Frances Anne's marriage was equally controversial. She first met Lord Charles Stewart, the British Ambassador to Austria and half-brother of the illustrious Foreign Secretary, Lord Castlereagh, in 1818. However, their first meeting, which occurred at Frances Anne's mother's house, was far from encouraging. When her mother, anxious to push this match, asked her daughter what she thought of Lord Stewart, Frances Anne replied 'not much … [he] looked as if he had false teeth'.[8] So much for first impressions as

Frances Anne soon found both him and his manner pleasing. Charles Stewart was twenty years her senior and a widower with one son, but the objections made by Frances Anne's guardian aunt stretched beyond this, being convinced that he was a fortune seeking philanderer with a family pedigree of mental instability. Financially Frances Anne's wealth easily outstripped that of Stewart, but he was far from impoverished – possessing an estimated annual income of £18,000. In addition to this, he was heir to the Londonderry estates with a fairly distinguished military career and ambassadorial and royal household appointments behind him.

A three month court case ensued as Frances Anne's aunt tried, without success, to prevent the marriage. The couple finally married in 1819 and aged nineteen Frances Anne was thrust into the diplomatic limelight, as the wife of the British Ambassador to Austria. She accompanied her husband to Vienna to host innumerable entertainments for Europe's royal and political elite. But she appears to have coped admirably with her new station. To give just one description of Frances Anne at this time, Martha Bradford, a vicar's wife stationed in Vienna, described her in the following terms:

> 'tis plain she is not free from caprice, and 'tis equally plain that she is a complete spoilt child with fine natural qualities and excellent abilities, and with a quickness of perception and a sense of the ridiculous which makes her at once entertaining to a degree and perhaps a little dangerous ...[9]

Like many other women of her class and position, Frances Anne harboured serious political aspirations for her husband and three sons, and consequently for herself. These aspirations also extended to the marriage matches of her three daughters as consideration was not only given to a suitor's financial and social standing, but also to the political capital which could be attained by marriage – essentially, aristocratic marriage was a way to improve or at least maintain a family's social standing. For instance, Frances Anne's eldest daughter married the seventh Duke of Marlborough and was mother to Lord Randolph Churchill and grandmother to Sir Winston. However, Frances Anne's ambition stretched beyond the confines of her immediate family into the echelons of society. Indeed, one of the reasons for this may be that her husband did not hold political office again following his resignation as British Ambassador to Austria in 1822.[10] From this date he remained in the House of Lords, where his parliamentary performance was often a source of derision, even amongst his party colleagues. To cite just one example, in 1832 the press noted that Lord Londonderry 'said a good thing the other day, which, if only on account of its rarity deserves to be chronicled'.[11] Although Lord Londonderry wanted to be appointed as either Irish Lord Lieutenant or French Ambassador, he was appointed to neither as he effectively alienated much support by disagreeing with many Tory policies and by frequently threatening to go into opposition.

In spite of Lord Londonderry's dubious parliamentary abilities, both he and Frances Anne were ambitious and were determined to make their presence felt both on the social and the political scene, which at this time were inextricably linked. There can be little doubt that their purchase of Holdernesse House in London's Park Lane at a cost of £43,000 in 1821, with thousands of pounds being spent on its renovation, the purchase of Seaham Hall in Durham in the same year and the rebuilding and refurbishing of Frances Anne's family mansion, Wynyard in Co. Durham in 1826 at a cost of £200,000, were representative of the Londonderrys making a serious social statement.[12] The London property became the focal point for Frances Anne's extensive and lavish political entertainments which continued over the course of several decades. With the close of the London season in July of each year, the Londonderrys, along with the rest of the aristocracy, left London to go to their country estates. For the Londonderrys this usually entailed stays at the Wynyard or Seaham estates in Co. Durham, with occasional visits to Mount Stewart in Co. Down, or, from the late 1840s, to Garron Tower in Co. Antrim. So, political entertaining did not end with the close of the London season, rather the location moved from the metropolis to the country estates. Indeed, the Londonderry's invitation lists for country house parties provide a valuable insight into who was closest or held in most esteem by the family and reveal that their circle included the royals, numerous visiting European notables with whom they had become acquainted in Vienna and leading politicians such as Peel, Wellington and Disraeli. And it was Frances Anne's relationship with the latter which extended her influence beyond that of her immediate family.

Frances Anne became one of several female confidantes of Benjamin Disraeli, the Tory statesman whose dependence on women was notorious. As Disraeli himself said: 'There is nothing like female friendship – the only thing worth having'.[13] Throughout his life he was never without female correspondents, who ranged from his sister to various aristocratic women, of whom Frances Anne was one. But the timing of Frances Anne and Disraeli's meeting in 1835 is crucial in understanding just how influential she was in his career. It is well documented that Disraeli was something of a wildcard by the standards demanded of politicians in the mid-nineteenth century.[14] Frances Anne, always aware of the sway of title and wealth, was intrigued by the reputation which Disraeli was establishing for himself. Although a relatively young man of thirty, he was not a complete unknown, having published three acclaimed novels and standing several times as an

MP, albeit unsuccessfully. Frances Anne's stepson, Frederick, was already acquainted with Disraeli through Lady Blessington's social circle and Frances Anne asked for an introduction. Their first meeting occurred at a fancy dress ball when Frances Anne was seemingly amused by Disraeli's wit and dandyism. Disraeli it seems was less impressed upon this first meeting, describing Frances Anne's Cleopatra costume as: 'literally embroidered with emeralds and diamonds from head to toe. It looked like armor [sic] and she like a rhinoceros ... I was with her a great deal'.[15] Disraeli was astute enough to realise the political potential of lionisation by one of the wealthiest and best connected Tory political hostesses of the time and he asked for permission to write to her. The impact of this acquaintance, which developed into patronage, quickly became apparent as Frances Anne introduced Disraeli to her most exclusive social set. This was of considerable significance to the young Disraeli. Indeed, it is hard to overestimate the importance of introductions within the strictly controlled confines of high society where admission to the private functions of the aristocracy were especially coveted. The introduction represented a form of social endorsement and patrons were responsible for those whom they introduced. Patronage was therefore something which was not hastily or ill-considered. Thus the speed of Disraeli's acceptance into the Londonderry's circle was all the more remarkable. Within weeks of his first meeting with Frances Anne he was invited to her public and private functions and was recording his intimacy with the Londonderrys in his correspondence. His recollections of one of the Londonderry's receptions is characteristic of many of his letters dating from the 1830s and the following extract highlights that attending such a prestigious event not only provided an opportunity for mixing with the socio-political elite, but also attracted publicity. As Disraeli wrote to his sister after attending a ball at Holdernesse House in London:

> Fanny [Frances Anne] was faithful and asked me, and I figure in the *Morning Post* accordingly. It was the finest thing of the season ... I think it was the kindest thing possible of Fanny asking me, and it was not to be expected in any way ...[16]

The sharing of information was one of the most important privileges of being in society.[17] It is therefore not surprising that Disraeli passed on all the latest political and social gossip to Frances Anne and that his letters to her were frequently punctuated with phrases such as '[I] write you a hurried line, as my news received this morning from the fountain head, may not be stale'.[18] So, in return for Frances Anne's patronage Disraeli kept her up to date with political developments, cabinet appointments and interparty wranglings, sometimes marking passages as confidential, or as Disraeli put it, 'under the rose', which meant that such information was only to be passed onto her husband.[19] Disraeli was also aware of the potency of using both flattery and humility when courting Frances Anne's friendship, stating, for instance, that he had nothing 'to offer worthy of your delicate ear, fed, I doubt not, by all the secret histories of the cabinets and saloons of Europe'.[20] He also regularly assured her of his devotion, claiming 'my greatest pleasure is to write to you'[21] and that he was so busy he would have to, 'forswear society, and shall certainly never pay another morning visit except to you'.[22] Their friendship was not, however, free of controversy as Disraeli had to defend his relationship with Frances Anne to his fiancée in 1838, stating quite categorically:

> I do not know what you mean by passing *so much* of my time with Lady Londonderry. I do not pass any more time with her than Lady anybody else.[23]

There was evidently an element of jealousy here which may explain why, after his marriage, the correspondence and contact between Disraeli and Frances Anne came to an abrupt end. Their association was, however, renewed at Disraeli's inclination in June 1845 when he sent Frances Anne a copy of his novel *Sybil*, in which he characterised her as the Marchioness of Deloraine, 'the only good woman the tories have'.[24] In an accompanying letter he stated his regret at losing touch:

> It often occasions me great unhappiness, that the personage to whose condescending kindness I am most indebted, and that, too, at a period in my life when it was doubly precious should be the only one to who ... it seems I never can have an opportunity of expressing my sense of her graciousness ... Yet life is not so long, and these feelings not so common, that I would willingly let them die ... I know from experience, that you have not only that great station, but that cultivated mind that prompts to sympathy[.][25]

Their friendship and correspondence was subsequently renewed and it seems that they grew closer during the 1840s. Frances Anne became Disraeli's only female confidante outside his family circle, and he described his visits to her as 'a pilgrimage of friendship'.[26] However, this friendship developed into a more reciprocal association, especially as Disraeli's political reputation grew. Not only was Disraeli a source of information, but having been elected MP for Maidstone in 1837, he also became Tory leader of the Commons and Chancellor of the Exchequer from 1854–61. Thus Disraeli was able to politically assist Frances Anne's step son Frederick, her sons, Adolphus and Henry and her son-in-law, John, Marquess of Blandford, later the seventh Duke of Marlborough.[27] It also seems that Frances Anne recommended people to Disraeli whom she felt were worthy of public appointment. But in addition to this, the benefits of Frances Anne's patronage became very apparent in 1850 when Disraeli opposed the Coal Mines Bill, less on a matter of principle and more on the basis of his friendship with the Londonderrys. They justi-fied their opposition to this legislation by claiming that this bill interfered with the rights of property in stipulating that mines would be routinely inspected by government officials. Although Disraeli was able only to delay the passage of this bill through the Commons, his actions underline the influ-ence which friendship could have on political decision making.[28] Disraeli, when the occasion demanded, would also communicate with the Tory party to add weight to Frances Anne's opinions or complaints. One of the clearest examples of this occurred late in 1861 when problems arose over Tory party candidature in Durham, where Frances Anne's sons, Henry and Adolphus, stood as MPs. Disraeli stepped into the fray, acting as a mediator and writing to the local Tory party to inform them that Frances Anne would withdraw her patronage if the Londonderry family interest was not respected. Disraeli also advised the notoriously headstrong Frances Anne that 'great tact and temper on ... [her] part were necessary. It is best to know nothing of all this ... He who gains time, gains everything'.[29] It is perhaps not surprising that this issue was subsequently settled in Frances Anne's favour.

Frances Anne was widowed in 1854, beginning what she referred to as 'a new and sad era'.[30] Although she continued to watch Disraeli's career closely and kept abreast of all the main political and Tory goings on, her main interest became business, taking over the running of the Londonderrys' extensive estates and coal mines. Her business acumen surprised even those who knew her well. Disraeli, for example, visiting her in 1861, remarked that she was:

> a remarkable woman ... surrounded by her collieries and her blast-furnaces and her railroads ... and four thousand pitmen under her control ... she has a regular office ... and here she transacts, with innumerable agents, immense business – and I remember her five-and-twenty years ago, a mere fine lady; nay, the finest in London! But one must find excitement if one has brains[.][31]

These business pursuits remained her main focus until her death in 1865. Frances Anne referred to her own life as a 'long brilliant existence'.[32] She certainly broke some social conventions with her active business involve-ments, delivering annual public addresses to both her tenants and her employees at a time when a woman addressing a public gathering was against convention. But her activities as a political hostess, patron and confidante aroused little contemporary comment, being seen, it seems, as part of an aristocratic woman's role. However, her early patronage of Disraeli was significant, accelerating his acceptance into high society and introducing him to those who could help fulfil his parliamentary ambitions. Frances Anne predicted that he would become Prime Minister, but she died before her prophesy was born out by reality in 1868 and again from 1874–80. Disraeli often referred to his gratitude for her patronage, especially in the latter years of his life. In 1874, several years after Frances Anne's death, he gave the Order of St Patrick to her son in recognition of the 'grande dame who was kind to me when I was a youth, though she was a tyrant in her way. But one remembers only the good in the departed'.[33]

It is clear from the life of Frances Anne Londonderry that personal acquaintance, correspondence and entertaining could be beneficial political tools in the mid 1800s. But after her death in 1865 the political profile of the Londonderrys waned. Frances Anne's step son Frederick, the fourth Marquess, was a Tory MP and, largely as a result of his family's Tory connections, he was appointed to several junior ministerial posts under Peel and Wellington. Frederick, however, suffered a complete mental breakdown and was eventually certified, thus removing him from the political running.[34] His half-brother, Henry, succeeded him as fifth Marquess, but it seems that he possessed few political ambitions, preferring instead to live on his wife's Welsh estate.[35] But it was not only the political fortunes of the Londonderrys which were undergoing change at this time. A series of Reform Acts altered the size and nature of the British electorate and the operation of politics, but did this undermine aristocratic women's political influence? It seems not as the career of Theresa, sixth Marchioness of Londonderry, effectively illustrates.

III

Theresa was the eldest daughter of the nineteenth Earl of Shrewsbury, a Conservative MP who was instrumental in arousing Theresa's interest in politics. She claimed that this interest began at the age of ten and that her father had taken her to hear all the best political speakers as a child.[36] Disraeli, upon meeting Theresa as a teenager, for instance, remarked on her ambition and in later life Theresa had to admit that 'he was not far wrong'.[37] Indeed, after her marriage to Charles, sixth Marquess of Londonderry in 1875, Theresa openly admitted that she was more ambitious for her husband than he was for himself. Like Frances Anne before her, Theresa was keen to promote her family politically, supporting her husband as a Unionist MP for Co. Down from 1878 until 1884 when he took his seat in the House of Lords and as Irish Lord Lieutenant from 1886–89.

The Conservative Party used social functions and personal association as party tactics for longer than the Liberal Party. This provided women like Theresa Londonderry with an opportunity to exert influence, glean information and rally support which was denied to their Liberal counterparts. From the late nineteenth century, for example, Holdernesse House, which was now known as Londonderry House, became not only the social hub of the Unionist party but also 'the centre and boiling-point of resistance to the Government's policy of Home Rule'.[38] Theresa was widely recognised as the leading Tory political hostess, a position from which she appears to have derived great pleasure. Known as a well-informed and useful ally who was well versed on developments within Unionist and Tory politics, she often passed information onto politicians from contacts within her own social circle and from an unnamed, but seemingly very accurate, informant in Dublin. As a result of her social standing and political interests Theresa Londonderry was respected, admired and feared in society. As she informed Margot Asquith: 'I am a good friend and a bad enemy. No kiss-and-make-friends about me, my dear!'[39] One contemporary went as far as describing her as a woman who 'went for life, hammer and tongs, she collared it, and scragged it and rooked it like a highwaywoman in a tiara'.[40] Certainly Theresa was renowned as 'one of the most stirring and dominating personalities of ... [her] time ... with unrivalled experience of men and things social and political'.[41] Indeed, by 1910 her political activities were being widely commended, as this letter from one ardent supporter illustrates:

> It is such a delight to ... see you more and more taking so prominent a part in affairs, for I truly think that no woman now living is to you equal in capacity for direct political energy.[42]

Theresa hosted an annual Tory reception on the opening of parliament and entertained on no less a lavish scale than her predecessor, Frances Anne. Her social circle included the royals and the majority of leading politicians – for example Arthur Balfour and Salisbury were frequent visitors to the Londonderrys' homes. And such was Theresa's position that she was taken, or perhaps worked her way into, the confidence of many politicians, including the Unionist leader, Edward Carson and the Conservative leader, Andrew Bonar Law.

Theresa first became acquainted with Carson when her husband was Irish Lord Lieutenant in a highly successful viceroyalty. She was the only person outside Carson's family circle with whom he regularly corresponded, and she remained his political confidante and one of his closest friends for over three decades. Carson obviously valued her friendship, writing of their relationship: 'You were always my best and kindest friend', 'No one is ever more helpful than yourself and you have indeed been ... kind and affectionate'.[43] As one of her political protégés, Theresa politically and socially groomed Carson, although she was often infuriated by his lack of self-confidence, which she believed prevented him from becoming Tory leader and prime minister. On one occasion she was so frustrated by his lack of drive that she compared him to 'a Derby favourite, who, when you have him saddled and bridled, and ready to lead out of the paddock, won't run'.[44] Their close friendship did cause tension between Carson and his first wife, Annette, who as a result of ill-health was unable to play an active role in promoting her husband's career. As Carson's political reputation grew, his wife became distinctly uncomfortable with the attention which he received from other women. Indeed, according to Carson's sister 'a great row' was caused by a letter from Theresa Londonderry which prompted Carson to have 'all his letters sent to the Club'.[45] But as the friendship between Disraeli and Frances Anne illuminated, patronage of this sort could be mutually beneficial to both parties. From Carson, Theresa gleaned information and enlisted political support for her family: he electioneered for her son at Maidstone in 1909 and provided Theresa with parliamentary reactions to her husband's and son's speeches in the Lords and Commons respectively.

The death of Andrew Bonar Law's wife in 1908 made him increasingly dependent on Theresa Londonderry as a hostess and she became responsible for organising the social niceties attached to his political statesmanship. Theresa, however, deliberately cultivated a closer friendship with Bonar Law following his accession to the leadership of the Conservative Party in 1911. This was an attempt to ensure that he would protect Unionist interests, because Theresa was concerned that he was 'not as interested in the various principles of the Tory Party as I should have liked, such as Church, Education and Home Rule'.[46] After 1911 Bonar Law was, therefore, regularly invited to dine at Londonderry House and stay at the Londonderry estates in England and Ireland. And it seems that he was only too pleased to let Theresa entertain on his behalf, actively seeking her advice and showing her draft legislation on more than one occasion.[47] Theresa was even responsible for bringing his daughter out as a debutante in June 1914. There were, of course, political implications to such contact, in that the Conservatives became more closely identified with Unionist opposition to home rule. Indeed it seems that this was a cause of some unease amongst the party.

But in addition to aristocratic women's role as political confidantes and hostesses, they were also becoming increasingly active in the public arena. Democracy was the cumulative result of a series of Reform Acts which transformed not only the size, but also the nature of the British electorate. These changes demanded new methods of political organisation. This was further reinforced by legislation like the Corrupt and Illegal Practices Act of 1883, which forbade the payment of political canvassers. Therefore an increasingly large number of unpaid party workers was required, many of whom were women. More and more women became politically active from the 1880s, joining associations like the Conservative organisation, the

Primrose League, which was established in 1883 and the Women's Liberal Federation, set up in 1886. However, female aristocratic influence was not diminished, as the leaders of these new political organisations were drawn from the upper-class elite. Theresa Londonderry, for instance, was a prominent member of both the Primrose League and the Ulster Women's Unionist Council (UWUC).

Theresa strongly opposed the first Home Rule Bill in 1886 and was the leading spirit in making Londonderry House a focal point of anti-home rule politics. Her opposition did not wane during the second home rule crisis of 1893, when she conveyed an Ulster women's anti-home rule petition with 20,000 signatories to London in her carriage to be presented to the Commons.[48] In 1911 the Ulster Women's Unionist Council was established to assist the all male Ulster Unionist Council, of which her husband, the sixth Marquess, was president, to resist home rule. Theresa was a vice-president of the UWUC for two years before she was appointed president in 1913 – which she later described as the proudest moment of her life.[49] By this time the UWUC was the largest women's political association in Ireland with an estimated membership of between 115,000–200,000 members. As a result of her political contacts Theresa was an inspired choice for president of the UWUC. She regularly corresponded with F. E. Smith, the principal Conservative spokesman on Unionism and frequently discussed Ulster and rallied support for Unionism with the editors of *The Times*, *The Morning Post* and *The Spectator*. She also corresponded with Arthur Bigge, private secretary to King George V, sending him newspaper articles on Unionism and photographs of Unionist demonstrations in order to convey the strength of anti-home rule feeling. Such were Theresa Londonderry's social contacts that she was able to ask Carson for advice and secure influential speakers for meetings. She was also a capable orator who effectively chaired meetings, canvassed and directed the policy of the UWUC by successfully urging the association to promote social, economic and imperial objections to home rule in a deliberate and astute attempt to avoid the charge of Ulster bigotry.[50] Moreover, in 1912, in the midst of the third home rule crisis, she was instrumental in establishing a pro-Unionist committee of women in London. Indeed, the UWUC admitted that their Ulster-based organisation was able to act on a much wider stage as a result of her influence:

> amongst leaders of the Unionist Party in England, and her unceasing efforts[,] that the Council was able to obtain so many openings in Great Britain for its workers during the third home rule crisis.[51]

But Theresa Londonderry's position as hostess, confidante and party activist was not unassailable. The death of her husband in 1915 caused serious displacement. The strictures of inheritance meant that Theresa's eldest son,

Charles, now the seventh Marquess, controlled the family's estates and property, whilst the strictures of high society meant that Theresa was effectively usurped by her daughter-in-law, Edith, as the foremost Tory hostess. The political focus which dominated Theresa's life was now gone and her years of widowhood, which lasted from 1915 until her death in 1919, were undoubtedly difficult. Lunching at Londonderry House in 1915, which was now under Edith's command, she noted: 'It gave me a terrible pang to see someone else in my place'.[52] Much of the correspondence from the last years of her life highlight just how isolated she felt. In 1917, for example, she wrote:

> London is very different to me now that I am not so to speak, really mixed up in politics ... Verily, being left by one's self and cut off from one's interest, if one cares for public affairs and interests is very hard, but if I really did as I did before there is not much room for two people of the same name to act independently. With a husband you discuss everything with him but with a son, though you do so when you meet, you cannot keep telephoning to know his point of view.[53]

Although she still entertained, promoted her son's career, attended the Commons and saw much of the royals and her closest political friends, such as Carson, Bonar Law and Salisbury, nothing was the same. As Theresa herself said, 'no one likes stepping down from a throne'.[54]

Following her death in 1919 Theresa Londonderry was remembered as a woman who 'used her political influence and wonderful social gifts unsparingly'.[55] And as she said of her own career: 'I worked as hard as any woman could do' by public and private means, 'for the preservation of the Union'.[56] But what occurred during her lifetime was an expansion of aristocratic women's role. Not only did women continue to act as hostesses and confidantes, utilising existing friendships and cultivating new acquaintances for political ends, they also adopted an increasingly public role: canvassing, addressing political meetings, writing to the press on political topics and playing a prominent part in the new political associations which were established in an attempt to educate a mass electorate.

IV

The career of Edith, seventh Marchioness of Londonderry was no less illustrious than that of her predecessors. As the daughter of Sir Henry Chaplin, a Conservative MP, Edith possessed a good political pedigree.[57] She was also interested in politics from an early age. Indeed, from her 'youth upwards' she 'heard politics discussed, and met all the prominent politicians of the day'.[58] She married Theresa Londonderry's eldest son and heir to the

Londonderry titles, Charles, in 1899 and openly admitted that her ambitions for her husband were more dynamic than his own. It was Edith, for instance, who used her political contacts to secure cabinet appointments for Charles and, on the outbreak of World War One, successfully persuaded the London-derry's family friend, General William Pultney to appoint her husband, who at this time was a Unionist MP for Maidstone, as ADC Captain in Pultney's regiment.[59]

During the war Edith established the Women's Legion, a semi-military organisation designed to free men for active service by training women to replace them in employment.[60] She also established The Ark, a club which met at Londonderry House from 1915 with the aim of continuing the socio-political entertaining of the pre-war era. The Ark was very exclusive and its total membership of approximately fifty included all the leading political figures. Each member was given a fictitious name, thus Edith was known as 'Circe the Sorceress', her husband as 'Charley the Cheetah', Edward Carson as 'Edward the Eagle', Arthur Balfour as 'Arthur the Albatross', Winston Churchill as 'Winston the Warlock', and so on. But behind this light-hearted facade, what was Edith's aim? The Ark, which continued its activities into the 1930s, effectively maintained personal contact between politicians and in founding it, Edith not only secured the Londonderry's place at the centre of politics, but also her own.

It was during World War One that Edith Londonderry really came to the fore, not only in establishing The Ark but by succeeding to Theresa's position of social and political prestige. Edith became the leading Tory hostess following the death of the sixth Marquess in 1915. Initially she was not entirely comfortable about assuming this role but ultimately she resigned herself to accept circumstances 'over w[hi]ch one has no control one is forced to step into other people's shoes'.[61] It was now Edith, and not Theresa, who organised the annual Conservative party on the eve of the opening of parliament. But Edith did share her mother-in-law's political enthusiasm and her ambition to shape events, direct careers and adopt the role of political confidante. In pursuit of these ends Edith corresponded with many leading political and influential figures, including Queen Mary, Stanley Baldwin, Bonar Law, Neville Chamberlain and Harold Macmillan.[62] Indeed, it seems that such was Edith's political empathy that her advice was actively sought, a fact which Samuel Hoare, the British Home Secretary, emphasised:

> You must let me talk over these ... political questions with you ... Your mind is so fresh and vigorous that it does me a great deal of good to discuss politics with you.[63]

Edith's consuming political interest, coupled with her position of social privilege, also enabled her to effectively negotiate between leading political figures. In 1922, for example, she was actively involved in trying to establish a die-hard Conservative Party as a result of growing unhappiness with the coalition government. She co-operated with Carson, Salisbury and Ronald McNeill to attain these ends and her efforts in this direction were highly commended by the Duke of Northumberland:

> I am so glad you are taking the lead in getting all those who think like us to me. It is not at all pushing and there is nobody else who could do it as well as you.[64]

In addition to this private influence, Edith was also politically active in the public arena as a vice-president of the Ulster Women's Unionist Council for forty years and as president of Newtownards Women's Unionist Association. She also became one of the first female magistrates, serving in counties Durham and Down from 1919. Furthermore, in 1922 the Northern Ireland cabinet asked her to organise an Ulster Women's Volunteer Association to enlist and train a body of women to replace men called out for active service from government departments, the police and organisations such as the St John's Ambulance and the Red Cross Association in an emergency situation.[65]

But it was Edith's relationship with the premier of the first Labour government, Ramsay MacDonald, which really captured the attention of politicians, the public and the press. This relationship also illustrates how aristocratic women's role as political confidantes remained potent. Widowed in 1911, MacDonald came to rely on Edith as his closest friend and confidante. They met for the first time in 1924 at a Buckingham Palace reception, when Lord Londonderry was Northern Ireland Minister for Education and leader of the Northern Ireland Senate. A close friendship between Edith and MacDonald ensued, which lasted until MacDonald's death in 1937. This, of course, was not without serious political implications.

The Boundary Commission was established in 1924, in accordance with Article 12 of the Anglo-Irish Treaty, in order to consider the geographical definition of Ulster. The commission seriously unnerved Unionists, raising doubts about the future of Ulster. Edith Londonderry's association with Ramsay MacDonald enabled her to exert considerable influence on him to ensure that Unionist interests were protected in the commission's report. The significance of this influence was arguably heightened by the Northern Ireland government's refusal to appoint a delegate to the commission. During 1924 Ulster's boundary became a common topic for discussion in both letters and conversations between Edith and MacDonald as she outlined Unionist fears, the importance of maintaining Ulster's territory and the need for compromise and trust between the London and Belfast administrations:

You ask me to do my poor best to help towards peace and get my friends to meet you reasonably. But to enable us to do this, you must be reasonable too and keep the faith with Ulster ... extend to us the ... hand of fellowship ... and throw to us the olive branch? This is my request to you ... You may rely on my helping you all I can to keep the peace, only you must help us too.[66]

When the commission finally reported in 1925, Ulster's territorial boundaries were unaltered. It is difficult to ascertain the exact impact of Edith Londonderry's influence in securing these ends, but her persuasive arguments and tempered reasoning with MacDonald seem, at least, to have helped to maintain a Unionist perspective in the commission's deliberations. The settlement of Ulster's boundaries did not mark an end of Edith's association with MacDonald, as their correspondence continued throughout the 1920s. Indeed from 1926 the tone of their now weekly letters grew more familiar as Mac Donald wrote: 'How I miss you, dearest of all friends and most desired of all companions'.[67] MacDonald joined The Ark in 1929 under the assumed name of 'Hamish the Hart', in recognition of Edith's nickname for him. This friendship was certainly beneficial, as it was largely due to Edith's relationship with MacDonald that her husband, having resigned from Ulster politics, was appointed first Commissioner of Works in the British cabinet in 1928.

However, the association between Edith and MacDonald became increasingly controversial following his appointment as Prime Minister of the national government in 1931 and especially after he appointed Lord Londonderry as Secretary of State for Air. There were rumours in society and in the press concerning the influence which Edith exerted as 'the Mother of the National Government ... [with MacDonald] as her tame lion'.[68] In the early 1930s Edith hosted functions at Londonderry House on MacDonald's behalf and became a frequent visitor to Chequers.[69] All concerned were aware of the gossip and rumours which abounded. Indeed, MacDonald's concerns were such that he was worried about compromising Edith's position: 'My fear is that you may be injured amongst your folk for asking me to sit at your table'.[70] Her husband expressed similar sentiments:

I am really rather frightened at the gossip and believe there has been some talk in the papers about petticoat influence: the P.M. said something about this at lunch ... you must remember that everyone is ready to gossip and say unkind things.[71]

Stanley Baldwin was prominent amongst those cynics who questioned Edith's motivation for befriending MacDonald. In a letter to Edith's son he stated outright that he believed her association with MacDonald was an act of 'political expediency'.[72] But MacDonald's resignation in 1935 made Lord Londonderry's position far from safe, underlining the insecurity of patronage in an increasingly meritocratic world. Baldwin replaced MacDonald as premier and swiftly demoted Lord Londonderry, appointing him Lord Privy Seal and Leader of the House of Lords, but only for a matter of months. Londonderry was soon dropped from the cabinet altogether, an act which Londonderry believed effectively wiped him 'off the face of the political map'.[73] After his ceremonious sacking in 1935, Lord Londonderry retained his seat in the Lords and the only other political activities which he undertook were the now notorious visits to Nazi Germany in the years preceding the outbreak of the Second World War. This was a well-meaning, though perhaps politically myopic, attempt to promote better understanding between Britain and Germany. However, these visits prompted severe criticism to be directed towards the Londonderrys, whom many now branded as Nazi sympathisers.[74] This may help explain the Londonderrys' fairly low political profile during the 1940s. Edith was widowed in 1949 and lived the last ten years of her life quietly on the family estates of Mount Stewart and Wynyard, with occasional visits to Londonderry House.

V

To conclude, although the Londonderrys' financial position was affected by increasing tax and death duties and by problems in the coal industry during the interwar period, they survived the financial crisis which affected so many aristocratic families.[75] Indeed, Londonderry House was one of the few great aristocratic London houses which was not sold during the 1930s. This was a position which the Londonderrys were all too well aware of, as the seventh Marquess noted: 'I cannot help feeling that the so-called big houses are becoming in a sense, anachronisms'.[76] But what about the family's political position? The changes which occurred in the political system as a result of an increasingly democratic electorate were undoubtedly momentous, but this did not lead to the immediate erosion of aristocratic influence. Indeed, Edith Londonderry's relationship with Ramsay MacDonald reveals the potency of the political influence which aristocratic women could still exert through friendship and entertaining. This, coupled with women's heightened public profile, meant that there was an enduring undercurrent of aristocratic female influence, which is crucial to gain a fuller understanding of the working of politics, not only in the nineteenth century, but also into the twentieth century. But times were changing and Edith Londonderry was undoubtedly the last great political hostess. By the middle of the 1930s, critics were labelling Edith's political receptions as too ostentatious during a time of economic depression, deeming them dinosaurs of a bygone era. Moreover, the role of familial patronage was clearly diminishing as Lord Londonderry tried in vain to persuade his cousin Winston Churchill to secure a cabinet appointment for him in the 1940s. Even the family's tradition of entering parliament was broken. Lord Londonderry successfully secured a seat for his son and heir, Edward Stewart Robert (Robin), in Co. Down in 1931, but he resigned this seat in 1945 and thereafter had nothing more to do with politics. In her autobiography Edith Londonderry could not ignore such significant changes:

> Society, as such, now means nothing except wealth and advertisement. The Peerage, to a great extent, has replenished its waning fortunes from the ranks of those who, before the War, would not have formed part of ... Society. Therefore, it ... does not represent what it formerly did.[77]

With these changes nothing was ever quite the same for the aristocracy, either financially or politically, and it is difficult to disagree with Edith Londonderry's assertion that nothing short of a 'revolution' had indeed occurred.[78]

Nurses, Nuns and Ladies:
A Study of Class, Ethnicity and Religion in
the Crimean War

MOIRA E. EGAN

I

In much of the literature about nursing in the Crimean War (1854–56), only Florence Nightingale's experiences are related. The image of 'the lady with the lamp' has become a symbol of nursing, a symbol however, whose connection to the realities of military nursing is almost lost. By analysing the experiences of upper-class women, the Sisters of Mercy, as well as Nightingale's, it is possible to give a more detailed picture, reflecting more than one group's experiences and connecting those experiences to the realities of nursing in the Crimea and to other experiences of mid-nineteenth-century women.[1]

On one level, women's work during the Crimean War can be seen as part of the British war effort. Conditions in the military hospitals in Turkey were terrible and the government desperately needed nurses. Florence Nightingale and those whom she recruited, including some Sisters of Mercy from Bermondsey in England, were the first to answer the request of the War Office. However, a second group of Sisters of Mercy, whom Florence Nightingale did not recruit, also came out to the Crimea from Ireland. The presence of these women raised questions about religion and ethnicity which complicate the picture of nurses' experiences in the war. The sisters' work reveals that there was more at stake in the Crimea than patriotism. They wanted to assert their respectability, their rights as Catholics and women religious, their nursing abilities and their autonomy. Their diaries reveal that they were conscious of the high stakes and knew that their work could advance the nursing profession and ensure that the terms 'Catholic' and 'British citizen' were not mutually exclusive.

Before discussing the central questions of this essay, it is necessary to provide some information about the women involved, the war itself and the history of nursing. Despite their differences of religion and ethnicity, women working as nurses during the war actually had much in common. Florence Nightingale, whose life story is most well known, had a comfortable childhood. She grew up in a wealthy, well-connected family in which she learned the traditional female role from her mother and a series of governesses, but was given an academic education by her father.[2] Florence excelled in her studies and wanted to put them to more use than the gender constraints of her class and time would allow. As a teenager, she longed for some meaningful work and lamented the fact that she would probably have to lead a life which she saw as frivolous.[3] Despite her family's strong opposition, she became convinced that she should become a nurse. Nightingale had little access to formal training, only making two brief visits, in 1850 and 1851, to a hospital run by a Protestant community of women religious in Germany. After this, she took an unpaid position as superintendent of the Institute for Gentlewomen in Distressed Circumstances in London.[4] Unlike the novitiate of the Sisters of Mercy, this experience did not prepare Nightingale for the cholera, typhus and typhoid she would encounter in epidemic proportions in the Crimea. After the war, Nightingale continued to work for sanitary reform in British military hospitals and established a training school for nurses.[5]

In addition to Nightingale's background, it is also crucial to give some general information about some of the Sisters of Mercy, since their presence in the hospitals and their relationship with Nightingale illuminate the issues addressed in this essay. Like Nightingale, the sisters all had a sense of mission. Their biographies reveal their desire to do work which was beneficial to society and their commitment to professionalism. Both Mary Clare Moore and Francis Bridgeman, the leaders of the two groups of sisters, came from comfortable backgrounds, where they received relatively good educations and would have been expected to follow middle-class women's roles. Like Nightingale, these women longed for something more and entered the convent as a way of pursuing a different model of womanhood. Unlike Nightingale, however, all of the sisters had previous nursing experience, which was why they were chosen to accompany her to the Crimea. Their order had been established, amongst other things, to care for the poor and the sisters from Ireland had ample experience of dealing with cholera and typhus from their earlier work in famine hospitals – diseases which they also encountered in their work in the Crimea. Those sisters from England possessed similar nursing experience, having worked during cholera epidemics in the 1830s. They had also continued to tend the sick until they were sent to the Crimea.[6]

II

The Sisters of Mercy and Florence Nightingale had different views of nursing. Nightingale believed that only surgical cases needed nurses, while the sisters felt that fever patients also needed attention. In addition, they differed over the question of night work; Nightingale did not want nurses to be in the wards after 8.30 at night and the sisters thought that it was important to make rounds at night and to sit up with cholera patients.[7] It has been argued that no one at the time understood the medical problems faced in the hospitals. Although contemporary accounts are filled with descriptions of rats and fleas, their authors did not realise that these were more than an annoyance, but the cause of many of the illnesses that they were treating.[8]

The Crimean War lasted from 1854–6 and posed a threat to the balance of power in Europe established by the Congress of Vienna in 1815. Russia attempted to gain more influence in Turkey in order to gain access to the Mediterranean. The British government perceived this as a threat to its interests in the Middle East and, with other western European countries, formed a coalition to stop Russia from conquering Turkey.[9] Although religious conflict was not the primary cause of the war, it did play a role. Influenced by the French and despite the objections of the Tsar, the Sultan of Turkey gave greater control over the holy places in his empire to Roman Catholics than to Orthodox Christians.[10] Whilst it is clear that political and not religious concerns caused the war, it is important to understand that religious differences and assumptions about them could affect politics. Ultimately Russia lost the war, but it was fought at great financial and human cost to all the combatants. In all theatres of the war, the allies lost 253,000 men and the Russians 256,000. However, it is unclear whether these figures include those who died of diseases such as cholera and typhus in the hospitals or only those who were killed in battle.[11]

Fanny Taylor wrote an account of her experiences as a nurse in the war, *Eastern Hospitals and English Nurses: The Narrative of Twelve Months Experience in The Hospitals of Koulali and Scutari by a Lady Volunteer*, which was published before the cessation of the conflict.[12] Her descriptions of the condition of the hospitals caused a public outcry about the need for nurses and prompted many women to offer their services. In early October 1854, Thomas Grant, the Bishop of Southwark, arranged with the War Office for a group of Sisters of Mercy from Bermondsey to go with Nightingale to the Crimea. He approved the rules established for them by the War Office:

> the first of which was that the sisters should attend to the corporeal wants of the soldiers, but that they should never introduce religious subjects except with patients of their own faith.[13]

The first group of thirty-eight nurses under Nightingale was made up of nurses from hospitals, 'lady volunteers', Sisters of Mercy and members of Anglican religious communities.[14] A second group was assembled by Mary Stanley and included Fanny Taylor and Sisters of Mercy mainly from convents in Ireland. Taylor indicates that the agreement between Florence Nightingale, under the direction of the Principal Medical Officer and the individual nurses, stipulated that the Secretary of War would pay a specified weekly salary, all expenses of transportation and lodging in any hospital and then cover the expenses of her return to England, unless she was discharged for neglect of duty, immoral conduct or intoxication. In the case of such a discharge, the offending nurse would forfeit any claims on Nightingale or the British government. With respect to the nurses' responsibilities, the agreement stated:

> The said [nurse] hereby agrees to devote her whole time and attention to the purposes aforesaid, under the directions and to the satisfaction of the said Miss Nightingale, the whole of whose orders she undertakes to obey until discharged by the said Miss Nightingale.[15]

Taylor did not discuss the conditions under which the Sisters of Mercy were to serve, except to say that in the case of volunteers, which they were, the statement about specific wages was omitted. For Francis Bridgeman, leader of the second group, the most difficult part of the agreement was its granting absolute authority over the nurses, both lay and religious, to Nightingale.

III

At the centre of the disagreements and misunderstandings between Nightingale and the Sisters of Mercy was the question of religion. Like many in the mid-nineteenth century, Nightingale and the British government officials, under whose auspices she worked, were very fearful of Irish Catholic sisters. It is tempting to dismiss these fears as merely irrational and based on stereotypes, but they must be taken seriously, since many actions either stemmed from, or were intended to alleviate, these fears. For example, concerns about religious instruction were not limited to the hospitals and their administrators, but were expressed to government officials and even to Queen Victoria.[16] During the war, religion was integral to patients' experiences in hospital. Taylor noted that above each patient's bed was a card listing his name, regiment, age, date of admission, disease and religion. Furthermore, Taylor claimed that once the religious affiliation was noted on the cards, their nursing work went much more smoothly, since previously all nurses had to ask a patient's religion before offering to lend a book or 'offering any religious consolation'.[17] Although not stated explicitly, Taylor probably intended this to refute accusations of proselytising made against the sisters, but it is interesting that her description of the cards indicated that all of the nurses were concerned with meeting the spiritual needs of their patients. This is perhaps not surprising. Nightingale, for example, believed that religion had a significant place in the professional work of a nurse, since she saw her own decision to break with her family and with the customs of the day to follow a nursing career as a call from God.[18] The contract between the Sisters of Mercy and the War Office did not expect them to work as secular nurses, but acknowledged their religious framework and permitted its exercise in specified cases. They were, however, instructed to discuss religion only with Catholics and were to be under the direction of medical officers for their work, but under the direction of their religious superior in religious matters.[19] In all accounts of the sisters' work it appears that they complied with these conditions. Indeed, some indicated that these conditions were actually beneficial to their work. Bishop Grant, writing to Mary Clare Moore, who led the first group of sisters which left from England in 1854, was pleased that the government had agreed to hire 'nuns as nuns'.[20]

Despite the agreement and the sisters' sense of its importance, all did not run smoothly, as Nightingale and others were not convinced that all of the sisters were honouring their contracts. Throughout the war, Nightingale frequently corresponded with the Secretary of War, Sidney Herbert, who was also a family friend. On hearing that a second group of sisters would be arriving from Ireland, she warned Herbert that there was no room for any more nurses, although she had previously expressed concern to him about a staff shortage. She also said that, unlike Moore and the other sisters from Bermondsey, the group from Ireland had an ulterior motive in offering their services, namely to gain converts to the Roman Catholic Church.[21] Unlike the nuns from Bermondsey, Nightingale had not personally recruited the second group of nuns led by Bridgeman. It is clear from Nightingale's letters that there was, in addition to religious disputes, a great deal of concern about authority.[22] There were, for instance, numerous personal conflicts between Nightingale and Bridgeman. One manifestation of the conflict between these two women was evidenced in the many times Nightingale compared Bridge-man unfavourably to Clare Moore. For example, Nightingale asserted that the group from Ireland intended to instruct non-Catholics in religious matters, a problem which she stated never occurred with the Bermondsey sisters.[23] Although the Irish sisters denied these charges and others asserted their innocence, the second group of nuns was charged with attempting to convert soldiers.[24] The issue of religious instruction was also related to the question of respectability. Though Nightingale does not elaborate this point, she seems to have been upset with the sisters for instructing even the mobile

Catholic soldiers and felt that they should confine their work, nursing and instructing, to those who were bedridden, while the ambulatory patients were to be seen by the priest for instruction.[25]

Initially, these religious disputes were handled internally. From the attention given to them in many of the sisters' accounts, it appears that much effort was expended in investigating the charges of proselytising or so-called 'religious interference'. This diligence was probably as much to ensure adherence to the agreement with the British government and forestall any justification of the fears of senior members of the military about allowing civilians to work in military hospitals, as it was to acquit the sisters of any charges of wrongdoing. Mary Joseph Lynch, a member of the group sent out from Ireland who, in addition to writing her own memoirs, served as Bridgeman's secretary, described several investigations of charges against the sisters. In one case, a young soldier had asked a sister if he could speak with the priest. Word of this reached one of the Protestant nurses as well as members of the clergy. The young man was questioned repeatedly (indeed, Lynch reported that he objected to telling his story so often) about his state of mind, the content of his conversations with the sisters and with the priest and his religious beliefs before coming to the Crimea. The matter seemed to have been put to rest once the soldier asserted that he had been baptised a Catholic, had not practised his religion for some years, but had decided to return to the Catholic Church whilst serving in the army.[26] One of those involved in questioning the soldier, the sisters and the Protestant nurses was Mary Stanley, a Protestant upper-class woman who was recruited by Nightingale. As Lynch and other sisters recalled, Stanley was thorough in her investigations and was free of any anti-Catholic prejudices. However, what the sisters took to be impartiality exposed Stanley to some criticism in other quarters; Lynch and others believed that she was perhaps considering converting to Catholicism, which she eventually did.[27] One reason for the deep concern about the question of proselytising was that it could be seen as a breach of contract. The agreement signed both by the group from Bermondsey and by Bridgeman, on behalf of the group from Ireland, made it quite clear that the sisters were to restrict their religious duties to Catholics.[28]

Bridgeman took accusations of 'religious interference' quite seriously, often investigating the charges herself rather than waiting for the superintendent to learn of them. In one case, she was able to discredit Kate Anderson, a persistent critic of the sisters, by asking for specifics of her complaint. Anderson was unable to give the name of the sister who had unlawfully instructed a Protestant soldier, the content of the instruction, or the name of the soldier. Bridgeman asserted that, as Anderson was willing to accept the word of this man that a sister had attempted to convert him, then the unknown sister should be given the same benefit of the doubt. There were witnesses, some of them 'lady volunteers', who testified to Anderson's unreliability and to the sisters' faithfulness to their contract, so the super-intendent of nurses stopped the complaint from going any further.[29] How-ever, this was not the end of the matter. In the spring of 1855, the War Office, probably as a result of the accusations of proselytising forwarded by several chaplains, reaffirmed its earlier contract with the sisters. But Lord William Paulett, commander of the hospitals, construed the latest War Office directive to say that the sisters were to give no religious instruction, even to Catholic soldiers. This dispute nearly led to the departure of the group from Ireland.[30] Bridgeman did not take the charges lightly, making it clear that she resented both the implications that the sisters had broken their agreement and what she took to be Paulett's attempts to change the terms of their agreement. Although not a diplomat or politician by training, Bridgeman's response to Paulett was worthy of both. In a letter to him, sent according to the proper protocol through Father Ronan, the Catholic chaplain, she hinted that, if he persisted, she would have no choice but to make arrangements for the sisters to leave since the terms of their contract were no longer applicable. She further added that she felt confident that Paulett's own sense of justice and honour would help him to recognise his mistake. Bridgeman went so far as to issue a thinly veiled challenge to Paulett's interpretation of the agreement and his authority as the representative of the British government, by assert-ing that no 'free government' could possibly deprive citizens, who were then risking their lives for the government, of their religious freedoms.[31]

As the commander of the entire Crimean operation, Paulett was clearly making decisions which would govern all nurses, not just those working with Francis Bridgeman. There is no evidence, however, that the Bermondsey group either objected to his statements or that they were named in the charges of proselytising. Nor is there any evidence to suggest that Moore was willing to cease instructing Catholics as Paulett wanted. It is reasonable to infer, therefore, that Moore felt the same way as Bridgeman about the importance of the sisters remaining free to instruct Catholics, but that she expressed her concerns in a more conciliatory manner than Bridgeman. In fact, Nightingale and Moore worked quite well together and remained friends after their work in the Crimea was over.[32]

IV

Using only Florence Nightingale's experiences to understand nursing in the Crimean War ignores the issue of class, both in its economic sense and its social connotations. One might argue that class must be considered in any analysis of work or of gender, yet it is particularly important when discussing the history of nursing. Many at the time, including Nightingale, held the view that nursing was not something that a respectable woman would do. In 1852, for example, a writer for the *Medical Times* and *Gazette* referred to a paid nurse as:

> a hard minded, ignorant, lazy, drunken woman, who upsets the whole establishment with her whims; sleeps when she should be awake; is cross when she should be patient; and is constant only in a persevering attempt to make the job as lucrative as possible.[33]

Educational reformer Emily Davies also criticised nurses, but her objections were gender based. She resented women's relegation to a subordinate position within the medical profession and wanted to ensure that women with the inclination and aptitude to become medical doctors were afforded the opportunity.[34] Both the notion that nursing was not respectable and the middle-class bias implicit in Davies' objections reveal the close connections between gender and class. This link was especially evident in the discussions of whether nursing was a calling or a profession. On one hand, those who deemed it a calling were attempting to change the view that nursing was distasteful work which was not suitable for women. Yet this view ignored the fact that working-class women, no matter how strong their desire to serve others, could not afford to view nursing as a calling, since that term implied that the work should go unpaid.[35]

Accounts written by Sisters of Mercy and Florence Nightingale's letters indicate that attention to class distinctions is not limited to present-day interpretations. These mid-nineteenth-century women also commented on these distinctions. Mary Joseph Lynch provides a good example. In her memoir it is clear that social position was of consequence.[36] Lynch's account contains many descriptions of the daily life of women working in the hospitals and by prefacing her descriptions with phrases like 'the nurses', 'the ladies', or 'the sisters', she distinguishes between the different groups of women. At one point in her account, she gives a lengthy and detailed description of a visit which some of 'the ladies' made to a Turkish home. They observed boys in a schoolroom and a dance performance, and were then invited to drink coffee with the Turkish women. Lynch reports that during this and other excursions which the ladies made during their time in Turkey, the sisters cared for the ladies' wards. Here and in many other places throughout her account, Lynch stresses the unity between the ladies and sisters. She mentions the fact that the sisters took over the ladies' wards not to condemn the ladies for shirking their duty, but to show that the different groups of nurses worked well together. And the 'ladies' Lynch writes of were all Protestant middle-class women.[37]

In the case of the Sisters of Mercy, and presumably of active women religious in general, class barriers were somewhat permeable. They had chosen a life of work among the poor and were, therefore, more in the public arena than those middle-class women who did philanthropic charitable work in addition to their work in the home. On the one hand, the sisters rejected the traditional feminine role of caring for a family, yet in their accounts, they asserted that their choice to work in the public arena did not imply that they rejected traditional middle-class standards of women's behaviour. Instances of this are numerous, but two particularly clear examples may suffice. On the voyage to Turkey, there were not enough berths in first class for the ladies and the sisters. Bridgeman was offered a place in first class with the ladies, whilst the rest of the sisters would be in second class along with the paid nurses. Bridgeman declined the offer, choosing to sleep in second class with the rest of the women religious. She did object, however, to the sisters having to eat with the paid nurses and other second class passengers. A courier offered to bring their meals to the sisters' cabin and the account indicates that many on board respected the sisters for remaining aloof from their lay and working-class companions.[38] Another example illustrates the sisters' acceptance of a traditional domestic role, even under very difficult circumstances. During the course of the war, most of the sisters remained in the hospitals in Turkey, but several went to nurse very close to the front. After reporting on the difficult conditions at the front Carroll describes the sisters ironing a clergyman's collars with a teapot filled with hot water, because they had no iron. This service apparently increased the estimation of the sisters in the clergyman's eyes.[39]

It is impossible to discuss the interplay of class and gender without discussing the concept of 'moralisation'. Twentieth-century historians of gender have illustrated the ways in which women of the middle classes, through their charitable works, attempted to inculcate women of the working classes with their values. While at times these were practical and beneficial suggestions about child care, hygiene and other health issues, working-class women believed other suggestions to be unwarranted interventions in their lives.[40] Florence Nightingale was quite explicit in her writings on nursing about the need to instil proper morals in working-class nurses and their patients. She was very concerned to preserve the morality of the nurses, even suggesting that doorways to nurses' rooms should be visible from any point in the hospital and that there should not be too many closets or dark hallways. As with the fears about religious differences, it is tempting to dismiss these vague, unnamed fears, which clearly had something to do with sex, as irrational or ridiculous. However, they must be taken seriously, as they informed Nightingale's views of training schools for nurses, which was one of her major contributions to the history of the profession.[41] Nightingale's beliefs about the need for close supervision of working-class women were not merely personal idiosyncrasies, but were typical of women of her class. The following passage from Fanny Taylor not only reveals something about the daily life of the nurses, but it also reveals a great deal about class perceptions in the way that Taylor speaks of the paid nurses, who are usually silent in the available accounts:

> At the ladies' home we assembled at eight o'clock for prayers, read by our superintendent, then followed breakfast. At nine the bell for work rang. We all assembled; each lady called the nurse under her charge to accompany her to her ward, or kitchen, or linen stores (we never allowed the nurses to go out alone, unless with special permission); and in five minutes all the different groups were on their way to the hospital ... At half past two we dined, the ladies in one room, the nurses in another, with a lady at the head of their table. The ladies took it by turns, a week about, to superintend all the meals of the nurses ... At seven we returned to tea; then one lady – we took it in turns – went out with the nurses for a walk; now and then, for a treat, in caiques, to the sweet waters or Bebec. The day concluded with part of the evening service read by the Anglican chaplain.[42]

Mary Joseph Croke, one of the sisters sent from Ireland, left a similar account to that written by Lynch. Croke's account is also filled with details about the nurses' daily experiences. Whereas Lynch seems merely to note or present the distinctions based on class, Croke attaches more meaning to these distinctions. While sailing to Turkey, the group dined formally and Croke pokes fun, sometimes none too gently, at the paid nurses who were unfamiliar with some of the food and with the table etiquette expected in the dining room. Croke's tone suggests that she believed some moral deficiency could be inferred from this cultural difference.[43]

Since the women who worked as nurses during the Crimean war came from different religious and social backgrounds, their views of the work and of the war varied. Moreover, as Nightingale was sent by the War Office, her primary concern was her adherence to her government's wishes. As illustrated by the sisters' response to the charges of proselytising, they certainly shared Nightingale's loyalty to the government and her sense of mission. However, they had additional concerns. Their work had broad implications for Catholics, as the sisters were performing a service to the Roman Catholic Church by being of service to the government. It has, for instance, been pointed out in one contemporary account that since the sisters nursed in Turkey, there had been no talk of 'convent bills' in Parliament, which were proposals to investigate convents in the belief that young women were being held there against their will.[44] But in addition to government and/or church loyalty, all of the nurses expressed patriotic support for the soldiers and sorrow for the harsh conditions at the front. Yet the Sisters of Mercy, especially Lynch, had a special concern for the Irish soldiers as expressed in affectionate anecdotes about particular soldiers. As Bridgeman's exchange with Lord Paulett revealed, the sisters did not always completely conceal their nationalistic feelings.

V

All of the women working in the Crimea had a sense of history; they recognised that their work was important and should therefore be recorded. This is most obvious for Florence Nightingale, a voluminous letter writer who also wrote many reports to government commissions urging further reforms of military hospitals.[45] On a more personal note, in a recording made in 1890, Nightingale hoped that: 'When I am no longer even a memory, just a name, I hope my voice may perpetuate the great work of my life'.[46] Many of the sisters' accounts were not published and, therefore, were originally meant only to be read by members of the order. However, their accounts show attention to detail and a desire to record both official documents and procedures, as well as ordinary conversations and descriptions of scenery, comments on cultural differences, descriptions of different styles of nursing and copies of government directives. Since several of these memoirs were written many years after the events recorded, the authors themselves were not the only ones interested in their production; they must have relied on people such as convent annalists to save letters written at the time. Francis Bridgeman provides a clear example of this sense of history, since she states at the beginning of her account that it was meant as a guide for her superiors. Even the 'non-official' accounts reveal their authors' attempts to preserve their experiences. Fanny Taylor's account reveals a sense of history. Like others, she says that her account is intended to tell part of a story which might not otherwise be known: the suffering of the soldiers who did not die in battle, but of diseases while in hospital. Taylor also stresses the importance of the daily experiences of the nurses. Although she does express a great deal of patriotism when describing the grave wrong which would occur if the soldiers who died of disease should be forgotten, she hints at a concern which later generations expressed more explicitly, that is, the danger of glorifying, but not presenting the horrors or even the ordinary experiences of war. She was particularly moved by the stories of many young soldiers who enlisted without really considering all of the ramifications, then bitterly regretted their hasty decision.[47]

An examination of the experiences of nurses during the Crimean War is a way to explore issues and questions for the nineteenth century as a whole. Rather than putting aside fears arising from religious or class differences, these fears were ever present and fundamentally shaped women's experiences. In addition to their fears, Florence Nightingale, the middle-class women and the Sisters of Mercy all felt that their work in the hospitals could benefit them, as well as the wounded soldiers. Nightingale and some of the other middle-class women wanted to improve the image of nursing, believing that it should be seen as a respectable profession for women and one which required rigorous training, as well as middle-class morals. The Sisters of Mercy, especially Francis Bridgeman, knew that their work could help to reduce anti-Catholic prejudices of the time. The fact that Bridgeman was Irish added another dimension to the work. Other sisters were aware of the services they were performing for their Church, but Bridgeman and the other Irish sisters were also very conscious of and resisted any infringements of their rights and authority. Thus, in the final analysis, the work of these women and the records which they have left provide us with multi-faceted views of British and Irish women's experiences in the nineteenth century.

Isabella Tod and Liberal Unionism in Ulster, 1886–96

NOEL ARMOUR

I

In her recent article on the life of Isabella Maria Susan Tod, Luddy has recorded her justifiable surprise at the fact that 'someone of Tod's importance to the political and social life of Ireland could be so completely forgotten'.[1] In the process of rectifying that omission, Luddy has successfully managed to restore 'the best known Irish women's activist of her day' to her rightful place in the pantheon of Irish feminist icons.[2] Yet, in the last ten years of her life, from the advent of the first home rule crisis in 1886 to the time of her death in 1896, Tod was perhaps better known by her contemporaries for her committed and forthright defence of Irish Unionism than for her advocacy of the rights of women.

During that closing ten year chapter of her life, Tod appeared and made speeches on numerous political platforms, orchestrated and participated in anti-home rule letter and article campaigns in newspapers and journals, was the sole female member of the policy-making executive committee of the Ulster Liberal Unionist Association (ULUA) and was the moving spirit behind the foundation of the Ulster Women's Liberal Unionist Association (UWLUA). Despite this level of prominence, Tod has consistently failed to attract any serious or sustained consideration from the historians of organised Unionism and the memory of her contribution to the Irish Unionist cause – confined as it has been to a few disjointed and sporadic cameos – has been largely allowed to fade from the collective Unionist historical consciousness.

She was remembered, however briefly, by Fisher in 1914 in his idiosyncratic account of the ULUA in relation to her role as 'the founder of the first Women's Unionist Association'.[3] After a lengthy absence from the annals, she was again partially resurrected by Lucy in his quasi-official history of the Unionist convention of 1892, in specific regard to the *conversazione* which was organised by Tod and her fellow Unionist women as a prequel to the main convention and at which she was the sole speaker.[4] More recently still, she has merited a mention in Greenlee's thesis on Ulster liberalism in the home rule era, where the fleeting reference made to her is in the misspelt form of Todd which, in a sense, typifies the cursory treatment Tod has received over the years from the Unionist historiographical tradition.[5]

It is indeed unfortunate that Tod's involvement in Unionist politics from 1886–96 has failed to attract the attention it has merited. Any study of her involvement has invaluable insights to offer on two of the least studied – and hence least understood – elements of the disparate loyalist forces opposed to Gladstone's home rule proposals as they banded together to form the Irish Unionist Alliance: women Unionists and Liberal Unionists. Little has been written on the role and place of women in the Unionist movement during the first two home rule crises in spite of the fact that two popular women's organisations, the Primrose League and the UWLUA, were specifically created as vehicles for harnessing the energies of women to the support of the Unionist cause.[6] The long-standing popular view is that:

> the crisis brought about by Gladstone's declaration in favour of Home Rule instantly swept all sections of Loyalists into a single camp ... and [Liberal Unionist] co-operation with Conservatives was so whole-hearted and complete as almost to amount to fusion from the outset ...[7]

This view has been allowed to persist because of the relative lack of interest in Ulster Liberal Unionism as a distinct phenomenon, deserving of separate consideration. The Liberal Unionists of Ulster, the generic as well as the intellectual heirs of the Presbyterian radicals of 1798, have been grouped together with all shades of Unionist opinion and expression to produce the orange-tinted zealot of popular imagination: the Ulster Unionist. The primary aim of this essay is, therefore, to explore these 'Cinderella' areas of the Unionist past through the paradigm provided by the very doyenne of early Unionist women and one of the leading Liberal Unionists in the home rule era, Isabella Tod.

Before directly addressing that agenda, it would seem important to chart Tod's experiences before 1886 as these had a clear and decisive bearing on her actions and opinions during the age of home rule. It seems particularly necessary to emphasise that, from Tod's standpoint, 1886 did not represent a personal political watershed. In her view, she and her fellow Liberal Unionists continued to follow the true light of liberalism and it was the great mass of metropolitan liberalism, mesmerised by what she regarded as Gladstone's misguided sense of duty towards Ireland, which Tod disparagingly dismissed as 'cheap good-will … to pay English debts and do penance for the sins of Orangemen', who had crossed the constitutional divide.[8]

II

Isabella Tod was not a native of Ireland. She was born in Edinburgh on 18 May 1836. Her father, James Banks Tod, was a Scottish merchant to whom, according to a rather presumptuous obituarist, 'she owed much of the judgement and clear-headedness which characterised her'.[9] Her mother, Maria Isabella Waddell, was an Ulsterwoman from Co. Monaghan, to whom the same obituarist perhaps more accurately accredited 'all of her verve and enthusiasm [and] all her devotion to the cause of females'.[10]

In the absence of any substantial sources on Tod's private life it is difficult to be precise about why the Tod family chose to settle in Belfast in the early 1860s, but it does seem fair to presume that some combination of their personal connection with the province and the opportunities for business advancement offered by the then rapidly expanding industrial metropolis of Belfast, must have played some part in the decision. It also seems reasonable to speculate that they enjoyed a relatively prosperous bourgeois existence, as Isabella Tod's prominence in the upper echelons of Belfast's social, political and charitable circles demanded the kind of Victorian respectability and gentility which required a relatively solid financial background. Her precise sources of income are unknown and she does not seem to have ever owned a property, though she did earn at least some of her income from journalism, an impressive feat in itself for a self-educated person.[11] In her will, she bequeathed her entire effects, which amounted to the not insubstantial sum of £1,463 7s 6d, to her brother Henry, a merchant then domiciled in London, who was also involved with the Liberal Unionist party.

Tod's links with Ireland and the province of Ulster through the maternal line were lengthy and deep-rooted. She took an immense pride in the legacy of her Ulster-Scots cultural heritage, which included one of her maternal ancestors signing the Solemn League and Covenant in 1646. Following in the family tradition, Tod was an active and devout member of the Presbyterian Church and she practised her faith as a leading lay member of the Elmwood Presbyterian Church in Belfast. This, in itself, was significant. Elmwood, Duncairn, Belmont and Fisherwick Presbyterian Churches enjoyed close connections throughout the nineteenth century and their tight-knit congregations contained the overwhelming bulk of Belfast's Presbyterian Liberal elite.[12]

Tod was at the hub of many charitable endeavours and she was amongst the most committed of those actively engaged in voluntary work and philanthropic institutions.[13] She was involved in an eclectic array of contemporary causes, which included the employment of the industrious blind, the boarding out of pauper children and the prison gate mission. Her abiding areas of interest, however, were the education, welfare and suffrage rights of girls and women and the great moral crusade of Victorian nonconformity – temperance. Tod played a leading role in all of the major campaigns on women's issues from the mid-1860s to the time of her death. These included the property rights of married women, the repeal of the Contagious Diseases Acts and women's right to enfranchisement in both municipal and parliamentary elections. She also played a leading part in the temperance movement in Ulster and Great Britain. As a result of her endeavours on behalf of these various causes, Tod gained a formidable reputation as a talented public speaker and writer. In addition, she also made extensive and long-lived connections and friendships with members of the provincial and metropolitan political and social establishments.

It is difficult to date precisely Tod's involvement in Liberal politics in Ulster, though it would seem likely to have occurred sometime between 1874 and 1880. She does not appear to have played any part in the agitation for the dis-establishment of the Irish Episcopalian Church between 1868–69, nor to have taken part in the 1874 general election campaign. However, by 1880 she was appearing regularly as a platform speaker at Liberal Society (as the Liberal Party styled itself in Ulster) election meetings, and she advocated the pressing necessity for land reform along lines broadly similar to Gladstone's Land Act of 1881 to the Ulster Liberal Convention of 20 March 1880.[14] Tod carried this interest in land reform into her Liberal Unionist days and she never swayed from the conviction that 'there was only one question whose settlement would settle almost everything else, and that was the old question of the land'.[15]

It appears likely that Tod's interest in advancing the role and status of women played some part in her becoming involved in provincial Liberal politics. That is not to say that women's issues generated any great deal of interest in the north of Ireland at this time, and such interest as did exist was liable to cut across party lines.[16] The most committed local male campaigners for women's franchise and educational rights were actually the Conservative James Haslett, who later became a long-serving Unionist MP, and the great hero of militant plebeian orangeism, William Johnston of Ballykilbeg. But, on balance, most of those who took a positive stance on the advancement of the educational, social and political rights of women were liberals. The titular head of Ulster liberalism, Lord Ava (later the Marquis of Dufferin and Ava), the most distinguished of Victorian diplomats, took some modicum of interest in women's educational provision and Tod was keeping him informed of her efforts in that sphere from at least 1868.[17] Less exalted liberals played a more involved part in women's affairs, and many of Tod's political allies in the post-1886 period, including Thomas Sinclair, Robert MacGeagh and Thomas Andrews, the dominant triumvirate in Ulster Liberal Unionism at a local level, and the great Liberal Unionist maverick and the parliamentary face of Ulster Liberal Unionism, Thomas Wallace Russell, all campaigned for advancing the status of women.[18]

Tod was the only female to breach the male bastion of Unionist politics in Ireland at this time. In that respect she was unquestionably exceptional. However, the political stances which she adopted in that male-dominated world were totally in keeping with those of her closest male colleagues in the Ulster Liberal Society. They, in the main, were Presbyterians like Tod, or were members of the smaller northern non-Episcopalian Protestant churches, particularly the Unitarian and Methodist Churches. They were also, with several important exceptions, drawn from the entrepreneurial or professional middle classes. This personnel profile was not, of course, altogether dissimilar from Liberal Party organisations in the north of England and Scotland. Equally, the issues on which the Ulster liberals campaigned and the policy areas which most concerned them, such as land, government and franchise reform, temperance and non-denominational education, were broadly comparable to their counterparts in Great Britain. They also shared the same faith in Gladstone, the 'Grand Old Man', minimalist government, the concept of progress and the importance of individual responsibility tempered by, and conditional upon, communal participation, as mainstream English, Welsh and Scottish liberals.[19]

While it is apparent that the kind of liberalism which Tod and her colleagues in Ulster espoused clearly resembled the mid-Victorian British Liberal model, that it derived from similar ideological sources and that the Ulster liberals regarded themselves as the 'ambassadors of metropolitan Gladstonianism', it is rather more important to emphasise that Ulster liberalism faced utterly different challenges.[20] The vexatious nature of the land question in Irish politics and the presence of stark and occasionally violent sectarian divisions within Irish society, had long posed stern tests for local liberalism. Ostensibly, Ulster liberalism had proven itself equal to these challenges and the Ulster Liberal Society was bolstered by its best ever general election performance which it posted at the 1880 poll – taking nine of the province's twenty-nine seats.[21] By 1885, however, this rosy situation for the Liberal Society had been utterly transformed and they were annihilated in the general election of that year.[22]

The Ulster liberals had been effectively crushed between the jaws of a Parnellite and Conservative vice. The Conservative versus Liberal consensual dichotomy in Ulster politics was replaced by the conflicting polarities of loyalist versus nationalist. As a result, the Ulster liberals lost much of their traditional support base. The rural Catholic tenant farmers switched allegiance to Parnellite candidates, and their Presbyterian counter-parts supported conservatives who campaigned on a straight anti-home rule ticket, as did the 'improving artisans' of urban Ulster. The Ulster liberals' failure to take a firm stance on the issue of home rule undoubtedly contributed to their electoral humiliation. More importantly, in the short term, the Irish conservatives, with their close affiliations to the Orange Order, the Irish Episcopalian Church and the interests of Irish landlordism, had stolen a substantial march on their Liberal rivals in the race to forge a new anti-home rule alliance to meet the Nationalist threat.

The internal divisions within Ulster liberalism over the national question reached crisis proportions by February 1886. The Liberal Society was caught between the conflicting extremes of full co-operation with their erstwhile opponents, the Ulster conservatives and their Orange allies or wholehearted support for Gladstone. In the face of that insoluble dilemma, the leadership of the society chose to prevaricate for as long as possible, hiding behind the soothing notion that: 'Mr. Gladstone had said nothing to imply that he intended to repeal the Act of Union',[23] or of 'granting Ireland an independent Nationalist parliament ... no matter what anybody might say or pretend'.[24]

Tod's status within Ulster liberalism had been significantly enhanced following the Ulster liberals' electoral demise and with that its direct representation at Westminster and its clearest line of communication with the Liberal Party's leadership. Tod, from December 1885 until the emergence of the ascendant star of T. W. Russell during the 1886 election campaign, was unquestionably the best-known and best-connected Ulster Liberal outside the province. She was also prepared to offer a virtually full-time commitment to political life, which stood in stark contrast to the majority of her peers, whose consuming business interests tended to take precedence over serious political involvements. Yet there is no evidence of Tod's support being enlisted by any of the competing factions or of her taking any part in the acrimonious public debate being conducted in the liberal press between those opposing elements. That situation changed dramatically at the cathartic Ulster Liberal Convention which met at St George's Hall, Belfast, to decide the future direction of provincial liberalism. This provided the venue for Tod to formally nail her colours to the Unionist mast.

The convention was held on 20 March 1886 and 600 delegates attended. Three motions were debated at the convention, which was brought together under the pretext of 'discuss[ing] the three questions specified by Mr. Gladstone in his letter to Lord De Vese [sic] ... for information upon the Irish Question'.[25] In reality, however, the convention marked the concluding act in the fractious struggle for the soul of Ulster liberalism. The first two

motions, which called for the introduction of no exceptional coercive legislation and for an advancement of Ashbourne's Land Act, were uncontentious
and received almost unanimous support. The third motion was still nomi-
nally supportive of Gladstone but, crucially, it specifically denounced the
concept of a devolved Irish legislature. Tod was called upon to provide the
concluding arguments in support of this third motion. Her appearance was
greeted by a mixture of hoots of derision and loud applause, but she does
not appear to have been unduly perturbed as she began her keynote address
by critically prodding the supporters of unfettered Gladstonianism who
were largely responsible for her raucous entrance:

> I have heard it hinted since entering this hall that some who have
> hitherto helped me in asking for the enfranchisement of women will
> draw back, because I have thought it right to speak here to-day. But I
> do not believe ... any ... of them would like to fall below the justice of
> a Tory member [William Johnston].[26]

Having subdued her detractors, Tod turned to the main body of her address
and provided a concise précis of the position of the majority feeling in the
hall:

> My presence reminds you how vitally interested women are in the just
> settlement of the question of government ... in my opinion anything
> larger than provincial councils would totally defeat the object of [good
> government] ... We all know quite well that the Dublin atmosphere
> even now is not by any means always congenial to business from Belfast
> and Derry and elsewhere. No harm in that; let them do their own work
> in their own way, but then let us do our work in our own way.[27]

With this address, Tod played her part in helping to administer the last rites
to the Ulster Liberal Society, which was no longer able to sustain the pretence
of unity in the face of the overwhelming imperative presented to it by the
constitutional question following the convention. Thereafter, Tod diverted
the bulk of her considerable energies into the forthcoming struggle against
the first and second Home Rule Bills and towards the creation of organisational structures which were primarily designed to provide a vehicle for the
exertion of Liberal Unionist influence within the nascent Unionist alliance.
Before considering Tod's role in developing the UWLUA and exploring the
role of women in the Unionist movement at this time, it would seem instruc-
tive to formulate an answer to the fundamental question of why Tod objected
so strenuously to home rule.

III

At the most basic level, Tod's opposition was firmly grounded in the belief that the Irish political infrastructure was underdeveloped to such an extent that it could not possibly sustain any system of government based on the accepted principles of a bourgeois democracy. For Tod:

> the conditions of a free democracy [did] not exist in Ireland. Before they [could] exist the two great training influences of widespread education and large local government must have room to be fairly brought into operation.[28]

That was reinforced by her belief that any conceivable future parliament in Dublin:

> would be unequally divided between two forms of Toryism: Parnellite Toryism, with its hierarchy of tyranny, its protective system, its hampering restrictions on trade, its use of questions of social reform as an engine for political purposes; and Orange Toryism, which can have no other mission but to fight and oppose.[29]

Of the two, however, it was undoubtedly Parnellite Toryism that Tod liked least. Tod particularly feared that much of her lifetime's work in the interests of women would be undone by any future Nationalist parliament. She made that point forcefully in a letter to the Liberal cabinet minister and intellectual, James Bryce, during the second home rule crisis:

> in the name of temperance workers, social purity workers, workers for justice to women in education, property, civil rights and political status … I resist [home rule] … the men who would be the ultimate rulers are not only unsympathetic with some of these reforms … but absolutely antagonistic.[30]

But Tod's objections to home rule cannot solely be attributed to her interest in women's rights. Her antipathy towards Parnellite Nationalism was inextricably linked to her negative views of Catholicism in general and Irish Catholicism in particular. She was convinced that:

> The same forces which have kept back the majority of women in Ireland, and would if parted from England keep them down permanently, would of course have retrogressive effects in other directions.[31]

'Home Rule means Rome Rule' echoed as the great rallying cry of Irish Protestants throughout the home rule era, and anti-Catholicism proved a highly durable bonding agent in the struggle to achieve and thence maintain a degree of unity of purpose in the potentially fractious Irish Unionist movement. Nevertheless, it would be impossible to dismiss Tod as an uncomplicated 'no Popery' agitator. There is no evidence of Tod publicly attacking the theological doctrines of Roman Catholicism in word or print. However, there seems no doubt that, as both a committed Presbyterian and a Liberal nonconformist, she strenuously disagreed with many of the fundamental tenets of the Catholic faith. Tod always confined the expression of her prejudices to the deleterious consequences of Catholicism in the temporal sphere. This was especially true of her views on the strong association between Catholicism, ignorance and poverty. That was bolstered by what she perceived as the marked contrast between the progressive bourgeois affluence of the rapidly expanding north-eastern economy with the retrogressive torpor and endemic agrarian poverty in southern and western Ireland. Expressed in its simplest form, Tod adjudged that this disparity in fortunes could be accounted for by what would later become the classic Weberian dictum that 'Protestantism [was] more favourable to the industrial virtues than Catholicism'.[32] Therefore, any parliament dominated by rural southern Catholic Irishmen with their naive and outmoded views on protectionism would naturally be inimical to the interests of the 'Presbyterian citadel' of Belfast with its export-orientated manufacturing industries. As with industry, so too with education. Tod, the great promoter of women's education, held the optimistic opinion that 'the one thing that Ireland is rich in is brains'.[33] Yet she also believed that:

> the thing which has been most hindered and weighted with extraneous considerations by the clergy of the popular [i.e. catholic] Church is general education. At this moment they are opposing a proposal of compulsion, although the proportion of illiterates in their flocks, after sixty years of an excellent system of education ... is painfully large ... their ideal is by no means universal education, but only high education for a selected number. In this number women are very rarely included.[34]

Tod's perceptions of Catholicism were closely connected to her views on race and ethnicity. She undoubtedly ascribed to the racial theories, which had reached new levels of popularity in the post-Darwinian period and were commonly held – from mutually antagonistic perspectives – by both Irish Unionists and Nationalists.[35] Salisbury's infamous 'Hottentot' (meaning barbarian) remark when referring to the fitness of the Irish to govern themselves during the debate on the first Home Rule Bill is perhaps the best known expression of that kind of Victorian racialism. Tod certainly did not place the Irish, by which she meant 'the majority of the people, wholly or partly Celtic, and chiefly Catholic', quite so far down the convoluted racial chain of traits and capabilities as the leader of the Conservative wing of the Unionist Party, but she did think that their 'special characteristics' meant that 'social forces affect them differently from the way they would affect Englishmen', and that 'their temperament is such that it is hardly able alone to create a quiet, commonplace prosperity'.[36] Given that, she somewhat patronisingly advocated that:

> the wise attitude towards them is not one which is easily assumed, or which costs nothing. It means respect for the Celtic people ... sympathy, endless patience, appreciation of their fine qualities; but no weak sentimentality, which only serves to relax the moral fibre ... nor wilful blindness to unwelcome facts, which encourages them to shut their own eyes.[37]

Tod's views on race and ethnicity underpinned her belief that:

> if a majority must be allowed to try so dangerous an experiment, then [the Ulster Unionists] must be allowed to carry out our own plans in our own portion of the country ... and ... refuse to submit to ... the reactionary rubbish which is called by the abused name of patriotism. It is bad enough to have an unprogressive community obliged to live ... by the ways of a progressive, but the reverse way is unspeakably worse ... we in Ulster must demand a separate jurisdiction, so as to keep our lives in our own hand.[38]

Tod stands out as one of the earliest and most consistent advocates of excluding Ulster from the provisions of any home rule settlement, and her readiness to put forward that solution provides a sound indication of her Liberal Unionist credentials. But the idea of exclusion was never more than a second best option for Tod or her fellow Liberal Unionists. She expressed this reality most succinctly at the *conversazione* of 1892, where she underlined that:

> it is necessary for Ulster to speak again, to speak unitedly and formally ... but let it be observed it speaks not for itself alone – no, nor chiefly – but as the first line of defence for the whole island ... it is as much from a sense of duty to Ireland as for the insistence for our own right to preserve our own civil and religious liberty that Ulster gives its vote of solemn warning.[39]

Although Tod propounded the notion of Ulster as a separate entity mainly as a wrecking measure ultimately designed to preserve the constitutional status quo, she undoubtedly derived a keen sense of her own identity from the province and from the ethnic group which she believed that she belonged to: the Ulster-Scots.[40] At the same time, she also regarded herself as an Irishwoman and took exception to those of her Nationalist opponents, like Michael Davitt, who accused her of not being fully Irish,[41] by arguing that:

> the prehistoric and unceasing intercourse between Scotland and the North of Ireland ... makes the gibe of Ulstermen as aliens about as wise as it would be to call the Irish-descended highlanders aliens in Scotland.[42]

Tod's sense of identity and her world-view was perhaps most profoundly influenced by her Presbyterianism. Tod's closest political affiliations were with the Presbyterian socio-economic elite who dominated both Ulster liberalism and Liberal Unionism. She shared their specific grievance culture, which had traditionally been focused against the Episcopalian landlord class and the viceregal authorities in Dublin for unfairly excluding them from the offices and rewards which their financial and social status merited. She also shared in the wider sense of Presbyterian grievance, which was largely the result of long-standing tensions between Presbyterian tenant-farmers and their mainly Episcopalian landlords. Those grievances and tensions remained, despite the coming together of Episcopalian and Presbyterian in the Unionist movement after 1886 and they provided Ulster Liberal Unionism with much of its *raison d'être*.[43]

The extent of Tod's Presbyterian particularism and her identification with the claims of the Liberal Unionist elite to their fair share of appointments was brought into sharpest relief by her efforts to secure a seat on the Irish Privy Council for William James Pirrie, the chairman of the shipbuilders Harland and Wolff and Ulster's 'Napoleon of Industry'. She pressed his claim in a letter to the Marquis of Dufferin and Ava thus:

> our excellent Lord Mayor, Mr. Pirrie ... [would like] ... a seat in the Irish Privy Council ... I cannot help thinking that in this matter we Presbyterians have something like a special claim. In all the two and a half centuries that they have lived and laboured in Ireland, not one was ever in that Council until the Gladstonians put Mr. T.A. Dickson there; which was certainly no pleasure to his co-religionists. Of course that is balanced now by our Unionist leader, Mr. Sinclair, but there is surely room for another. Although Mrs. Pirrie is a Unitarian, her husband belongs to us.[44]

IV

It has been argued that Tod became a Unionist because she 'viewed herself as British, rather than Irish'.[45] That, in part, is of course true. But, as I have hopefully demonstrated, Tod was a lifelong Unionist Liberal, who became a Liberal Unionist because of the interaction of a complex mixture of factors which defy convenient categorisation. Her denominational affiliation; her sense of regional and national identity and of group allegiance; her interpretation of Liberal ideals; her view of the other significant groups in her society and her interest in women's affairs, all contributed to her leaving the Liberal fold in 1886. Tod's abandonment of the Liberal Party has also been seen as part of the rightwards trend in late Victorian feminism.[46] Again, this seems to be largely a question of perspective, as Tod's stances would not appear to have shifted significantly on any major issue post-1886. She continued to press for the reform of Irish local government and the abolition of the castle administration; she continued to advocate the importance of incremental reform of the Irish landholding system; she remained a typically socially conservative Liberal in the Gladstonian mould and she promoted markedly similar women's issues, albeit in new political clothing.[47] Her desertion of the Liberal Party must, therefore, be attributed primarily to Gladstone's reframing of the Irish constitutional question.

That is not to deny that the Liberal schism in 1886 and the subsequent realignment in British and Irish politics had important personal and institutional consequences for the women's movement. At a personal level, for Tod at least, the actions of former Liberal suffrage colleagues such as Josephine Butler in supporting the first Home Rule Bill caused a 'bitterness ... the injury [of which] can never be cured in this world'.[48] At an institutional level, the traditionally Liberal feminist movement was fragmented into Conservative, Liberal Unionist and Liberal wings, which competed against each other to produce a series of new women's organisations.

Tod was instrumental in gathering together a Belfast women's group in April 1886. This organisation appears to have enjoyed only a fleeting existence. This can be mainly attributed to the fact that Tod spent much of her time from April to June 1886 speaking on anti-home rule platforms and election rallies in England in support of Liberal Unionist candidates, who included her friend and long-time supporter of women's suffrage, Leonard Courtney.[49] At the same time, she was also involved in organising the collection of 30,000 Ulsterwomen's signatures for a petition which was sent to Queen Victoria calling on her to refuse the royal assent in the event of the Home Rule Bill passing through parliament.[50] The UWLUA was established in May 1888 after:

a large number of liberal Unionist ladies throughout the kingdom ... decided to organise themselves in a central association with local branches ... the first committee formed was in Birmingham ... the next was the Ulster committee, to which nearly sixty influential ladies have already given their signature.[51]

The impetus to develop a national Liberal Unionist women's organisation was partly inspired by the success of the Primrose League, but was mainly a response to the formation of the Women's Liberal Federation in 1887.[52] Tod, inevitably, played a pivotal role in both the local and central bodies and she represented the UWLUA, alongside Mrs T.W. Russell and Mrs W.P. Sinclair (the wife of William Pirrie Sinclair, Liberal Unionist MP for Falkirk Burghs and the cousin of Thomas Sinclair) on the central committee of the Women's Liberal Unionist Association.[53] The high incidence of husband-and-wife partnerships in Liberal suffragism has attracted some comment, and any comparison of the respective memberships of the UWLUA and ULUA will bear out the veracity of that observation.[54] Indeed, it was not only the wives, but also the daughters and sisters of Ulster's Liberal Unionist elite who predominated in the upper echelons of the UWLUA. But whereas the senior male figures enjoyed dual membership and took an ever increasing part in directing the activities of the women's organisation, Tod was the only female to figure in the ULUA.

In the absence of precise admission criteria, it is impossible to establish whether Tod's fellow Liberal Unionist women were specifically disbarred from membership of the ULUA, were actively discouraged from joining or simply preferred to express their political views through the medium of the sister organisation. It is clear, however, that Tod's period of real prominence within the ULUA was brief and lasted only as long as she was the sole nationally recognisable figure amongst the local Liberal Unionist movement. With the rise of Russell, his parliamentary colleague Thomas Lea, and less acclaimed Belfast based Liberal Unionists like Sinclair, MacGeagh, Andrews, Duffin and MacKnight, that situation rapidly changed. As a result, Tod's status was much diminished within the male organisation. From 1888, she concentrated her efforts mainly within the sphere of the women's organi-sation. The primary directive of the UWLUA was:

> to spread information by voice, by pen, and by the distribution of literature; to give local help; and to give the moral support of members to the cause of the Union, which both in England and Ireland, but especially the latter, most deeply affects both their interests and their duties.[55]

In short, the women's association was conceived as being an appendage of the Liberal Unionist party in the on-going struggle against home rule and not as an agency for promoting the interests of women. It was relatively successful in carrying out that remit, which was pursued with renewed vigour during the second home rule crisis of 1892–93. Tod, as always, was to the fore. This was despite her growing ill-health, which was attributed to extreme over-work during the first home rule controversy.[56] She conducted a speaking tour on behalf of the UWLUA to support Liberal Unionist candidates in Scotland during the 1892 general election campaign,[57] and was chairperson of the joint committee formed by the UWLUA and the dames of the local Primrose League to support the successful candidature of the Liberal Unionist, Hugh Oakley Arnold-Forster, in West Belfast.[58] She was also the chief speaker at the first ever all-women's Unionist demonstration to be held in Ireland, in the Ulster Hall on 6 April 1893, where she repeated her oft-mooted assertion that the:

> One great enemy was the ignorance of the people of Great Britain on the question [of home rule], and it should be the aim and object of every one of them to do what they could to remove that ignorance.[59]

That demonstration, 'quite unique in [its] composition', marks out the degree of advance made by women within the Irish Unionist movement from 1886–93.[60] From an extremely low starting point, Unionist women had unquestionably managed to carve out a distinct niche for themselves as a useful force of canvassers, fund-raisers and, most importantly, propagandists. They had become an important and overt arm of organised Unionism. Supporting the Unionist cause also seems to have proven more attractive to the middle-class ladies of urban Ulster than the pursuit of women's enfranchisement. That said, there were highly committed exponents of women's franchise rights within the various Unionist women's organisations, but the constitutional issue tended to overwhelm all other considerations in the 1886–93 period. Clearly, in view of the political and social disabilities of the late-Victorian period, women were unable to occupy the highest offices of the Unionist Party and only Tod managed truly to transcend the gender mores of the day. However, it is equally clear that relatively few Unionist men enjoyed or even aspired to attain those offices, and the types of political activities undertaken by active Unionist women were distinctly comparable to those performed by the bulk of active Unionist men.

The last mention of the UWLUA which I have managed to find was in 1896, the year of Tod's death. With her passing the organisation seems to have petered out. This, however, was probably no more than coincidental, as many of the institutional structures created by Irish Unionists to resist home rule between 1886 and 1893 lapsed into abeyance in face of the much reduced indigenous threat from the fragmented post-Parnell Nationalist movement, and Rosebery distancing the Liberal Party from Irish home rule. Those structures were not resurrected until the devolution crisis of 1904–5 with the formation of the all-male Ulster Unionist Council. A specific women's organisation, the Ulster Women's Unionist Council, was formed in 1911 in the midst of the looming constitutional crisis and 'with the incipient intent of supporting male Unionists' opposition to home rule for Ireland'.[61]

V

Isabella Tod died on 9 December 1896. In a life devoted to public service, she made an immense contribution to the varied causes which attracted her interest. The Presbyterian Church, the suffrage movement, the campaign to increase educational provision for girls and women, the temperance movement and a host of charitable institutions all benefited from her services. Yet in death, she was chiefly celebrated as a heroine of the successful 'crusades' mounted by Irish Unionists and their British allies to resist Gladstone's home rule bills.[62] Her funeral was attended by virtually all of the leading provincial figures in those crusades and the route from Elmwood Presbyterian Church, where her funeral service was held, to her final resting place at Balmoral Cemetery, was thronged by an 'immense concourse'[63] moved to pay silent tribute to the woman 'who ... [had] done more than any other person whatever for the cause of the Union'.[64]

Tod had indeed campaigned tirelessly for the Unionist cause throughout the last ten years of her life. She had taken a prominent part in the death of Ulster liberalism and had performed the role of midwife in the birth of Ulster Liberal Unionism. Her colleagues were convinced that:

> so great was her influence and the importance attached to her opinion on the Irish question that she was instrumental in preventing several persons of importance in public life from following Mr Gladstone.[65]

She was instrumental in providing the Unionist movement with an efficient and energetic women's auxiliary wing, which provided a sound model for later Unionist women's organisations.[66] Most important of all, however, she had been one of the earliest and most articulate of the Irish Unionist missionaries to Great Britain. There, as an Ulster Presbyterian with impeccable and well-established Liberal credentials, she concentrated on attempting to woo the crucial nonconformist vote away from its support for the Liberal Party by playing on that constituency's traditional fears of Catholicism and by stressing the dire consequences for their Irish co-religionists in a home rule parliament, ultimately bent on complete separation and dominated by men who had 'shown utter indifference to all the canons of the Moral Law'.[67]

It seems surprising then, given the strength of her commitment to the Unionist cause and the degree of contemporary prominence which she enjoyed, that Tod has been denied her place in the Unionist pantheon. This, of course, can be largely explained by the long-standing gender bias which has been as prevalent in the Unionist historiographical tradition as in many other forms of Irish historical scholarship. Yet it has also been brought about by the failure of Unionist historians to recognise sufficiently the contribution made to the Irish Unionist alliance by Ulster's Liberal Unionists. Tod was an archetypal Ulster Liberal Unionist and the source of her success within the Unionist movement lay in her ability to enunciate the concerns and interests of the Presbyterian business and tenant-farming communities, who provided the Ulster Liberal Unionists with the bulk of their adherents. Indeed, so central was Tod to the Ulster Liberal Unionist experience that no study of that phenomenon could possibly be considered complete without lengthy reference to her.

New Battlegrounds: The Development of the Salvation Army in Ireland in the Nineteenth Century

GRÁINNE M. BLAIR

I

Money is the sinews of war; and, as society is at present constituted, neither carnal nor spiritual wars can be carried on without money. But there is something more necessary still. War cannot be waged without soldiers ... More than money – a long, long way – I want men; and when I say men, I mean women also – men of experience, men of brains, men of heart and men of God.[1]

The Salvation Army, as it became known in 1878, grew out of the earlier work of the East London Revival Society, later called the East London Christian Mission. It was the theory and practice of such work, led by William Booth, his partner Catherine and their eight children, which provided the focus for the development of the army. The army considers the British Isles as one complete salvationist territory, with its overall command located in London,[2] and, prior to this research, no separation of Irish and British data has existed.[3] Worldwide territorial decisions and ideology were formulated in the London headquarters and the theory and practice of the army's work influenced, and was informed by, late nineteenth-century public opinion and politics.[4]

This article explores 'new battlegrounds' for the army in the nineteenth century. In particular, it focuses on two aspects of the salvationists' work in relation to nineteenth-century Ireland: Irish women who used the army's English rescue network and the expansion of the army into Ireland from the 1880s onwards.[5] The role of some of the first women salvationists responsible for the development of the army in Ireland is also highlighted. In its expansion the army frequently encountered serious opposition. These publicised 'battles' served to establish the army in the popular imagination as reports of events were carried regularly in both salvationist and non-salvationist publications.

II

Catherine Mumford Booth was directly responsible for influencing her husband, William, and her children in establishing the ethos of the army. Indeed, the distinct beliefs and enduring work of the army owed more to her than to anyone else. The Booths set out on a crusade to wage war on behalf of London's slum-dwellers and the so-called 'sunken tenth' of the populace. Neither Catherine nor William Booth accepted that such appalling social and economic conditions were necessarily the will of God, the lot of the poor or the deserved results of personal sin. In this they were well ahead of most of their contemporaries' Malthusian and *laissez faire* beliefs on the status of the deserving poor. The Booths were appalled by the extent of homelessness, so the first Salvation Army shelters were established and a new era in social reform began. They aimed to help young women of the kind which William Booth described as:

> The bastard of a harlot, born in a brothel, suckled on gin, and familiar from earliest infancy with all the bestialities of debauch, violated before she is twelve, and driven out into the streets by her father a year or two later, what chance is there for such a girl in this world ... I say nothing about the next?[6]

Findings like this fired the Booths' convictions that they were duty bound to change social conditions in order to help people towards salvation. By choosing an army and its militaristic language and methods, William Booth clearly belonged to the Christian militaristic tradition, arising out of the Crimea War and other strands of romantic imperialism. The army believed that the message of God was not accessible to everyone, especially the lowest orders of society who were excluded from traditional church services by their dress, language and lack of money for pew seats.[7] Salvationists believed that the rescuer and rescued were equally sinful and that people found it difficult to maintain a Christian life. The army actively recruited amongst all classes, offering both hope and support to those in need. This was the real strength behind the development of their early rescue work. Furthermore, effectiveness was ensured by exchanging the democratic conventions of Methodism for a Booth autocracy. The unity of the army in the early days of its rapid growth was one of its strengths, but the central authority held by William Booth's autocracy was to prove difficult for some of his followers to accept. As the first general of the organisation he legally controlled all the army property, commissioning officers and defined the orders and regulations by which salvationists lived. This autocracy was approved by an act of parliament in 1878, which gave Booth the right to designate his successor. Only another act of parliament in 1931 finally revoked these powers. William Booth's son, Bramwell, succeeded his father and remained in control until he was deposed in 1929. With Bramwell's sister, Eva, serving as general of the organisation from 1934–39, an element of continuity was ensured. Indeed, there was a Booth at the helm during the majority of the army's formative years.

The army set out to win converts from all walks of life, the majority of whom were from the slums and the growing working classes. The newly converted salvationist was immediately recognisable, due to the army's distinctive uniform. Converts changed their way of living, which often resulted in conflict with family, friends and employers, as they moved away from their old patterns of behaviour. Conversion involved living a new life based on the creation of solid family life, the encouragement of temperance and thrift, a stable relationship with the army and strict observance of Sunday as a special holy day. This moral transformation had direct cultural implications as the lower classes moved away from their old 'vices' to the 'virtues' of the middle classes. Furthermore, converts were saved to save and having been saved, were ready to rescue others.[8]

III

It was Florence Soper, wife of Bramwell Booth, who commanded and expanded the army's Women's Social Services, ensuring its position as the largest, most effective and perhaps most innovative rescue organisation worldwide. The rescue network provided women with refuge, employment, friendship, education, training, lodgings, childcare, adoption, fostering, medical care and spiritual guidance. Many Irish women used the Salvation Army's rescue network in the nineteenth century.[9] Indeed, out of a total of 2,891 records on women using the network during the period 1886–92, 233 Irish women are included.

How did these women become involved in the rescue network? Twenty-one per cent of the women included in the Irish sample went to a meeting or spoke to a salvationist in the street. Once a woman professed she would be brought from a local corps meeting to the area receiving house. It seems that the support of other women was very important to many of these Irish women. There were, for example, cases of older women sending younger women directly to army homes: 13 per cent of applications were referred by previous users of the army's rescue network. Named individuals, such as matrons of non-salvationist institutions offering refuge or hospitalisation, accounted for 37 per cent. It is clear from this high referral figure that there was an institutional network which would refer women from one institution to another. In spite of this, the salvationists' preferred method of application was self-referral, as it implied that a woman wanted to change her own life. Salvationists believed that these women stood a better chance of staying saved. Such was the case of Rosie, an orphan who had spent some time in a convent (probably a Magdalen home) in Waterford. From there she travelled to Cork and then to Dublin, where she worked in laundries before going into a non-salvationist refuge in Baggot Street. However:

> before leaving Baggot Street she heard of the Bethel from other girls. She had a strong desire to come to us and at last in spite of all persuasions, she left Dublin and walked to Belfast, came direct to the Home saying 'If you haven't a vacancy for me now, I am going to the workhouse to wait until you have'.[10]

The salvationists made room for her. Other women who sought refuge in the salvationist homes just needed a safe place to go. To cite just one example, Emily needed 'a quiet safe refuge' after her brother's sudden death, which left 'her alone, friendless and ill'.[11] How successful the salvationists were in their endeavours to spiritually save these women is illustrated in Table 1 below.

The figure of 60 per cent for women recorded as being saved in Table 1 may be particularly high because many women may have felt that they had to make an effort to be seen to change their lives to benefit successfully from

Table 1: *Numbers of Irish Women Using the Salvation Army Rescue Network 1886–92, who were Listed as Saved in Salvationist Records*

Category	no.	%
Women recorded as being saved	141	60
Women initially recorded as being saved but then became backsliders	7	3
Women not saved	52	22
Women who professed but were not saved	11	5
Women not saved but wished to be	3	<2
Women not saved as they were Roman Catholics	3	<2
No information	16	7
Total	233	100

the rescue network. Four women from this sample eventually became salvationist soldiers. The struggles to get saved are well recorded and although some women ran away, got drunk and backslid, they were re-admitted to the rescue network and were eventually saved. From this sample two women were dismissed for unspecified 'bad conduct', another two ran away and a further thirteen were recorded as returning to their 'sinful lives'. Some of these women had other problems such as mental disorders, which may have been associated with sexually transmitted diseases. Others had serious alcohol problems. Such inmates must have made life difficult for all women living together in the rescue homes.

Of the 233 Irish women surveyed, 120 or 52 per cent required medical attention for a variety of complaints. Not all of these women were treated in hospital, but rather in a variety of institutions which provided medical attention. Illness kept a woman from working and after a stay in hospital, many were destitute and needed refuge for temporary convalescence. Ninety-three of the 120 women needed immediate hospitalisation. A detailed examination of their illnesses clearly identified certain complaints such as rheumatism and chest problems. Other women were suffering from pleurisy and bronchial illnesses which, combined with inflammation and lumbago, could have been caused by working in textile industries or laundries. Whatever their origin, all of these illnesses were closely associated with poverty. Confinements and gynaecological complaints were the second highest admission, recorded at 23 per cent. Many of these women were admitted to local infirmaries and workhouses, a considerable number of which had a hospital section by the late nineteenth century. The majority of these women, thirty-nine, representing 33 per cent, were admitted because of syphilis and many of these were multiple syphilitic admissions. Indeed, three of the women in the sample died from syphilitic aggravated causes. One of these cases was that of Agnes who left home after her father's re-marriage and ended up in a brothel. Illness sent her to a lock ward, then to domestic service where she was accused of stealing a watch. She was subsequently imprisoned. From prison Agnes went to Tudor Lodge, a non-salvation refuge, which provided her with some care. She was then admitted to an infirmary suffering from rheumatism. By the time this woman reached the salvationists, she was dying of consumption, with an abscess in her side and the worst kind of syphilis. Another woman, Ellen, was fifteen when she was forced onto the streets. She eventually turned up at a salvationist meeting many years later, aged thirty and very ill. Ellen had eight children, seven of whom had died. Initially cared for in the salvationist home, extreme illness sent her to the infirmary. Two weeks later Ellen brought her daughter with her and they both stayed in the home for approximately three weeks. Unfortunately Ellen was now dying and had to return to the infirmary. The salvationists visited her there until she died, granting her last request to have an army funeral: 'She is one of the brightest examples we have had of the wonderful power of God to work a complete change in the very vilest'.[12]

Table 2: *Continued Contact of Irish Women with the Salvation Army Rescue Network in the British Isles, 1886–92*

Nature of contact after leaving refuge	no.	%
Still in contact	84	36
Still in contact as re-admitted to SA rescue network	15	6
Still in contact as sent to another SA home	4	2
Still in contact now an SA soldier	4	2
Not in contact as died	3	1
No information if still in contact	123	53
Total	233	100

Almost half of the Irish women recorded in Table 2 were in contact after they left the rescue network. The salvationists understood the difficulties women experienced in striving to maintain their new, reformed lifestyle outside the confines of the refuge. As a result, women were encouraged to spend Sundays with the salvationists – attending meetings, subscribing to a fund and acting as role models for women who were still maintained in the rescue network.

IV

During the late nineteenth century, the army seemed to be incredibly successful with its membership growing from 5,000 in 1887 to 100,000 by 1901.[13] Further evidence of the organisation's popularity is provided by sales figures for the army's newspaper, *The War Cry*. This paper, selling at a halfpenny per copy, had a circulation of approximately 17,000 copies per issue by 1879, increasing to about 200,000 copies per issue by 1881. Such figures are perhaps not surprising, given that the *Christian Mission Magazine* in 1878 recorded that expansion was the main aim of the army. This was to be achieved through winning new territories. Instructions for this expansion were specific and were detailed in *Orders and Regulations of the Salvation Army*.[14] Spontaneity was not encouraged. Instead military precision was favoured and the areas chosen for a so-called salvationist invasion were scrutinised to ensure success.

However, opposition to the salvationists' work came in many forms. The apparent success of the army incited many, including a considerable number of religious notables, to discuss the vulgarity of a group introducing religion in public houses, on the street, in theatres and other easily accessible public venues. Such discussions invariably missed the point of the salvationists' aims – to save the lower classes.[15] Others did not express their opposition verbally. During the 1880s much physical violence was also directed towards the newly formed army.[16] *The War Cry* of January 1882, for example, stated that twenty-three children had been injured in various battles, as well as recording adult soldiers' loss of life, limb and liberty. Assaults were common-place in these years and the police did little to prevent attacks. But ultimately the persistence of the salvationists won through a barrage of insults, attacks, rotten eggs, dead fish, lime, tomatoes and potatoes.

Women were constantly involved in the army's work as leading mission-aries and administrators. Indeed forty-one of the ninety-one first salvation officers were women. It was Caroline Reynolds, a veteran officer from the Christian Mission days in Whitechapel, who was entrusted with the 'invasion' of Ireland. On 3 May 1880 she accepted the Army's Colours for the 1st Irish Corps to be formed in Belfast and the 2nd Irish Corps to be formed in Londonderry from Catherine Booth.[17] Reynolds said she was not afraid to go to Ireland as she had 'put [herself] in the hands of God and the General, and [had] given [herself] to be led by them'.[18] Reynolds also believed the Irish to be 'naturally a religious people, you know'.[19]

The salvationists arrival in Ireland was eventful to say the least. They came virtually unprepared for the cultural, religious and political differences which existed in that part of the British empire. To Ireland, the salvationists brought a treasonous flag and 'orange' hymn books which simultaneously both appealed to and divided their congregations depending on their reli-gious denomination. At their first outing in Belfast the salvationists were surrounded by a large group of working-class people. Once they finished singing and praying they moved to 'a room called the Bethel in Craven Street'. There 'the place was so full we would have got more [converts]'.[20] That first weekend the salvationists continued to hold open-air meetings and indoor meetings in the Bethel. They also conducted some home visiting. They attracted some recruits and, by trial and error, discovered better places to attract crowds and their packed meetings were attended by many from different religious congregations. Relating her early experiences in Belfast, Caroline Reynolds stated:

> the people seem all so kind. When I got to the hall I found brethren keeping the doors, brethren to make the collection, and do anything I wanted; in fact I don't think we ever have been received with such a welcome as we have here. I believe the Lord is going to give us Belfast![21]

Soon their meetings were drawing crowds of over 1,000 and these numbers continued to grow. For instance, when the salvation general visited Belfast in October 1886, 10,000 people attended the meeting. There are also examples of open-air salvationist meetings held each Sunday on the steps of the Custom House in Belfast regularly attracting congregations of 2,000–3,000 people. These meetings were conducted by the Belfast Citadel Corps which had been active in the city since 1881. In addition to this corps, the salvationists had branches scattered throughout Belfast. For example, their main barracks of Belfast I was located at Blackstaffe in the centre of the city; Belfast II was situated in the Shankhill area of West Belfast and Bally-macarret Corps was in the south of the city. Indeed, the enthusiasm of the latter was such that it was described as 'a true hot-bed of Salvationism'.[22]

Due to the success of the army in Belfast and the establishment of a salvationist network in Ireland, the first Irish rescue home opened at 63 Great George Street in Belfast in 1887. In keeping with salvationist practice, the home was located as closely as possible to the communities they aimed to assist. In order to offset the home's expenses, fine sewing of linen and handkerchiefs as well as the finishing of shirts provided both cash for the home and employment for women leaving the refuge. By September 1889 the Belfast home had dealt with 250 cases, with most women leaving the refuge to take up employment or to return to family or friends. By 1901 Belfast was the Irish Provincial Army Headquarters with fourteen corps, two societies and a demand for more. By this date, after nearly twenty years in the city, the parent corps, known as the Citadel, was prosperous and making 'substantial progress'.[23] Indeed, such was the progress of the army in Belfast that one 'old and experienced officer' claimed that she had 'never laboured in a town where the general public were more friendly and well-disposed towards Salvationists'.[24]

It seems that the salvationists' success in Belfast spurred them on to further expansion. *The War Cry* for 12 June 1880, reported that Major Caroline Reynolds and 'three of The Army had gone to lay siege to London-derry' some days earlier on 1 June. However, the reception the salvationists received was marred by violence as the same column in *The War Cry* also reported that 'Heavy Fighting in Londonderry' had occurred. The salvation-ists got off to a quiet start in this predominantly Catholic city by holding an open-air meeting. However, later on they began to sing hymns and had:

> only sung one verse when young men came running from all sides – regular Fenians! I thought, here's a beautiful lot of people to get saved! They yelled-danced-spit-hooted – everything! We couldn't get a hear-ing at all ... We saw we couldn't have an open-air at night, so we came straight back to the Rink. Never, the longest day I have to live, shall I forget that sight! The police wouldn't let the crowd in, so they had formed a circle round the Rink to yell! And they did yell![25]

The Rink was reportedly surrounded by 'two to three hundred of the roughest men you could find'. Inside, the hall was filled with people who were truly interested in the salvationists' work, but the back rows were full of men of all ages who were determined to disrupt the service: they sat with their hats on, smoked, hooted, groaned and hissed until it was almost impossible to begin the meeting.[26] Four policemen saved the day and the meeting continued in some semblance. It was like this in Londonderry for the next five days as the salvationists sought to save their first five 'souls', who 'are all standing to-day, except one who died a triumphant death'.[27] But in spite of these initial problems in Londonderry the salvationists, as in Belfast and other areas of Ulster, gained a foothold and by 1888 twenty-eight army corps were open and operating in the province. The next stage of their campaign was to move into Dublin.

The battle to establish the army in Dublin was as, if not more, difficult as the problems which the organisation initially faced, for instance, in the east end of London and in Londonderry. As was common worldwide, these pioneering salvationists were physically and verbally attacked. However, in comparison with other cities, it seems that Dublin was particularly danger-ous: missiles were hurled in and out of windows and salvationists were pelted with stones, dead rats, fish bones, rotten fruit and horse manure. *The War Cry* of July 1901 even went as far to describe Dublin as a city:

> whose women are said to be treated with a courtesy unsurpassed in any other part of the world – strange to say, the sight of a woman wearing an Army bonnet in the streets acts upon the crowd like a red rag to an infuriated bull ...[28]

The strength of opposition to the army in Dublin was undoubtedly fuelled by fear and ignorance as to the real nature of their work, especially at a time when the Catholic Church was trying to establish its own charities and warning against proselytism. Proselytism was a reality in eighteenth and nineteenth-century Ireland. Government supported institutions, such as charter schools and foundling hospitals, were seen as highly suspect by the Irish Catholic population.[29] This can be explained by the fact that the majority of established state-supported institutions were managed and governed by those who believed in saving children from 'popery, beggary and idleness'.[30]

Even though many Irish Protestants deeply resented this new wave of souperism and continued to live in harmony with their Catholic neighbours, this did not halt the antagonism. Protestant and other missionaries of any form were anathema to many Catholics. Local Catholic clergy often led the battle against Protestant bible societies preaching and distributing tracts.

These battles took on a new form when bible societies offered free education, food, clothing and shelter to alleviate the growing wretchedness of the Irish from 1830–60, thus creating the reviled 'souper'. From the 1850s it was the particular methods of the Church Mission Society, under the leadership of Reverend Alexander Dallas, that aroused most anger amongst the Catholic population and strengthened Catholic opposition to bible societies.[31]

Dr Paul Cullen, the Catholic Archbishop of Dublin, spearheaded such religious opposition campaigns. Cullen issued many pastorals on the evils of proselytism, including in the 1860s, his opposition to the workhouses and the Poor Law in Ireland. The Protestant Archbishop of Dublin, Dr Whately, also publicly condemned Dallas' organisation and practices, whilst privately subscribing. By 1862, however, the bible societies dwindled to fourteen in number and, as a result, their activities were greatly reduced. The Salvation Army, although coming in the wake of this religious hostility, denied proselytising. Instead the army described itself in the following terms:

> We have no politics, and therefore cannot enter into discussion or arouse enmity between man and man on that point. We do not contend with other religious bodies or attack their creeds. We are not a sect, but an Army of peace, whose one duty is to preach … Our religion is plain, practical, happy and bubbling over with songs.[32]

The first salvationist corps in Dublin opened in South Richmond Street on 31 May 1888.[33] Major Adelaide Cox, writing in 1889, noted that the salvationists made significant progress in their first year in Dublin:

> three hundred and sixty-eight men and women of every class have knelt at the penitent-form in token of their desire to obtain forgiveness and power to live a better and truer life … A most impressive meeting was held on Sunday morning, at the close of which the soldiers of the Corps rose to yield themselves up for a new years service, and pledged themselves to go forth with new determination to win the multitude around them for the King of Kings …We were urged upon by many who have the work at heart to open a Rescue Home in Dublin. There, as in all our large towns, is to be found a multitude of poor girls, dragging out a miserable existence upon the streets, and numbers of warm-hearted friends gathered round me to speak of our Rescue Work and to urge me to represent the need at our Rescue Headquarters …[34]

By 1889 Earlsfort Skating Rink had become the army's Dublin Headquarters and many open-air meetings were held at this location. Large numbers of people continued to attend their meetings. For instance, in 1906 *All the World* reported that street meetings starting at the Bank of Ireland, College Green, which was part of the Dublin 1 corps, moved on to George's Hall for seated meetings for audiences of over 600 people. By this time the army's Dublin headquarters had moved to Lower Abbey Street.

However, in spite of the apparent public interest in their work, salvationists still met resistance in Dublin. Towards the end of the 1890s their work in the city was described as a 'battle still raging'.[35] Colour Sergeant Treacy described the open-air meetings held on the steps of the Custom House as a time when:

> you couldn't hear the strongest voice ... a woman could not attempt to speak ... [the] Army isn't known [here] yet, of course, and the great desire of all our people is for Rescue and Social Work to be started. Meanwhile, the open-air work is the chief weapon, and ... [I] and [my] flag will go, as long as there is a sinner to be reached, or a salvation message to deliver ...[36]

While Treacy was carrying the colours in a salvationist procession in the city, she was attacked by one of the queen's soldiers, who tried to take her flag. However, Treacy held on and although a pitched battle ensued, with the crowd joining in and many missiles being thrown, the salvationists escaped unscathed and were escorted safely to the police station. Undaunted, the salvationists held a prayer meeting in the police yard.[37] But in Dublin, the continued hostility meant that most ranks of the salvationists could not wear their uniforms in public. As *The War Cry* explained:

> [in] most districts, if we visited in uniform, before we left the house, probably every window in the place would be smashed, they say, and much as they dislike it, they are obliged to visit out of uniform.[38]

On other occasions salvationists were punched and kicked, or were deliberately ignored in shops. This gave them all the more reason to gird their loins before re-entering the fray and strengthened the determination of the army to wear their uniform whenever possible, despite the consequences.

In addition to this high level of determination, salvationists also recognised that there were particular social needs to be met in Dublin. In 1914, for example, they drew attention to the fact that:

> There are at least two Dublins, as two Edinburghs or two Liverpools. There is the Dublin comprised of those who are well clad, well housed, and well fed, and there is the ragged, ill-sheltered, and starving Dublin with which we are here concerned ... Of course Dublin is not the only

city with slums of which its inhabitants are ashamed. Indeed, it would, we regret to say, be hard to find a single big city where many of the poorest are not crowded together in a most unwholesome way ... The Army is confronted with peculiar difficulties in the South of Ireland in general and Dublin in particular.[39]

Nineteenth-century Dublin was the unhealthiest city in the British Isles, with the highest rates of death and endemic disease. Deaths from typhoid continued to rise from the 1880s, so that by 1890 the mortality rates from typhoid were higher in Dublin than in any other city in the British Isles, with the exception of Belfast. Continuing problems of overcrowding in unsanitary housing, as well as undernourishment, was the backdrop to life for the majority of unskilled Irish people. Thus salvationists felt that:

Social Work is greatly needed in Ireland. The police of Dublin and Cork say the quays, alleys, and open passages are crowded night after night with penniless sleepers. Out o'works throng the streets. Hunger hides under good clothes ... children ... beg at the Army barracks for a bit of bread.[40]

Slum-Captain Wellbeloved described the city's specific problems, stressing the point that the salvationists' social work was so stressful that officers occasionally had to be called away from the seat of war in order to recuperate. Indeed, conditions were so bad that:

There is enough work in Dublin for half-a-dozen Slum Corps – if we could get to work. An old woman I'm tending has lived fifteen years in a cellar. Such a place! Filled up with rags, ashes and filth. How do I manage? I do my best for them, nurse and clean them and their homes, pray, talk about Christ, and when they are better say right out 'I am a Salvation Army Officer'. Sometimes they let me come back after that, but generally it is the door shut in my face.[41]

Even when the salvationists attempted to address social need with slum work, regularly sending women to the Belfast home, they often came under fire from protesters. The Dublin slum corps were restricted to Smithfield Market and Pill Lane, the back of the slum barracks which was located at the rear of the Four Courts. The latter was a particularly violent area for the salvationists to march through and every time they held meetings in this area, there was a police escort waiting. Both the police and the salvationists faced barricades of barrows and boxes, not to mention all the buckets of water and general refuse thrown at them and the usual ruckus that prevailed.

Despite this opposition to their slum work and their open-air meetings, by December 1913 the army had managed to establish four corps in Dublin and an additional corps in Kingstown (now Dun Laoghaire). Salvationists had also set up a Men's Home which was located in Albert Hall, Peter Street, housing 119 men in need. Open-air meetings continued to be an important facet of their work and were commonly held at Charlemont Bridge, Portabello Bridge, Harold's Cross Bridge and the Phoenix Park. Always looking on the bright side, salvationists like Major Caroline Reynolds, who had successfully opened sixteen stations in Ireland by 1886, reported that:

> although there are great difficulties in the way, there are at the same time some advantages in Ireland which we have not on this side of the Channel, and I feel confident that ultimately The Salvation Army there will be a brilliant success.[42]

This optimistic spirit prevailed. Salvationists writing in 1902, for example, believed that the difficult conditions they had to endure would ensure that: 'Out of Ireland … should come battalions of mighty Salvation Soldiers!'[43]

V

In conclusion, the Salvation Army brought a new way of providing care for those in need. Based on an interactive response to the wants and desires for social betterment of marginalised people, the army developed practical, skilled and cost-effective ways to care. Despite the initial naiveté of the salvationists in expanding their territory and the opposition and difficulties of establishing salvationism in Ireland, their nineteenth-century efforts paid off – they are still providing service and care to various communities in both the north and south of the country.

The reality of the lives of the lower classes did not match the ideals of nineteenth and twentieth-century moralists, economists or politicians. With regards to women, for example, it was a popularly held belief that they had to be protected for their own good, as they were weak and could easily fall victim to the dangers of an immoral life. Factory work was often cited as an excuse for making young women crude and vulgar, as well as providing them with an independent income. This was in spite of the fact that many Irish women's wages did not provide them with enough money to survive. Salvationists understood the lack of self-esteem of the women who presented themselves for help and their particular response of shelter, training, employment, personal development and the support of new friends and a family group, if desired, was unique.

But in Ireland there were specific problems associated with working with women. This was often religiously based, as the issue of proselytism ran deep. Proselytism also has much bearing on contextualising the problems associated with the development of the army in Ireland. The army, with its new type of religion, was particularly foreign to Catholic communities. In addition, salvationists often had English accents and attitudes, which distinguished and alienated them from the native Irish population. The army's religious meetings were noisy, lively affairs, where congregations were encouraged and expected to participate and where women preached publicly and conducted services. These factors may partially explain why the Salvation Army met such resistance in Dublin and Londonderry. Moreover, the army records show that Catholic women left or were removed by their families from the salvationists' rescue home because they had been advised by the local clergy to do so or because they feared that these women's souls were in peril. Throughout Ireland the Catholic clergy preferred women who were at risk or in need to be treated by Catholic agencies and not exposed to other religions.[44] The army did not distinguish between women on religious grounds to the same extent. They believed that the needs of the woman came first and only later encouraged a woman to find her own path to God, even if that was not via salvationism. Most of the other homes open to women in need in Ireland in the nineteenth and early twentieth century were refuges like Magdalen homes. Many of these were places where women had to commit themselves for at least two years or until they were considered fit to return to the world after having undergone a regime of moral education and industrial training. The army provided Irish women with non-judgmental refuge, employment, friendship, education, training, lodgings, childcare, adoption, fostering, medical care and spiritual guidance. During the nineteenth century the provision of such non-judgmental care was innovative to say the least. Furthermore, this approach was obviously effective. The majority of Irish women using the army's rescue network stayed in the refuge only for a short period of time of between one to ten months. These women left to take up employment usually gained for them by the army. Only 6 per cent remained in the rescue network for a longer time ranging from fourteen months to a maximum of three years. This latter group was made up of women who entered the network early in a pregnancy, who stayed for their confinement and subsequent employment and arrangements for their child. Other women were either simply too ill to leave, or chose to live and work with the salvationists.

The primary task of the salvationists was to evangelise the masses and conducting women's social work was one method of achieving this. Moreover, salvationists recognised and publicised the economic inequalities and vulnerability of all women. They, like other rescue networks of their time, reinforced the whore/madonna dichotomy. However, the salvationists believed that, no matter how dreadful the sin, everyone was entitled to help, even if they found it difficult to stay on the path of righteousness. Time and time again army records list the same women being assisted. The salvationists identified themselves with the Irish women they helped and, unlike many other organisations, offered the women the opportunity to become the rescuer rather than the rescued. Within this philosophy, all women were equal and in this the Salvation Army had something unique to offer the women it strove to save.

'Let the Girls Come Forth':
The Early Feminist Ideology of the Irish Women Workers' Union

ALISON BUCKLEY

I

'Let the girls come forth in their lovely garb and take their rightful place as the stars and ornaments of the earth'.

With this rhetorical flourish, a columnist, known only as 'E.A.M.', called on the working women of Dublin to organise themselves in the newly-formed Irish Women Workers' Union (IWWU). The article appeared on 16 September 1911 in the 'Women Workers' Column' of the *Irish Worker* newspaper, the organ of the Irish Transport and General Workers' Union (ITGWU), led by Jim Larkin, the ITGWU's founder and General Secretary. The 'Women Workers' Column', edited by his sister, Delia Larkin, was established as the voice of the IWWU. It provides an invaluable window through which to observe the sorts of issues, interests and the feminism which shaped the early Irish labour movement.

At 8 o'clock on the evening of 5 September 1911, at the Antient Concert Rooms in what is now Pearse Street in Dublin, a group of labour militants, suffragists and revolutionary nationalists gathered to inaugurate the IWWU, Ireland's first labour union exclusively for women.[1] The headlined speaker of the meeting was 'Big Jim' Larkin, founder of the ITGWU and other instruments of Irish working-class action.[2] In rapid succession he set up, as instruments of liberation and the vehicle of his own syndicalist vision, firstly the ITGWU, then the Irish Trade Unions Congress (ITUC) and the Irish Labour Party (ILP).[3] Sitting beside Jim Larkin on the platform that September night was his younger sister, Delia, whom he had just appointed as General Secretary of the IWWU. Alongside her were Constance Markievicz and Hanna Sheehy Skeffington, whose presence was particularly significant. Markievicz was primarily a revolutionary nationalist, while Sheehy Skeffington was an activist for women's higher education and a leader in the suffrage movement. Both shared the hope that the new union of women workers would be a valuable ally to their respective causes. From its foundation, the IWWU was an ardent partisan of the women's suffrage movement. Indeed the *Irish Worker*, almost alone amongst working-class newspapers, supported even the militant actions of the Pankhursts and the Women's Social and Political Union (WSPU). Markievicz, the first speaker at the meeting, promised that the new IWWU would improve women's working conditions and help them to win the vote '... and thus [she promised] make men of you all'. This rally, according to the *Irish Worker*'s account of the meeting, provoked cheers and laughter from the crowd. Sheehy Skeffington, who spoke later, was reported to have 'dealt at some length with the question of Women's Franchise, which seemed to have the support of all present'.[4]

Delia Larkin had come to Dublin early in 1911 from Liverpool, where she had been working as a nurse. Presumably, her brother intended from the first that she should take over the leadership of the projected IWWU and, as a step to that end, act as the spokesperson for the organisational drive necessary to establish the new union. The first step in preparing her for this role would be to let her familiarise herself with the ITGWU staff and programmes and become known to the union branch leaders. A position on the staff of the union's paper gave her the opportunity to do both. By June 1911 she was writing for the *Irish Worker* as a staff correspondent. Her early columns dealt largely with working-class 'social' problems. It is very significant that, from the start, she wrote as an advocate for the wretchedly poor children of Dublin. Delia Larkin saw only one remedy for their sufferings – Irish workers must join in 'one great organised body united and firm'. Only then would the unemployed:

> be granted the right to work and not only to work, but also to receive proper return for their work – that is sufficient wages to make it possible for them to live.[5]

This was clearly a version of the syndicalist creed which she shared with her brother, which Dublin employers would soon label as Larkinism.[6] Nevertheless, for Delia (and probably for Jim Larkin as well) her indignation at the plight of Dublin's poor at this time owed more to Charles Dickens than to Georges Sorel or any other continental social theorist.

II

In establishing the IWWU, Jim Larkin was setting up another instrument of class action. The new IWWU was to take over the ITGWU's task of recruiting women members. Whether he chose to make the IWWU structurally separate from the ITGWU because he believed that women would be more effective in organising other women or for another reason, we do not know. We do know, however, that shortly afterwards the ITGWU leadership in Belfast, under Larkin's deputy, James Connolly, took an opposite line on this. However, neither Connolly nor Jim Larkin ever explained their differing choices.

During the first year of its existence the IWWU played a role in a few industrial disputes and strikes. These mainly occurred in the Dublin area and Delia Larkin reported them in her column. However, one brief and unsuccessful strike took place in Belfast among the semi-skilled textile workers a month after the IWWU was established. It was not an IWWU strike, as James Connolly had organised an Irish Textile Workers' Union, among the predominately female workforce of the Belfast textile industry, as a branch of the ITGWU. The decision to do this hard on the heels of the foundation of the IWWU seems significant in itself. It clearly suggests that Connolly did not accept Jim Larkin's view that women workers could most effectively be organised in a union of their own with women leaders. Connolly, a Marxist, may have preferred a single organisation to represent the working class.[7] In his view, the broad umbrella of the ITGWU should give that representation. Alternatively, he may merely have been unwilling to trust the direction of the effort to a new and untried group centred in Dublin. Connolly claimed to have believed from the outset that the strike would not succeed, stating that he had reluctantly agreed to organise the women and call the strike at their own request so that the women workers of Belfast could 'learn the power of organisation'.[8]

Delia Larkin needed an avenue of communication for the new union, distinct from the *Irish Worker*, for which the parent union would not be legally responsible. The IWWU, in short, needed a voice of its own. To serve this need in August 1911 she announced that she would be editing a weekly 'Women Workers' Column'. She asked for contributions from her readers and, in doing so, defined the column's aims. It would deal, she said, with:

> (I) The house: hints on how to keep it clean and lessen labour; (II) The home and its comforts; (III) Cookery hints; (IV) Dress and dress reform; (V) Women Workers grievances; (VI) Then a little article on women, their mission and work in the world, will be acceptable either in prose or verse. Now there is plenty of brains among the women-workers and here is a splendid opportunity for using those brains, so send along anything you think will benefit the cause of labour, lighten the burden of the toiler, or help build an Irish-Ireland.[9]

She clearly envisioned her column as a working-class equivalent of the advice columns in the magazines directed toward middle-class women. Indeed, many labour activists of this period found it useful to similarly emulate middle-class interests.

The following week Larkin set out in her column her first call to women to join the new IWWU. No IWWU records for the years before 1918 have survived. There are no minute books, membership rolls or correspondence files. All have disappeared and, what is more remarkable, have disappeared largely without comment, explanation, or even notice.[10] Therefore, Delia Larkin's columns survive as the only known record of her concerns and those of the IWWU leadership in these formative years. During its first years, until the lockout of 1913 crippled the Irish labour movement, the IWWU tried to deal with a number of agendas: union organisation, suffrage, Nationalism and economic and social reform. An understanding of how the leadership – mainly Delia Larkin – addressed these issues offers us a more nuanced understanding of Irish labour history and Irish women's history.

The early columns were largely devoted to discussions and debate on broad 'women's issues'. By this, Larkin was referring to matters which would concern working mothers, rather than more narrowly focused trade union issues such as industrial dispute tactics or grievance representation. Larkin may have felt that she had more to contribute on social issues, while she was still mastering her brief in the fields of union recruitment and organisation where she was a relative newcomer. Later, as her experience grew, she paid increasing attention to industrial disputes and to their resolution. More interesting, however, is how Delia and her guest writers used the column as a forum to discuss and debate women's issues. Questions of equality and difference, of equal and comparable pay and the problems rising out of the dual responsibilities of working mothers were discussed. The contributors came to no firm or common conclusions. However, that is hardly surprising, since the issues raised are still matters of feminist debate.

A reader of these columns cannot escape the feeling that Larkin herself seems to have been a reluctant trade union organiser. Perhaps she initially saw an exclusively female union as a contradiction of the 'one big union' ideal of syndicalism. In her first column as general secretary of the IWWU, published on 9 September 1911, she wrote of her 'surprise' at the success of the founding meeting: 'I myself, have always felt that women were apathetic in their attitude towards their own betterment'. She went on to describe her own surprise that 'each speaker was listened to in a most intelligent manner'.[11] However, she was not above hectoring her readers when recruitment went poorly, stating: 'It is no use whining and lamenting your wretched condition ... when deliberately and with your eyes open you place yourselves in the position of slaves'.[12] Indeed, frustrated by the fact that women would not report Insurance Act violations, she suggested they be fined for not doing so.

Apart from the issue of suffrage, which the labour movement supported in general as part of its reform agenda, in what sense and to what extent was the IWWU a feminist organisation? This question is not easy to answer. For years, social historians saw the granting of the vote to women in 1918 as marking the onset of a decline for feminism. More recent scholarship, however, suggests that women activists in the early years of the twentieth century were not unified on a single feminist agenda.[13] Feminists disagreed on such issues as equality of treatment, some insisting on gender blindness and others demanding accommodation for particular needs. They differed, for example, over equal pay as opposed to comparable pay. In brief, the suffrage campaign strove to maintain an appearance of unity which was largely illusory. The fragmentation of feminist agendas in the years following women's enfranchisement was therefore merely the natural result of dissolving alliances as underlying differences surfaced.

The 'Women Workers' Column' never found an audience as a 'Ladies' Help' column. Yet by looking at those columns which dealt with the social concerns which were important to Delia Larkin and her contributors, we can detect an ideological framework for the labour and social reforms they sought. When Larkin first invited readers to contribute to her 'Women Workers' Column' she stated that the column's interests would not be confined to, or even primarily concerned with, the problems of trade union organisation. Her agenda was one of broad reform, aimed at securing a better, richer life for working-class women and their families. For Delia, the primary means of fulfilment for a working woman was not her work, but her home and family. Work was seen as a necessary means to that end. There is no evidence that Larkin ever wavered in this deeply traditional view. She believed that the first duty of a married woman (and she seemed to think that most women *would* marry) was to home and family.[14] However, she felt that a working woman could discharge that duty most effectively by actively participating in a trade union. A woman's primary loyalty was not to class or union, but to home. Implicit here is the corollary that a trade union could justify itself to working women as long as it served this interest of its members.

For Delia, the social ills of the Liverpool and Dublin slums were the result of an evil and exploitative capitalist system. She believed that the squalid living conditions in Dublin's decaying and overcrowded tenements were powerful obstacles to a working mother's efforts to create a 'home' environment. A woman's view of her house, she said, was essentially different from a man's. Where a man saw a building, a woman saw a potential home. Home and family were the centre of a woman's life and a work of her creation. There, rather than in the workplace or the union hall, could she find human fulfilment of the deepest level.[15] Indeed, Larkin's concern for the slum children and their need for a decent family life formed the basis of her commitment to the union cause. This is the starting point in understanding her work. She came to the labour movement because she believed it was a necessary means to effect social change. Her goal, however, was not a classless society, but the goal of an enriched domestic and family life for her members. Her early columns reflect this in their repeated inclusions of housekeeping tips and recipes. Because Larkin prized these things so highly, she could not but believe that her readers felt the same. But as Larkin's confidence in her ability to handle the challenges of union organisation grew, her column gradually changed. Its early focus on practical advice about running a working-class home while holding a full-time job shifted to new concerns with trade union organisation and recruitment problems. She still continued, however, to write about ways to reduce the time women spent on routine housekeeping by forethought and organisation. Delia never thought this an unworthy topic for a General Secretary's attention. Repeatedly, her column insisted on order and method in domestic chores: 'It is a well known fact', she states, 'that surroundings either elevate or denigrate'.[16] A woman had a duty to keep her home as clean and pleasant as circumstances permitted and to work with other women to change those circumstances.

Larkin suggested ways for working women to find more free time for their betterment. Housework was drudgery which had to be done and should be done well. Done efficiently, it could be completed quickly and thereby create time for a woman's self-development.[17] If homes were run efficiently, she urged, there would be more time to rest, walk and foster good health.[18] Above all, this household efficiency would afford time to read. Larkin showed the special passion of a self-taught person for books and language and evidenced a profound belief in their liberating power. Among her first acts as the IWWU's General Secretary, was to set up a library, a literacy class and Irish language classes for the members at Liberty Hall, headquarters of the ITGWU and the IWWU.[19] This concern with the domestic aspects of the life of the Irish woman worker was not unique to Delia Larkin. Other contributors to her column echoed similar views. In February 1912 'W.F.C.' wrote an open letter to the readers of the 'Women Workers' Column' calling them to action in the IWWU to better their conditions, but also sounding a note which would be heard with increasing frequency in the next decade, that of national militance:

> You are the mothers of the Ireland that is to be – Ireland that is in the making – in short the future of the Irish Nation rests with you.

Opinion in the IWWU, to judge from other contributors to the column, also reflected this view. Men and women, they believed, had radically different viewpoints and aims. Some contributors on this topic are difficult to interpret in a way consistent with 'emancipation'. Delia Larkin and her fellow activists not only accepted the differences in gender roles; they exalted in them. But views such as these did not change their conviction that the working class would be free only when society accorded women the same basic rights as men. This view was clearly expressed in March 1913: 'No people can ever be free while one-half of them are bound with the chains of slavery'.[20] It is crucial to note, however, that they also believed that women would exercise these rights very differently from men and it was also their right to do so.

III

For women labour activists in 1911, as for most radical religious and conservative reformers of the time, alcoholism among the poor was a central social problem. The distiller and his public house were the enemies that had to be fought every day. Like many social reformers, Jim Larkin, James Connolly and Delia Larkin were total abstainers and prohibitionists, ready to use the force of the law against the liquor trade to whatever extent the public would support. In the place of drink Delia offered a vision which would offer her readers hope, self-discipline and direction – a motivating vision of a good life. She proposed this in one of her columns which dealt with drunkenness among poor women.[21] She believed that women bore the greater familial responsibility. Therefore, when women sought to escape from the burdens of family life in the slums by a temporary escape into drunkenness or the permanent escape of desertion, the failure of the mother was more destructive to the children than a similar abandonment by the father.[22]

Dublin custom forbade respectable women from entering a public house without an escort. It frowned on women drinking in public bars, but this was tolerated in working-class neighbourhoods if women were escorted. Delia rejected this practice, not because she thought it limited women's freedom, but because she thought it too permissive. Indeed, to her mind, it was bad enough that men had the opportunity to become drunk. The social consequences of a mother's drunkenness on her children were so dire that society should protect women from the temptation to drink and bar them from pubs altogether. As Larkin noted:

> I cannot see why a woman should not be served with drink when alone but that she should be served with it when accompanied by her husband. For my own part, I wish the law would make it a criminal offense to supply women, [whether] alone or accompanied ... intoxicating drink.[23]

Larkin saw prohibition only as a stop-gap measure to deal with an immediate and pressing problem. The long-term solution to the problem of drunkenness and the harm it inflicted on women, families and above all children required a fundamental change in the present 'acquisitive society' driven by profit. Larkin interpreted the fact of drunken women on Dublin's streets as symptomatic of social corruption:

> But as well as making this law, [i.e., prohibition] it is also very necessary to find out if there are any reasons which are the cause of so much drunkenness amongst women ... [that] are ruining the home life, [causing neglect of] the children, and branding the future generation with ill-health, disease, and [an] inherited taste for intoxicating drink. Although condemning the women who have allowed themselves to become slaves to the drink mania and saddling [themselves] with the awful results which arise from their indulgences, still there is some excuse for them, when one knows the awful conditions under which the majority of these women live.[24]

In her view, three factors largely accounted for the problems of drunkenness among working-class women: public houses and publicans, the wretched squalor of living conditions and the economic necessity which drove women into the workplace in a desperate effort to secure the minimum income which they needed to feed themselves and their children. With regard to the former, Larkin felt that:

> a woman who staggers [from] one public house into another and who asks for and is supplied with drink is not nearly so much to blame as is the publican who serves her. The drink she has already taken has made her irresponsible ... [The publican who serves her is] committing a criminal act by supplying the woman.[25]

Even more to blame for the scourge of drink, however, were the tenement slums, the only housing which the working poor could afford. To Larkin these tenements were: '... without a doubt [among] ... the greatest causes which help to make drunken slaves of the women who live there'. Women moved to the tenements 'having never tasted drink', only to find a way of life where the only opportunity for friendship, the only place for socialisation or recreation, was the public house. To avoid such temptation, Larkin's basic demand was that 'each married woman have a house of her own' and by this she did not mean a tenement flat.[26] But it was the third cause of women's drunkenness which Delia highlighted that is, perhaps, the most fascinating. She blamed the wage system itself. This had long been a view of many revolutionary theorists and was a fundamental tenet of both anarchists and syndicalists. It was also the view of British guild socialists and their ideological enemies, the Marxists.

If trade unionism was to succeed in Ireland, at some point it would have to capture a significant portion of middle-class opinion. Delia Larkin's social agenda offered the broad outlines for an appeal to this section of the populace. Ireland at this time was an agricultural country, where wealth was in land. Since the passage of the Land Acts of the late nineteenth and early twentieth centuries, land effectively came into the hands of small holders. What Irish industry there was, was largely located in the mainly Protestant north of the country. It had become increasingly clear that Jim Larkin's 1906–7 success in the Belfast dock strike was due to a temporary relaxation in the city's communal tensions. These tensions had since revived with greater fury as the Liberal Party's promise of home rule moved slowly toward fulfilment. James Connolly, directing ITGWU operations in Belfast from 1908 until 1913, could not hold the gains which Larkin had made in Belfast. In the mainly Catholic south of the country, winning popular opinion meant gaining, if not support, at least acquiescence from the socially conservative Irish bishops. Jim Larkin made no effort to find support or even detente with them. His eloquence was vivid, powerful, always militant and often inflammatory. Amongst Irish Catholic bishops, already predisposed to believe that any 'socialist' was also hostile to religion (and especially toward the Roman Catholic Church) Jim Larkin also had a reputation as an outspoken anti-cleric. The bishops themselves had little understanding of urban industrial labourers or their plight. Moreover, neither the Catholic Church nor the trade unions had the lines of communication needed to ally each other's fears.

Delia Larkin, a relative neophyte to the trade union movement, put her finger on the themes that might have allowed labour to open the door to a tactical *démarche* which could win support from the middle class and the Church by finding common ground. She raised what became a central issue in the Irish debates on social policy between the 1920s and the 1960s – the issue of a family wage and the place of women and their special problems in the workforce. In the decades after Pope Leo XIII issued an encyclical letter, *Rerum Novarum*, on the problems of industrial workers and the Church's position on modern social developments, much was written by Catholic social theorists on the issues which the letter raised, including the rights of labour to organise and bargain. The English-speaking world paid little attention to this theory.[27] Therefore, Delia Larkin's call for wages which would enable a worker to raise a family in what European Catholic theorists of the time described as frugal comfort ran the risk in Ireland of being judged a dangerous novelty.[28] But Larkin possessed a remarkable ability to find strength in an adversarial position. It was widely known that Irish wages lagged behind those in Britain. Employers of unskilled and casual labour in Dublin paid subsistence wages.[29] The small, but growing, Irish middle class knew and resented this and condemned those who profited from such a practice. If the only means of supporting a family in such conditions was for a mother to go to work for less than subsistence wages and if a trade union could make the public see their struggle in these terms, strikers would have a powerful claim on public sympathy. With this in mind, Delia Larkin's indictment of the wage system was a powerful one which had the potential to appeal to a variety of listeners:

> What a crime this system of married women going out to work is. It is a crime against the woman herself, against the husband and against the children … [It] has a bad effect on the whole community of workers; it keeps women's wages at a starvation rate, men's wages low and is the means of making drunkards of both men and women. The woman goes out to work the same as the husband and works as many hours. There is no home life for them, and no meals are prepared. Therefore the temptation to indulge in strong drink is very strong. A married woman's duty is not to help the sweater [i.e., the sweatshop employer] and [the] publican, but to look after her home and those who live there. This can only be done when the men's wages are of such a standard as will enable them to live in decent houses and provide in a right manner for their wives and children.[30]

A foreshadowing of later controversies over 'equal pay' as opposed to 'comparable pay' and other contemporary issues such as 'hostile environment' and 'quid pro quo' sexual harassment were also discussed in Delia's column. In discussing the working conditions of women in factories, she argued that women needed a union to give them an effective means of complaint against such harassment. She also never advocated a marriage bar or other device to make it impossible for married women to work. She knew enough of the economic realities to see that such a measure would be unworkable and that industrial work was often vital for a woman to support her family. But she believed it was an unfortunate necessity and a departure from her social ideal.

Delia Larkin wrote with eloquence, but she had a more effective gift – a sense for those themes which would engage and move her target audiences. In essence, she recognised that there were many audiences whose support would be valuable, if they could be reached and won over to endorse some, if not all, of labour's aims. Larkin addressed each of these audiences in terms which they would value – of family, children, national pride and resentment at poor working conditions and wages. She spoke of the fears women shared and with which all could identify – the loss of a husband dying young and the dread of raising a family alone with no one to help. She moved from one vivid image to another, using concrete examples to dramatise the plight of the poor working woman. Thus, Delia Larkin spoke to the hopes, dreams and nightmares of her listeners.

IV

To what extent was the IWWU a 'feminist' organisation? Cott offers a three-pronged definition of feminism. Feminism, in her view, opposed a sex hierarchy and subordination, saw gender roles as social constructs and therefore alterable and promoted a consciousness of group identity. In many ways, therefore, the IWWU was a feminist organisation and yet in these early years it offered a feminism which had the potential to appeal to both a significant portion of Ireland's radical and reform minded individuals and to many of the socially conservative, Irish middle class as well. The unifying characteristic of the feminism of the IWWU was based on the role of women in the home and as mothers. Regardless of differences on specific issues, all of the contributors to the 'Women Workers' Column' saw, as Delia Larkin did, the primary characteristic of motherhood as defining their feminism. Irish labour feminism was essentially *grounded* in an ideal of separate spheres, domesticity and motherhood.

How effective was such an ideal in mobilising support for the IWWU? By early 1913, membership was growing rapidly. It was making strides, for instance, in organising the confectionery makers, one of the larger Dublin industrial enterprises and one whose employees were almost all female. But in that year union organisation met with disaster, the great Dublin Lockout. The story is a tangled tragedy. In brief, the Dublin employers agreed amongst themselves to break Jim Larkin's ITGWU, which they felt was becoming too popular with the city's workers. They demanded from every worker in the city a signed and enforceable promise never to join a Larkin union and to resign from one if they had already joined. This was a declaration of war on organised labour. When workers refused to comply they were locked out. The Dublin municipal government disrupted union meetings and on a so-called 'Bloody Sunday' they opened fire to disperse a group of workers listening to Jim Larkin speaking from a hotel window. Scores of people were killed and wounded in police gunfire, nearly all of them leaving Sunday mass at a nearby church. That night, the police were hunted through the streets and killed.

In a few months the Lockout brought Dublin to the verge of starvation and revolt. A soup kitchen, organised and managed by Delia, provided the only food for many of the city's poor. For most of 1913 the workers, their wives and children, survived through the generosity of British trade unions and their members. Welsh miners, for example, though themselves in need, gave thousands of pounds a month to feed Dublin's poor and the British Board of Trade held hearings, flatly condemning the efforts of Dublin's employers to break unionisation. For over nine months Delia Larkin was at the centre of the struggle and with some British volunteers, devised a plan to send Irish children to stay with British families until matters were resolved. This was the 'Save the Kiddies' programme which brought ruin in its wake. Many were to blame for this. Delia was so overwhelmed with running the soup kitchen and conducting other relief work that she relied on well-intentioned British volunteers, who unfortunately had no understanding of Dublin or the complexities of Ireland. Meanwhile Jim Larkin was barnstorming Britain, calling for a general strike, attacking his allies and benefactors by name and alienating every supporter his union had in a hurricane of wild and senseless eloquence. To further complicate matters, the Catholic Archbishop of Dublin chose to see the 'Save the Kiddies' project as a Protestant attempt to proselytise Catholic children. Amid this angst, the growing support for the worker's cause collapsed and the strike was broken. This reduced the membership of the ITGWU and IWWU to a handful in a matter of weeks.

In the aftermath of the Lockout Jim Larkin appears to have suffered some sort of nervous breakdown. In the autumn of 1914, he left Ireland for the United States to raise money for the Irish Labour Party, leaving Connolly as Acting Secretary General for a proposed period of a year. But it was 1923 before Jim Larkin returned. In the interim Connolly found more to interest him in the small union self-defence unit Jim Larkin had organised to defend his meetings – renamed the Irish Citizen Army, it made Connolly a player in insurrectionary politics. His leadership also had implications for Delia Larkin. She was eased out of her position in the IWWU within a few years by the women Connolly had brought with him from Belfast, the leaders of his Belfast women's auxiliary. His auxiliary leaders got on well with their counterparts in Dublin. These women of middle- and upper-middle class origins were first active in the revolutionary Nationalist movement. Thus by July 1915 Delia Larkin was no longer a factor in union affairs. In that month she left Dublin for Liverpool. She returned to Dublin in 1918, but was never able to successfully apply for membership of the IWWU again.

Hearths, Bodies and Minds:
Gender Ideology and Women's Committal to Enniscorthy Lunatic Asylum, 1916–25

ÁINE McCARTHY

I

Towards the end of the eighteenth century a fundamental change occurred in the way madness was perceived in Great Britain.[1] Until this time 'lunatics' were considered to be unfeeling, ferocious animals who needed chains, straitcoats, bars on locked cells and physical brutality to keep them in check. However, under new ideas of 'moral management' implemented throughout the British Isles in the nineteenth century, the mad came to be regarded as sick human beings, objects of pity, not fear and capable of defeating their madness if subjected to kindly surveillance and care in comforting surroundings. Reformers posited 'asylums' as a suitable environment for this care, not the jails, workhouses or private madhouses in which the mad had previously been housed.

Alongside the ideological changes of moral management came a fundamental shift in the symbolic gendering of insanity, from male to female. The repulsive madman who had been the prototype and cultural representation of the lunatic was replaced by the youthful, victimised and sexualised madwoman.[2] As the nineteenth century progressed asylum doctors, eager for scientific legitimisation in an increasingly positivistic age, linked their classifications of insanity to discoveries about women's reproductive systems, so that several distinctive forms of female insanity were 'diagnosed' at this time – puerperal mania, ovarian madness, insanity of lactation and climacteric melancholia.[3]

Ireland, under British rule during the nineteenth century, experienced these developments and the fact that fewer women than men entered Irish asylums did nothing to dissuade Irish doctors that women were more vulnerable to madness. The first Irish doctor to write a major treatise on insanity and the most prominent of the early Irish disciples of moral treatment was Dr William Hallaran of Cork. Hallaran was thoroughly convinced of female susceptibility to madness, writing in 1818 that:

> This cannot be wondered at when we take into account the many exciting causes to which females are more particularly exposed ... Those arising from difficult parturition [or] the sudden retrocession of the milk, immediately on delivery ... [or menopause]

Men however, even when predisposed to insanity through heredity or other factors, would find that 'their superior powers of resistance' would overcome any latent tendencies they might have.[4] As the century wore on such concepts began to be taken for granted, so that by 1874 a standard textbook on psychological medicine could affirm the connection thus:

> Women in whom the generative organs are developed or in action are those most liable to hysterical disease. Indeed, the general fact is so universally acknowledged and so constantly corroborated by daily experience, that *anything in the nature of proof is unnecessary* [my emphasis].[5]

This medicalisation of madness and its gendering as female took place within a society which was developing a highly regulated ideology about women's innate nature and appropriate behaviour. Ideology in this sense refers to a system of beliefs by which a group or society orders reality, the 'imaginary relation of individuals to their real conditions of existence' to use Althusser's succinct phrase.[6] Gender ideology with regard to women in early twentieth-century Ireland was located firmly in the domestic realm and had come to hold universal sway across different social classes and groupings.

This essay analyses the intersection between gender ideology and discourses of women's madness, in a particular place (Wexford) at a particular time (the early twentieth century), by focusing on the 356 women committed to Enniscorthy Lunatic Asylum during the decade 1916 to 1925.

At its most obvious, it is clear that the gender ideology which sustained the institution of the family in this time and place was rigidly patriarchal and that the asylum was the final destination for some of the female casualties of this system. Both those who rejected and those who wholeheartedly embraced their gendered role within society were vulnerable to committal. What also emerges from this study is that the asylum and the medical theories of madness which emanated from it, both reflected and reinforced the gender ideology favoured by society.

Enniscorthy District Lunatic Asylum, opened in 1869, was one of twenty-

Table 1: *Marital Status, Age, Religion, Education and Occupation of Inmates of Enniscorthy Lunatic Asylum, 1916–25*

	Female	*Male*	*Total*
Total Admissions	356	429	785
Marital Status			
Single	200	288	488
Married	120	109	229
Widowed	32	26	58
Not given	4	6	10
Age			
0 to 19	11	20	31
20 to 39	149	175	324
40 to 59	130	140	270
60+	64	91	155
Not given	2	3	5
Religion			
Roman Catholic	331	387	718
Church of Ireland	20	26	46
Not given	5	16	21
Education			
Illiterate/not given	78	95	173
Read only	7	18	25
Read and write	239	274	513
Well educated	32	42	74
Occupation			
Farmer/farm family	80	106	186
Labourer/labourer family	48	170	218
Servant	85	1	86
Housekeeper	70	0	70
Shopkeeper	4	3	7
Shop Assistant	2	7	9
Dressmaker/tailor	9	5	14
Fisherman	0	3	3
Publican	0	4	4
Soldier	0	14	14
Pensioner	5	14	19
Religious	7	6	13
Pauper/none	25	23	48
Other	21	73	94

one Irish Poor Law institutions built as part of the great wave of asylum construction in nineteenth-century Britain. Throughout that century accommodation in Irish lunatic asylums continuously expanded, so that by 1901 there were almost 17,000 inmates in asylums originally planned for less than 5,000. Enniscorthy Asylum also grew rapidly – first admission rates per 10,000 of the population increased from 3.69 in 1871 to 6.14 in 1911, an increase of 166 per cent. By 1916, there were 556 people in the asylum, 286 women and 270 men, and the institution remained full for the period 1916–25 (see Table 1).[7]

There are limits to the use of asylum records. The behavioural history of the inmate, the manifestations of madness and its causes, were supplied by the person who brought them to the asylum and the doctors made little attempt to verify the information. Similarly, behaviour within the asylum was described by asylum staff. Occasionally, one of the doctors would transcribe directly what he believed an inmate had said to him and while such quotations are illuminating, their accuracy is impossible to ascertain. In short, the history of women's experience of the asylum can be read only through the male medical discourse (the casenotes and medical theories written by men about women) which has created that history. But the value of these historical documents is the analysis they allow of the social and economic contexts within which committal occurred, an analysis which was entirely missing from theories of madness during the period.

II

Discourses of madness in early twentieth-century Ireland drew on theories which had first been promulgated a century earlier – the ideas of moral management summarised above. These were later modified by Darwinian ideas, which saw madness as the product of hereditary organic defect and the lunatic as a person from whom society must be protected. Common to both theories was a conviction of women's greater propensity to madness, a propensity rooted in female biology, which these 'experts' viewed as an aberration from the male norm. The discourses which regulate femininity and madness have been linked in Western culture since at least the end of the eighteenth century. While the categorisation of female 'symptoms' may change from one historical period to another, the gendering of madness has remained constant since that time. Thus madness, even when experienced by men, is metaphorically and symbolically represented as feminine – a female malady.[8] This feeds into another discourse which situates women on the side of irrationality, nature and the body and men on the side of reason, culture and the mind.

Men were committed to Enniscorthy Asylum in greater numbers than women during the period 1916–25. This represented a reversal of the situation in other countries like Britain, parts of Europe and the United States. Ireland has long been a statistical aberration in this regard, with more men than women being treated for madness before and since this period. But this fact has done little to challenge the link between femininity and madness, a link fully accepted by doctors at Enniscorthy who made careful notes in the casebooks about the biology of their female patients. One of the first questions put to a woman on committal was the pattern of her menstrual period, and details of regularity and quantity of the blood were duly noted: 'menses are on and very profuse'; 'says she has not been regular in this way for some months past'; 'menses regular but light'.[9] Such a focus on female biology placed the problem of madness within the woman's person, rather than the social reality of her life. Sis Berry's admission form, for example, cites 'Menopause' as her cause of insanity. However, a doctor's conversation with her sister suggests that life stresses, not biology, may have been the root of her trouble, as, according to her sister, Sis's husband 'never agreed with her and always gave her a hard time'.[10]

Many of those who were admitted with puerperal mania were suffering from physical gynaecological problems rather than mental symptoms. McGovern has written of how American asylums, because of the medical theory which assumed a physiological connection between the female generative organs and the nervous system, were seen as the appropriate place to send women suffering from gynaecological disorders.[11] This pattern also seems to have applied in Wexford. Anastasia Jones, a single woman of thirty said to be congenitally mentally deficient, related on admission how nine months previously she had been constantly 'annoyed' by a national soldier and that eight days before her committal she had given birth to an illegitimate child. She had experienced a very difficult labour with a forceps delivery, leading to severe puerperal rupture which extended to her rectum. The rupture had turned septic. Her physical condition was treated and she made a good recovery, leaving the asylum two years later.[12] Ellen Keelan was admitted 'very sickly, with sores on her teeth [gums?] and lips very dry and crusty. Pulse thready and very fast. Dazed and confused'.[13] She had given birth ten days before, but her baby died ten minutes after birth. She was treated for her physical problems, appearing to have little else to explain her committal. On recovery three months later, she was discharged.

Childbirth and miscarriage are, of course, life incidents with enormous psychological implications which can bring trauma, not just physical, but social and emotional, in their wake. Darwinian theories, however, left no room for understanding how social and emotional factors, or indeed poor health care, could affect mental well-being. So, for example, the interpretation of the case of Margaret Murphy, who came to the asylum having lost a baby some weeks before was that the miscarriage was the catalyst which allowed Margaret's inherent – and hereditary – tendency to melancholia to manifest itself. Margaret, a forty-five-year-old married housekeeper, had no other children, though she had miscarried before. In such circumstances, strong feelings of loss would be expected and in Margaret's case they seem to have been intensified by the pressures of a society in which the female function of childbearing and rearing was central. It is unsurprising that she was described as 'much distressed' by her loss and that she considered it a 'terrible calamity'. Unsurprising too is that she feared she was 'going to be punished' for her failure. She died in the asylum forty years later.[14]

Table 2: *Categories and Causes of Madness amongst Inmates of Enniscorthy District Lunatic Asylum, 1916–25*

	Female	Male	Total
Total Admissions	356	429	785
Category of Madness			
Mania	169	256	425
Melancholia	130	91	221
Congenital mental deficiency	31	37	68
Epilepsy	15	17	32
Other	11	28	39
Cause of Madness			
Not known or given	143	177	320
Heredity	89	88	177
Overwork	5	1	6
Drink	7	61	68
Mental stress	14	10	24
Politics	1	5	6
Military/shellshock	0	9	9
Domestic trouble	9	0	9
Epilepsy	15	17	32
Senility/age	15	15	30
Childbirth/miscarriage	15	0	15
Flu/measles/pneumonia	8	7	15
Menopause	5	0	5
Poverty/hardship	3	5	8
Death/illness of relative	9	0	9
Masturbation	0	2	2
Other	18	32	50

By the early twentieth century, the concept of insanity had become so flexible that it could be stretched to encompass almost any behaviour. In the period 1916 to 1925, the main 'Categories of Insanity' (see Table 2) ascribed to inmates in Enniscorthy Asylum were mania (54 per cent total, 47 per cent of women), melancholia (28 per cent total, 36 per cent of women), congenital mental deficiency (8 per cent total, 8 per cent women) and epilepsy (4 per cent total, 4 per cent of women). A small number were given another category like senile dementia. These classifications – particularly those of mania and melancholia, which between them accounted for the vast majority of admissions – were vague in concept and had little scientific basis. Effectively they could mean whatever the asylum doctors wanted them to mean. This nebulousness was convenient for those who wanted to emphasise women's instability and inability to take part in public life. As medical professionals took control of the mad, the same discourse of biological inferiority which claimed women were more vulnerable to madness was also used in an attempt to exclude them from the emerging medical profession and any other form of public activity. As a Victorian psychology textbook stated:

> The [female] reproductive organs are frequently the seat of disease or abnormal function, [the] androgynous character is often accompanied by mental imbecility ... is not this a cogent reason why the women who have invaded the sphere of man's work and duty have as a rule proved such miserable failures?[15]

III

The family was the primary economic and social unit in early twentieth-century Ireland. The countryside had undergone radical transformation during the final decades of the nineteenth century, characterised by a move from pasture to large-field tillage. This, combined with the consolidation of smallholdings after the famine and various land acts, had created a rural landscape composed in large part of small, family-owned farms.[16] The declining economic and social position of women as land became the distinguishing criterion of status has been well documented. By the time of the 1926 census, the employment profile of Irish women was characterised by a low participation rate for both married and single women, a concentration of workers in agriculture and domestic service and a high proportion of women employed within the family economy.[17]

Eight out of ten people in agricultural employment worked not for a wage but by virtue of their family relationships. In these farm families, the farmer – most often the father, but sometimes a widowed mother or older son – had full control over the family members who worked on the land as unpaid labourers. The norm was for the eldest son to wait for many years before he would inherit from a retired or dead parent and for the eldest daughter to be dowered to a neighbouring farm. The other, usually numerous, children had essentially four options: emigration; a religious vocation; migration to the towns or cities for work (though there were few employment options open to women and even fewer which were well paid) or staying at home in indefinite dependence, a spinster aunt or bachelor uncle, contributing to the running of the house and farm, but with no income and little status. Independent behaviour was viewed as deviant and threatening to familial authority and individual needs were submerged in the interests of the family and the land.[18]

The acquisition and inheritance of land was based on the dowry system and the chastity of the woman was the basis of the contract, ensuring that only a legitimate male heir would have claim to the land. This socio-economic system gave rise to a gender ideology which, by the early twentieth century, had come to dominate Irish society. Though these values originated in the farm family, they spread to embrace all classes of the urban as well as the rural population. Many of those in the trades and professions in the towns, as well as the priests and nuns who controlled education and health services, were the daughters and sons of small farmers and were educated in institutions dominated by the farmer ethos.[19] By the period under consideration, therefore, notions of what was natural for women and what was appropriate female conduct had become a universal stricture, a system of beliefs ordering reality, in essence an ideology. According to this gender ideology, women had an overwhelming desire to marry and have children, remain faithful in a life-long union and remain subordinate and dependent in their marital relationship. Their sexuality was totally contained in marriage, with 'illegitimate' births even less acceptable in Ireland than elsewhere in Europe. Men, whose sexual urges left them with little powers of resistance, were dependent on women's superior moral nature, lack of desire and heightened sense of right and wrong to draw the line in sexual matters. Any transgressions were a woman's fault. Her natural sphere was the domestic and her role as mother was strictly defined. The social institution which gave most public and organised support to this ideology was the Roman Catholic Church, with its teachings on the role of women in the family supporting the socio-economic practicalities dictated by the farm family. The Virgin Mary summed up the requirements: virtue and chastity for the single, and self-sacrificing mother love for the married. Although the church preached chastity for both sexes, there was more public leeway for male 'indiscretions'.[20]

An ideology is not a blanket prescription, equally felt and experienced by all. For some women the prevailing ideological formulation of womanhood may have seemed so accurate as to be true, whilst for others it was a goal to aim for, something to resist or a judgement of their failure. But however an individual woman might react, it was impossible to escape gender ideology, mediated as it was through the widespread and interwoven fabric of social structures – from large institutions like the Church to less organised, but no less effective, controls like neighbourhood gossip. This gender ideology supported a harshly patriarchal system. Women's labour in the household, on the farm or in the family business was unpaid. A woman may have received maintenance for herself and her children in exchange, but not if her husband chose to spend the money on drink or something else instead. Marriages were 'matched' to the economic advantage of fathers and there was no escape if a marriage was brutal or miserable. There were few other ways for women to earn a livelihood, as gender ideology held that paid work was unseemly for married women. Unmarried women were pitied or reviled spinsters. Homosexuality, for either sex, was outlawed. A sexual double standard meant ostracisation from family and community for the woman who 'erred', while her male sexual partner received no such punishment. Male violence against women and children was hidden and condoned by a state which did nothing to intervene against it, except in the most exceptional circumstances. Analysis of Enniscorthy's records makes it clear that many casualties of this system ended up in the asylum.

IV

Unmarried women were of little benefit to a household, indeed they were often a financial burden if money was short. Socially they were objects of pity, ridicule or even revulsion. Unsurprisingly, the casebooks show that many single women, adrift and purposeless, ended up in Enniscorthy Asylum. Fifty-six per cent of women admitted to Enniscorthy Asylum during this period were single. In some instances of single women's committal, evidence of madness was scant. Annie Stafford and Mary Cullen, for example, both single women who complained about 'persecution' by family members who wanted them out of the house, were committed for expressing their anger and despair – Annie for threatening to kill her sister, Mary for threatening to end her own life, because 'her father treated her so badly'. Both were noted in the casebooks to be 'quite rational in manner', but both lived the remainder of their long lives, and eventually died, in the asylum.[21] Mary Sinnott, to cite another example, said she:

> was never so surprised as when her mother and brother came and dragged her out of bed and brought her here [to the asylum], as she doesn't know what she did.[22]

She told the doctor that she did not get on with her mother and brother, who wanted her out of the family home. The doctor concluded:

> It is impossible to know how much truth there is in her statements. Probably she has a bad temper and gives her relatives a time of it but it is quite possible there are faults on their side as well as is often the case.

Indeed, but it was Mary who ended up in the asylum, though it was noted that she spoke 'quite rationally and coherently and was perfectly quiet and collected in manner'.[23]

The lunacy committal could also be an instrument of domination, a reinforcement of power within the family, or a coercion into the 'good' behaviour expected of women. Lucy Dwyer, a young single woman, believed she was committed because she would not acquiesce to her father's demands. Described on admission as 'wild and restless' she insisted she would not stay, 'she intends going to Dublin, that her father cannot stop her, as she is twenty-three years of age now'.[24] A similar case, but much more fully documented, is that of May Ryan, a twenty-six-year-old typist, which is related here in detail as it reveals how the asylum committal could be an instrument with which to control women who transgressed their gender role by showing independence and spirit rather than docility and submission. May's admission form cites the following as 'Facts Indicating Insanity':

> Wanting to get out of the house and could [only] be kept in with difficulty; bought a great deal of articles of clothing today which she did not require; threatened to commit suicide; she broke lock in door endeavouring to get out of the house.

The casebook continues:

> Brought in by the guards and both she and they stated that the father being an RIC pensioner was very down on the Free State or anybody connected with it and she states that her father is just punishing her because she was going with a Free State officer from Kilkenny.

The asylum assistant medical officer, Bernard Lyons, was not convinced of May's madness and interviewed her repeatedly. After an in-depth interview he reported that:

> she answered everything very intelligently. She explained about the vermin on her clothing by saying that for past few weeks they [her parents] kept her clothes locked away, even her underclothing and she

could not get a change. She said they did that so as to keep her from going to meet her boy and to keep her from going to the job in the YWCA because of her threat to change her religion. She said that they were giving her such a bad time that she casually threatened to do away with herself just to see if it would make them more lenient with her. The only harm she did at home was to break open a lock to get her clothes. The only clothes she bought was a pair of boots costing 18/-. She wanted them badly as she was going to Dublin to her new job ... she promised to pay for them soon as she would be earning 55/- weekly at her new job. She speaks intelligently and well and so far it is impossible to find anything wrong with her mental condition.

A few days later, Lyons reported:

I tried every way I could to upset her and I could not find the least thing wrong mentally. She said she occasionally bought things and the bill went home but her parents had given her some years ago everything she wanted in the line of clothes and the habit of buying things she occasionally fancied continued as she got older. She did not want to be at home as she was having constant trouble with the parents, especially the father.[25]

May was discharged as not insane and wrote to her mother to take her home. This is the reply which she received:

Dearest May

I have learned you could now be discharged if we were willing to take you out and take charge of you but we cannot undertake to do so unless we get a promise of your future good behaviour – it would be out of the question to think we could look after you, unless you feel you have rid yourself of these false ideas of doing as you please. So if you are willing to make a promise to give no further trouble re. running bills – of course I have discovered where those presents has [sic] come from – and you must give a further promise to cease been [sic] so untruthful. We cannot see any hope for you only under lock and key unless there is a complete reformation. A reply to every question in this note will be considered as what we will do. Your loving mother[26]

Aged twenty-six, May was still expected to follow the dictates of her parents whose emotional and financial support was conditional on her conforming to their gendered code of 'good' behaviour.

Behind this code lay the fear of 'illegitimate' pregnancy, and those who found themselves in this plight were thrown back on the mercy of their families for economic survival. Many parents, particularly those of the middle classes – fearful of public contempt or reluctant to support the economic burden of an unmarriagable daughter – cast their daughters from their homes. Many of these castaways ended up in the workhouse or worked in prostitution. Another option was the asylum.[27] Almost half the women in Enniscorthy whose admission forms or case records make reference to childbirth or miscarriage were single. Some of them never left the asylum afterwards and no mention is made of what happened to their children.

Many of these women were troubled by thoughts of their sexual 'misconduct' and real or imagined slights about alleged illegitimacy. Ellen Morris was so disturbed about what her neighbours said about her that she kept a knife under her pillow. She told a doctor 'she never had a bastard and always was decent and respectable'.[28] Mary Cox refers to 'jealous' people who claimed that her children were illegitimate and made other 'false statements' about her.[29] Margaret Cummins told the doctor on admission that it was 'love for the boys' which had brought her to the asylum.[30] Whatever the truth about their mental condition, one consequence of labelling these sexually nonconformist women as mad and locking them away in the asylum was that their threat to the ideology of femininity was neutralised.

V

Though women who married and had children were conforming to their gender role, this did not leave them immune from unhappiness, the taint of madness or the fate of the asylum. It appears that marriage was less advantageous to women's mental condition than men's – 34 per cent of women admitted to the asylum were married, compared to 25 per cent of men.[31] The disparity between the ideal of marriage perpetrated by gender ideology, that marriage was a loving, trusting relationship, the pinnacle of a woman's achievement, the fulfilment of all her desires and the source of her security, and the reality often experienced has been explored at length in feminist theory. The reality in early twentieth-century Ireland was that a married woman was expected to submit to her husband and husband's family, to bear and care for children, to look after the home and any other duties which might be allocated to her. Women who failed on one or all of these counts could find themselves committed to the asylum. Women such as Joan McCarthy, described as 'flighty, cheeky and resistive' on admission, who had 'threatened violence to her husband' and 'will not mind her children' was committed for 'trying to get away from home'.[32]

The trouble could begin as early as the 'match'. In Wexford during this period the marriage match was the basis of acquisition and consolidation of land, with fathers deciding who was 'suitable' for their sons and daughters, with suitability being defined in the sense of economic advantage.[33] Margaret Doyle, on admission, told the attendants that she hardly knew her husband before marriage and that she had been forced by her people to marry him. When her father and brother called to see her, she became 'very excited and screamed at the top of her voice', telling her father that 'he forced her to marry against her will and that the result now was that she was in the asylum with her mind lost'.[34] The night following this visit she attempted suicide by tying a sheet around her neck.

Though patriarchy paid lip-service to the notion of husband as provider, should he fail to fulfil his obligations, it was his wife, not he, who suffered the consequences. Such privation appears to have been a route to the asylum. Some of the women admitted were said to be hungry, though their husbands worked. Drink was often a culprit. Mary Ellen Doyle, for example, was in poor physical health when admitted and her house was said by the RIC to be very damp. When her sister visited the asylum she reported that Mary Ellen's husband drank and that she was left very little to live on and was often 'almost in want'.[35] Elizabeth Walsh's admission form gave 'doesn't wear sufficient clothes' as her symptom of insanity. The RIC officers who brought her in stated that she had a bad husband who had deserted her and their children and that she lived with her father who was 'also a bad lot'.[36] But with patriarchal fatalism about the distress of women and children, this was seen as Elizabeth's hard luck, with no suggestion from either the police or the asylum doctors that her husband or father should be called to account and no concern about how her committal might add to her and her children's troubles.

Conflict between spouses could also lead to committal. Anastasia Hogan was admitted with 'delusions with reference to her husband being unfaithful to her. She frequently gets fits of violence, striking her husband and accusing him of unfaithfulness'.[37] The police who brought her in stated that her husband claimed she had attempted serious assault on him, struck her child and accused him of unfaithfulness 'without any cause'. Anastasia alleged that her husband beat her, called her names and was unfaithful. It was a case of his word against hers, but it was she who was committed.

In both farming and working-class communities, the woman usually 'married in' to her husband's family and she had to adapt to their ways. This made conflict with in-laws extremely common. The story of Sarah Ryan is an illustration of this, as well as the way in which the asylum could be used as a dumping ground for the unwanted. Admitted to Enniscorthy because her husband considered she 'romanced a lot, does not speak a sensible word and believes if at home she w[oul]d be a danger to herself and children',

Sarah was found to be quite rational and was let out on probation a couple of months later. Her husband, however, re-admitted her within two weeks, with her weeping that she would 'never forgive' him. The casebook recorded her as saying her in-laws are:

> very interfering, [she] thinks they look on her as inferior and are always finding fault with her. Thinks her husband is fond of her and they could live happily if it wasn't for his relatives. He more or less assents to her in-laws poor treatment of her and it upset her a good deal and made her depressed and given to brooding over things.

Eight months later Sarah was again given probation, but once again returned within a few days. She was said to have abused her sister-in-law, claiming she had tried to keep Sarah's husband away from her and had not looked after their children properly while Sarah was in Enniscorthy. She was very distressed at being brought back and blamed her sister-in-law. Sarah's repeated probations when her family was unwilling to take her out are an indication that her mental condition had little to do with her committal. This was confirmed by reports over the next two years, which found her to be rational in manner and conversation. However, it was not until February 1923, six years after her initial admission, that the doctor tried again. He noted that:

> She is anxious to get home and I wrote to husband saying I thought she ought to give it a trial. [However he appeared] to be afraid to venture on taking her out as he said she would probably get upset again and he has no house of his own now as he is living with his mother, the children being with his sister.[38]

VI

The ideology of the Roman Catholic Church emphasised the 'natural' female virtues of obedience, servility and self-sacrifice for women and repressed the reality of female sexuality. At the same time, there was an undercurrent of obsession with women's bodies as a source of sin, by which was meant sexual misconduct. The admission forms of many women admitted to Enniscorthy during this period quoted 'symptoms' which exaggerated the religious devotion expected of them to an unacceptable extent. Bridie Hayes, for example, was admitted for not staying in her bed because God had directed her to go out; Nellie O'Keefe because she had a vision of the Sacred Heart; Margaret Butler for singing hymns and believing that the Devil told her she was going to be damned and Teresa Nolan for feeling 'hopeless' over concealing a 'sin' in confession, that she had pre-marital sex the previous summer. She had been too ashamed to tell the priest and now lived in fear of being 'damned forever'.[39] Under Catholic and patriarchal ideology, women could never be good, pure or holy enough. This was internalised by women and manifested itself in those suffering from religious symptoms. Sr Mary McDonald was firm in her belief that she was not pure enough to receive holy communion, as she feared she was going to commit 'a great sin', that she often thinks of 'queer things and wants to give up prayers and religion'.[40] Another woman, Mary Sinnott, 'imagines that she has done everything wrong and that her soul is lost and she is deserted by God Almighty'.[41]

Some of the women with religious symptoms had rejected religion outright and it seems that this alone could be reason enough for their committal, especially if it was a deviation from previous behaviour. Mary O'Neill, a fifty-six year old farmer's wife, had been 'formerly of a very devout disposition, now she won't pray at all'.[42] Bridget Welsh was admitted weeping incoherently and saying 'I'm a virgin like the mother of God and my husband is like St Joseph'. She had been a devout Catholic all her life and her madness manifested when she engaged in 'unseemly conduct' during divine service and began cursing, blaspheming and refusing to go to mass on Sunday.[43]

Many of the women who suffered religious 'symptoms' also refused food. Katie Quigley, for example, believed that every time she ate she was committing a sin.[44] This linking of eating and sin was not uncommon. Hannah Riley was admitted because 'it was nearly impossible to keep her away from the chapel' and she stated that the 'only food she lived on was the Blessed Sacrament'.[45] With her reluctance to feed her bodily appetites and her overwhelming devotion to the Roman Catholic Church, Hannah exemplified the physical and spiritual ideal demanded by the prevailing gender ideology. This all too wholehearted embrace of her gender role was her route to the asylum.

VII

'A lunatic asylum is a large home', proclaimed a psychiatric journal in 1858.[46] Under moral management, the regime adopted by asylum authorities mirrored the behaviour and beliefs of the typical Irish farm family, with the social structure of the family reconstituted symbolically in the asylum. The most important feature of any asylum, argued one doctor, was its 'homishness', as a setting within which madness could be domesticated, tamed, controlled and converted into behaviour which the authorities considered 'moral', that is, normal according to their gender and class values.[47] Many commentators have noted the patriarchal nature of psychiatric institutions, with the superintendent as father, matron as mother, the attendants as older siblings and the inmates as the young children, dependent, sexually chaste, subject to constant paternal surveillance and in need of authority and control. However, as Chesler has pointed out, the experience of the inmates in the asylum replicated the female, rather than the male, experience within the family.[48]

The idea of the asylum as a replica of the family home was still adhered to in Enniscorthy in the early twentieth century, if only as an aspiration. But ideals of domestic containment had long been found to be unworkable. Moral management was a failure, with the practice falling very short of the theory. Committal under the Dangerous Lunatics Act of 1837, for example, meant that the mad, very few of whom were dangerous, were committed by a magistrate and transported – often roughly – to the asylum by the police. One annual report bemoans the fact that of the sixty-three patients admitted in the previous year, thirty were sent in on magistrates' warrants as 'Dangerous Lunatics', a situation described by the medical superintendent as 'little short of deplorable'.[49]

Once in the asylum, the overcrowded conditions rendered moral treatment, which required a close one-to-one relationship with a therapist, impossible. A contemporary account sums up the conditions in Irish district asylums:

> Our asylums are in a bad way. They are over-crowded. They are both understaffed and inefficiently staffed. Curable and incurable cases are herded together. There is practically no treatment. The percentage of cures remains at a very low figure. Public money is wasted. The asylums are unsuited for their purpose in almost every respect.[50]

By the early twentieth century, the financial burden of the institutions was weighing heavily on local management boards. Within Enniscorthy Asylum, like the other district asylums, this translated into a bare, unadorned environment, with few comforts. Basic neglect was sometimes in evidence – unpainted walls, worn floors or bedsteads which needed cleaning and enamelling.[51] Diet was basic, mostly bread and potatoes, and followed the usual practice in rural Ireland of giving more food to men.

The inspector in 1925 recommended introducing plants, flowers, more books and papers to create a more homelike appearance in the asylum. However, the utopian vision of domestic harmony was a fantasy which gave the controlled environment of the asylum – where eating, sleeping, dressing, working and relaxation were strictly regulated – a benevolent gloss. Just as the reality of women's subordination within marriage was disguised by a gender ideology which painted it as the fulfilment of all feminine desire, the reality of domination within the asylum was concealed within roseate domestic imagery.

Communal asylum life was supposed to promote reintegration into society. This was dependent on the patient's ability to relate well to other inmates and staff. An asylum inspector summed up the expectations of the system: 'The conduct of the patients was admirable. There was no noise or excitement'.[52] Any noise, heightened emotion or violence was seen as a failure, and the casenotes show that doctors found such behaviour particularly unacceptable in women. The assistant medical officer, or sometimes the superintendent, would walk the wards talking to attendants and patients, making notes in the casebooks as the regulations demanded – frequently at first, annually after the first year. The attitude of the doctors to the inmates varied, sometimes affectionate and kindly, sometimes barely disguised disgust, but always paternal. 'Progress' was carefully observed and recorded and case histories read like behaviour reports from a refined convent school, with complaints about the noisy or 'troublesome' and approval for those who were docile, self-controlled and hardworking. As well as being submissive, inmates, especially the women, were expected to be neat and tidy in dress and personal habits. Margaret Hicky's 'untidiness and dishevelled hair', for example, were enough to secure her committal, even though the doctor admitted that she 'did not show much signs of insanity further than [that]'.[53]

There is no reference to theories of madness in the casenotes, no consistent framework within which the 'progress' of an inmate was evaluated, only the doctor's own values and prejudices. The casenotes on May Ryan, whose parents put her in the asylum as a threat to make her behave herself, as discussed above, provide a telling illustration of this. From the notes we learn that May was high-spirited, extravagant, mischievous and untruthful. But mad? Dr Lyons was convinced that she was not and arranged for her discharge. But another entry in the casebook, signed 'HJ', questioned his judgement. When the day came for May to leave the asylum, he recorded that she:

> refused to go home with a nurse and another patient – said her clothes were too shabby (not a fact). She wrote to a sister to send her a lot of clothing and told her to send new underclothing. She is very high in her ways and ideas. Does no work. Sits at fire in workroom reading a book or paper. At first I thought there was nothing wrong with her mentally but her conduct would make me doubtful as to her true mental state.[54]

HJ's attitude shows the way in which the asylum could support social ideas of control and appropriate behaviour for women. Although a convincing case for May's sanity was made, it was a small step from finding fault with her 'high' ways and her refusal to clean the floors or wash the laundry, to questioning her 'true mental state'. Fortunately, his doubts came to nothing and May was discharged as 'recovered' (presumably in her new underwear!) a week later.

Only those who conformed were considered to be improving and would therefore stand any chance of release – those who protested their lot of being deprived of liberty and subjected to a barrage of rules were considered to be still suffering from their madness. Six months after her admission, for instance, Elizabeth Kearns was said to be 'somewhat better in mind'. The reason? 'She is not so full of complaints and is doing a little work'.[55]

Work was presented as therapy and the inmates in the asylum received no payment for their labour. Although doctors were aware of the economic benefits of having inmates employed without pay, they tended to be silent about this aspect and extolled its therapeutic benefits. Work was allocated on strictly gender divided lines, with men working on the farm, in the Kilcarbery vegetable garden or in the workshops and women dressmaking, repairing stockings and underclothing, working in the laundry, the kitchen and dining hall.[56] Not to work, as in the case of Elizabeth above, was to get a black mark. Work, general behaviour and privileges were related, with inmates being treated like children. Those who did not work or who 'mis-behaved' could find they were not allowed social breaks, or treats like tobacco. For serious misdemeanours – like being boisterous, aggressive, out of control or violent – moral treatment allowed for mechanical restraint and seclusion, but by 1916, it seems that mechanical restraint was no longer used in Enniscorthy.[57] Seclusion, however, was widely used. In 1917, for example, the inspectors reported that it 'was found necessary' to seclude four men and two women on thirty-two occasions, for an average period of about ten hours on each occasion. Five years later, twenty-four people were secluded on 171 occasions. In 1925 the inspector complained that the number secluded was 'very large' and recommended that alternative methods should be found 'for the treatment of these refractory or troublesome cases'.[58]

Drugs were rarely used, but were prescribed more frequently to women than men. A 1905 review of sedatives and narcotics used in the treatment of the mad agreed with the contemporary opposition to 'drugging'. However, it made one exception: the use of a depressant in cases of 'moral insanity' which in the writer's experience were 'always female'.

> Such patients, when found to be getting out of hand and kicking against the rigid discipline of asylum life, are benefited considerably by a short course of hyoscyamus [which would transform a] termagant into a useful and obliging patient.[59]

Celibacy was strictly enforced in the asylum and there was strict segrega-tion of the sexes into separate wards, dining halls and dayrooms, to the extent that a female attendant could not enter one of the male wards without special permission. Any expression of sexuality was feared, mocked and punished and it appears that not even the 'lunatic balls' with their chaperones, curfews and sexual frustration which were such a notorious feature of asylums in Britain, Europe and the US, were permitted in Enniscorthy. The inmates came into intensive daily contact with the attendants, whose job it was to focus on correction of behaviour – uncleanliness, slovenliness, disorderliness, bad sexual habits and destructiveness were all to be eradicated. It is difficult to ascertain exactly how the attendants treated the inmates; no doubt that varied with the individual. But it is obvious that ideas of moral management meant a struggle between the attendants and the 'troublesome'. Bridie Hayes, for example, was reported to be 'quiet and harmless' from her admission in 1920 until an incident six months later when she 'attacked' an attendant. Another attendant intervened and Bridie was put in a single room for the night. The next day she 'refuses to get up and says they "murdered" her'. Bridie's conflict with her attendants continued. Eight months later the casebook reported that 'when she gets upset she thinks the attendants are doing her harm and keeping her food from her'. Were they? The nature of the records means we cannot know. Three years later, there was still conflict between Bridie and those who were meant to care for her: 'Today (19.1.1923) she became excited and violent at breakfast and struck attendant Annie Cooney a severe blow with a bowl on the ear, cutting her'.[60] Complaints about the attendants, like any other complaints, were rarely given due attention and could instead be interpreted as an indication of continued madness. Elizabeth Kearns told her husband and sister that 'she was beaten and generally ill-treated by the nurses'. The doctor, however, felt that her statement was 'quite untrue' and concluded that Elizabeth's complaints meant she was 'no better in mind'.[61]

VIII

Once committed to the asylum, an inmate could leave only with the permission of the authorities and often the agreement of family too. Many railed against their incarceration, as this [undated] letter from Elizabeth Nolan, known as Elsie, who was committed to the asylum in 1923, shows:

My dear brother

Just got your letter and am glad you are well its high time I left here as the time is up so you had better write to the doctor to make some arrangement about bring me back every day I expect to get back and it ends just the same till, I know nothing about the place except that you at least should bring me back or tell me why you put me here … It's the same thing day after day. I can hardly write with everyone speaking and I think it very unfair of you to leave me here so long. I'm glad you enjoyed yourself in Galway though if you are always thinking of me how is it you only came once. The Dr said that I would soon go home conditionally and anyhow I am tired of being here and want my own home and I'll be just the same as ever when I get back ... Anyhow the sooner you get me home the better it will be for me unless of course you want to get rid of me altogether[.] Yours Elsie [62]

On the other hand, a number of women were discharged even though the authorities still considered their mental condition to be troubled. This was almost always because they were required for domestic duties at home. Katie Grant had been in the asylum for seven years when her brother took her out. His wife had died and he needed 'someone to keep house for him'.[63] The authorities let her go, but her housekeeping skills must have left something to be desired, because she was back within a week. The asylum doctors seemed to have little regard for the feelings of their patients in such circumstances, or little to say about what was best for them. Agnes Whelan was sent home on probation for four weeks, six months into her third stay in the asylum. The casebook recorded 'she is not well but her husband who is in bad health wanted her home'.[64] So home she went, even though an earlier note had acknowledged that a visit from her husband seemed to distress her. This category made up only a small minority – just 6 per cent of the women discharged. While we know that 44 per cent of the total sample died in the asylum (see Table 3), 40 per cent were discharged and of these, the vast majority were said to have 'recovered' (70 per cent) or to have been 'relieved' of their symptoms (24 per cent). Some of these, fewer than 10 per cent, returned to the asylum later in life but the vast majority did not. It would be a misrepresentation to say that the asylum provided a cure in such cases. Rather, the asylum was the context within which an inmate learned to readjust their social and mental world in a way which allowed for discharge.

In many ways, therefore, the asylum mirrored and helped to reinforce and reproduce the gender ideology favoured by society. The rules and regimen in Enniscorthy Asylum allocated inmates an exaggerated and bureaucratised version of women's social role. Inmates were a source of free labour, expected to submit to the orders of doctors and attendants. Their lives were to be devoid of sexual expression, autonomy or independence. Violence or abuse was hidden, deemed not to exist by a domestic ideology which disguised the regime of domination and control in the language of caring and compassion. And just as those who transgressed the rules of society were secluded in the asylum, the punishment for those who broke asylum rules was further isolation, removal to solitary confinement.

Table 3: *Length of Stay and Discharge Records for Enniscorthy District Asylum, 1916–25*

	Female	Male	Total
Total Admissions	356	429	785
Length of Stay			
<1 year	149	216	365
1 to 5 years	82	75	157
6 to 10 years	29	35	64
11+ years	79	76	155
Unknown	17	27	44
Discharged			
Relieved	44	43	73
Recovered	96	131	227
Not improved	3	15	23
Unknown	54	49	103
Recordable escapes	3	3	
Died in Asylum	159	188	347

IX

A number of interlinking discourses framed knowledge about, and regulated the experience of, the women who were committed to Enniscorthy Asylum in the period 1916 to 1925: discourses of medicine, sexuality, femininity and domesticity as well as madness. But what all have in common is that they were patriarchal constructions of knowledge: created by men about women, to men's social, political and economic advantage. Women's madness and their committal to the asylum was, therefore, a key player in patriarchy, that system of social structures and practices by which men dominate, oppress and exploit women. A diagnosis of madness protected patriarchy by dismissing women's anger as illness, by locating the problem within an individual woman, rather than within misogynous social structures and by punishing, marginalising and silencing nonconformist women who gave lie to a gender ideology which failed to describe their lives. Cursory consideration of the male case records during this period suggest that gendering also played its part in male committals. Often, male and female paths to the asylum were different. When violence was a factor in committal, for example, men were more likely to have enacted the violence, women more likely to have been its victims. Mania attributed to alcohol abuse was a diagnosis almost nine times more likely to be attributed to a male admission than a female. A small number of men attributed their madness to their experience of war, either the First World War, the War of Independence or the Civil War, all of which occurred during the period under consideration. Of far more significance numerically were the many men who had been allocated a 'feminised' social role, as the socio-economics of large farming families created a pool of surplus sons who had little opportunity to live independent, autonomous lives. A conflict between religious prudery and an undercurrent of masculine codes of sexuality also seem to have been a factor in some male committals. However, whilst gender ideology can be constraining for both men and women, it is vital to recognise that in a patriarchal society it is not equally oppressive for both sexes.

To say that gender was a central factor in the dynamics of committal and incarceration is not to claim that it provides a full explanation of these processes. The people committed to Enniscorthy Asylum arrived there by a variety of routes and reacted in a variety of ways. Gender ideology interacted with a multitude of factors such as social class, physical illness, family circumstances, personality and many others to determine how each individual experienced her madness, the process of her committal and her time spent behind the asylum walls. But gender was a hugely important factor which has, until recently, been ignored by Irish historiography.[65]

What emerges most clearly from this study is the struggle endured by so many of these women who were labelled mad, as they tried to cope with familial misfortune, with codes of behaviour and with economic insecurity and powerlessness in a society which allowed little scope for independence or autonomy. Thus the gendered code of behaviour was for many impossible to sustain. Such factors were never acknowledged by the psychiatric literature of the time, literature which both reflected and reinforced the prevailing gender ideology. Consequently, it is only by extracting women from male medical treatises and analysing them in the contexts of their own lives that the historical range of meanings surrounding women's madness can be fully understood.

The Press, Police and Prosecution: Perspectives on Infanticide in the 1920s

LOUISE RYAN

I

> The nation, as an object of study, is as elusively complex as the ways in which it is defined discursively. The text of the newspaper and the newspaper's cultural project as narrator, educator and entertainer of a society make it a particularly important site for the scrutiny of this kind of subtle discourse.[1]

Despite the recent contributions of feminist researchers, women still remain largely invisible in mainstream texts in Irish history. The dominant focus of historical research and texts continues to exclude women's experiences and lifestyles within Irish society.[2] Consequently, there are many aspects of Irish women's histories about which relatively little is known. This essay addresses one under-researched area and explores some of the advantages and disadvantages of using newspapers as a source within such historical research.

To judge from the pages of the *Cork Examiner* and *Irish Independent* infanticide was a monthly, if not weekly, reality in Irish society. This essay examines what press reports tell us about *who* committed infanticide, *why* and in *what circumstances*, and the rates of detection and punishment of these so-called 'deviant women'. It examines the newspaper coverage of infanticide for the specific period 1925–26. Those particular years have been chosen because, following the War of Independence and the Civil War, they represent a period of readjustment and reconciliation, a return to 'normality' after years of uncertainty and unrest. While concentrating on the *Examiner* and the *Independent*, I will also refer briefly to the *Irish Times*. The purpose of this discussion is to examine the press reports on infanticide in the Irish Free State in the 1920s – the overall political ideologies of the particular newspapers is not my key concern. Nevertheless, it is important to note that while the papers addressed themselves to different audiences – the *Examiner* to a predominantly Munster provincial readership, the *Independent* to middle-class readers and the *Times* to affluent and largely Protestant readers – they shared a broad political outlook. As Brown writes: 'The ruling Cumann na nGaedheal party had the support of the major national dailies, the *Irish Independent*, the *Cork Examiner* and the *Irish Times*.'[3] Thus, all three papers were operating within the dominant ideology of the newly established state and shared a concern for the future order and stability of that state.

II

In analysing women's history, newspapers are a valuable source of historical data simply because they report a good deal of information about women in a given period. For example, within specific class parameters, fashion and society pages suggest something of women's dress and leisure pursuits. 'Women's Pages' indicate patterns of housework, child care and domesticity. In addition, advertisements provide information about the cost of living, the availability of labour saving devices, beauty aids and so forth. The employment advertisements are also helpful in suggesting wage levels and the types of jobs carried out by women and men. Women feature very strongly in press reports throughout the 1920s. A perusal of the newspapers reveals the multiplicity of roles which women played in the new state – as politicians, as activists and reformers, as workers and as philanthropists.[4] Indeed, this period appears to have very particular concerns about the roles which women could play in society. According to Valiulis, the 1920s gave rise to a particular gender politics in the Free State: 'In the government's definition of a post-colonial identity, women's roles would be restricted to the hearth and home wherein they could keep alive the traditional cultural values'.[5]

However, despite the best efforts of politicians to preserve the traditional roles of Irish womanhood,[6] the newspapers offer more complex and diverse accounts of women's day-to-day experiences. It is apparent that newspapers in the 1920s, in fulfilling what Conboy calls their roles of narrator, entertainer and educator,[7] reflected some of the harsh realities of life in the new state. Pastoral letters, extolling the virtues of Irish family life, were printed side by side with court reports on domestic violence and applications for judicial separations. The Catholic Truth Society's campaigns to protect innocent Irish women from the immorality of Hollywood films were printed in close proximity to gory accounts of infants' deaths in suspicious circumstances.[8]

However, as a research source newspapers are not entirely unproblematic. In using newspapers from the past to attempt to uncover an understanding of women's experiences of infanticide, one should be sensitive to the danger of merely reconstructing *a representation of a representation*. Clearly the newspapers reported particular things in particular ways. They offered a specific perspective on infanticide rather than an 'absolute truth'. Indeed, one of the most serious shortcomings of newspapers is that they reported only those infanticides which had been uncovered, and so tell us nothing about all those which may have gone undetected. In addition, using newspapers in this way, particularly in a historical context, raises significant methodological questions. How many layers of meaning and interpretation have to be unravelled? In a present day context, where access to contraception and abortion information, while still not widespread, is at least becoming easier, perceptions of infanticide are probably very different from those of the 1920s. Infamous infanticide cases, like the Kerry Babies case of the 1980s, stand out precisely because they are considered unusual and shocking.[9] By comparison, in the 1920s the discovery of infants' bodies merited little more than a paragraph in the local newspaper.

It is important to explore the processes through which the newspapers themselves actually reported infanticide cases. At first glance the reports outlining the discovery of infants' bodies seem surprisingly short, matter-of-fact and non-judgmental. This was, however, not unique to the Irish press. Rose's research on Britain in the 1800s reveals rather complacent social attitudes to infanticide: 'In the context of the high infant mortality rate the periodic discovery of a baby's body in the street or river was shrugged off as a grim inevitability'.[10] This was reflected in the press reports throughout the Victorian period which 'were not sensationalised, but tucked away on inside pages occupying one or two paragraphs of close print'.[11] However, by the 1920s, Rose claims that infanticide had declined dramatically to about twenty cases per annum as a result of the increased availability of birth control and improved adoption legislation. In Ireland, if one is to judge from newspaper reports, infanticide in the 1920s was still high. Although the press reports are short and unsensational, they do occur with considerable regularity.

While murder trials involving adult victims could receive up to two or three columns in the *Examiner* or the *Independent*, often carrying on over several days, infanticides usually received one paragraph with little or no follow-up on the case. But even within those short reports it is possible to detect a certain pattern. Journalists are clearly framing certain topics in very particular ways. In reading newspapers it is apparent that while some things are clearly reported as opinion, as in editorials, most press reports claim to be entirely factual. But to what extent can the reader accept these 'facts'? Do the reports themselves carry some clues as to how these 'facts' are constructed and from where their authority is derived? The Irish press coverage of infanticide is interpreted through a journalism which employs both medical and legal discourses to define its authority. In addition, the names of reporters are not provided so that the personality of the journalist and her/his opinions are apparently absent. The article thereby gains further authority by the discourse of impersonality.

III

Employing concepts like 'discourse' and 'representation' to examine the patterns in press reports does not deny the underlying reality of infanticide. Without doubt, infanticide did occur in Irish society and was prosecuted on a regular basis in the Irish courts. In the period 1925–26, the *Examiner* referred to approximately twenty-five cases involving infanticide or suspected infanticide. In August 1925, for example, the *Examiner* reported on the discovery of four infant bodies; in Midleton, Co. Cork an infant's badly decomposed body was found wrapped in blankets; in Kilmallock, Co. Limerick a man out walking discovered the body of an infant; in Nenagh, Co. Tipperary an infant's body was found in a local river and in Kanturk, Co. Cork a baby's body was found in a well. This represented the highest number of bodies discovered in any one month during the period of this study. However, the nature of the discoveries was quite common and was reflected in other similar discoveries reported in other months. For example, in February 1925 the *Independent* reported the discovery of the naked body of an infant on a Dublin train and in August 1926 the *Independent* reported that a baby's body was found buried in a field in Co. Longford.

In addition to these brief accounts of discovered bodies, the press also carried reports of the arrest and prosecution of the infants' mothers. These cases tell a great deal more about the circumstances under which infanticide was committed and under which it was likely to be discovered. Thus, although the following information is very useful, it can provide only a partial account of infanticide. However, in demonstrating how infanticide was reported, this material does suggest certain patterns and sequences of events. In a close comparison of the *Examiner* with the *Independent*, it is apparent that while both papers used a similar style of reporting infanticide cases, there were some significant differences. The *Examiner* not only reported infanticide more frequently, but also tended to offer much lengthier coverage with a fuller account of court proceedings. On 12 March 1926, for instance, the *Independent* gave a thirty-nine line report on a murder trial in which a young domestic servant from Co. Tipperary was charged with killing her baby. On the same day, the *Examiner* devoted seventy-two lines to this case.

Both reports provided accounts of the court proceedings. However, whilst the *Independent* merely summarised the details of the case, the *Examiner* provided a lengthy account of the case against the young woman and the prosecution's address to the jury. On 15 April 1926, a similar difference between the two papers is apparent. In reporting the murder trial in which a brother and sister from Co. Cork were charged with infanticide, the *Independent* gave a forty-three-line summary of the case. On the same day, the *Examiner* devoted a full column plus eleven lines to the story.

Both the number of infanticide cases reported in the *Examiner*, and the space devoted to such stories, far exceeds those reported in either the *Independent* or the *Times*. How can this be explained? As national broadsheet papers the *Independent* and the *Times* devoted space to a range of national and international news issues. As a provincial paper, the *Examiner* carried far more stories of local interest, especially those relating to the Munster area. The difference in focus between national and provincial papers has been analysed and it seems that provincial papers have a long tradition of reporting human interest stories, murder trials and criminal investigations, especially those of local interest.[12] It was in its capacity as a provincial paper, pursuing human interest stories with a local angle, that the *Examiner* reported so many infanticide cases.

In the *Examiner* infanticide reports between 1925–26 four of the women suspects were married, while twelve were unmarried. This suggests that either married women were less likely to commit infanticide or that perhaps they were less likely to come under suspicion. In fact, in one of the four cases involving a married woman the *Examiner* tells us that the 'gruesome discovery' in Co. Galway was made quite accidentally by a guard whilst searching a house for poteen. Thus, were it not for the guard's visit, this married woman may not have come under suspicion at all.[13]

From the press reports it would appear that infanticide usually came about in one of two ways. Some women did not conceal their pregnancies and delivered their babies in the local County Home (workhouse), usually with a nurse or midwife in attendance. Infanticide only became an issue later on, when their babies died 'in suspicious circumstances'. Other women, however, concealed their pregnancies and had their babies alone and in secret, disposing of the bodies afterwards. In order to successfully pursue the latter plan, a woman had to avoid seeking any medical attention. In several of the reported cases it was only the necessity of sending for a doctor which subsequently led to the investigation into suspected infanticide. The discovery that a woman was concealing her pregnancy was more likely to cause suspicion in cases involving unmarried rather than married women. Concealment usually meant keeping one's condition secret even from family members, neighbours and employers – although in several cases it was suspicious employers who alerted the authorities. Hence, women living under the close scrutiny of their employers made up a large proportion of those charged with committing infanticide.

In the *Examiner* reports, six out of the twelve unmarried women arrested for infanticide were domestic servants. Again, two conclusions may be drawn from this information. Domestic servants may well have had a high rate of infanticide – after all an illegitimate child could cost them not only their employment, but also the roof over their heads, leaving them at the mercy of the workhouse. There is, however, another possibility. Domestic servants had a high risk of getting caught. Living in restricted quarters in their employer's home they had little opportunity to conceal a birth.[14]

IV

Even in the early 1900s domestic service remained the second largest area of female employment, with over 100,000 indoor servants in the Free State.[15] Despite the stereotype of the large country house, most 'domestics' worked for middle-class employers as the only general servant. Indeed, it has been estimated that by 1911, 80 per cent of Dublin domestics worked in one servant households.[16] These servants were usually very young women: 24 per cent of servants were aged between fifteen and nineteen years, with a total of 47 per cent aged under twenty-five years. Unmarried servants were preferred and were expected to leave service upon getting married. Living in their employers' home with a demanding work schedule, these young women had little leisure time and almost no privacy. Employers, often middle class and keen to assert their own position in society, demanded 'respectable', 'clean' and 'sober' servants. Nevertheless, this frequently involved a double standard on the parts of employers. As Hearn points out in her study of Irish domestic service:

> Servants were particularly vulnerable to sexual exploitation by the master, sons and visitors to the house in which they worked. They were often regarded by the employing class as inferiors who could be abused with impunity.[17]

Hearn demonstrates the frequent hypocrisy of employers who showed little sympathy for the young servants who became pregnant. Once a servant was dismissed, she not only lost her job, but also her home and, without references, would find it impossible to secure another position:

> Prostitution was commonly regarded as the likely fate of domestic servants who were unfortunate enough to lose their situations ...

Crimes such as concealment of birth, infanticide and suicide often followed.[18]

The points raised by Hearn are borne out by two very similar cases of infanticide in the *Examiner*. On 30 November 1926, the paper reported that a young woman servant was charged with murder. The article described how the woman's employer, finding her unwell, sent her to hospital. The body of an infant was later discovered hidden in a suitcase. Although the woman was charged with murder, she was found guilty on the lesser charge of concealment.[19]

On 28 January 1925, the *Examiner* reported on a very similar story in Fermoy, Co. Cork. Carrying the bold heading **'Infanticide Near Fermoy'**, the report was a full column in length and gave a detailed summary of the inquest. The article illustrates how the *Examiner* presented 'factual' reports based on the 'reliable' testimony of 'experts', civic guards and doctors, as well as the testimony of relatives. The report gives the names of all the people involved, including the jury at the coroner's court. A Cork reader in 1925 may well have been able to identify some or all of those involved. The first witness was the young woman's father, who denied knowing that she had been pregnant. The *Examiner* reported the inquest almost as a transcript of the proceedings, implying that it is a word for word account. The journalist is entirely absent, as the following extract illustrates:

Coroner – Did you notice anything unusual about her then? No.
Foreman – Did she not say anything to you about her condition? No, sir.

The woman's employer testified that she had been employed as a domestic servant in his house for two years. His evidence is reported in detail and takes the form of a narrative of his actions:

He shouted at her room as there was unusual snoring. She made no answer. He shouted three or four times, and then with a lighted candle he entered her room. He asked her what was the matter and she replied that she had been vomiting all night.

This style of reporting puts the employer's evidence beyond doubt. It is simply stated as 'fact'. It is graphically described like a fascinating and very dramatic story. The employer went on to recount how he had gone for the priest who, on seeing the young woman, recommended a doctor be sent for immediately. The doctor's testimony is reported in the same factual narrative style:

The girl was lying in bed, very pale, pulseless and unconscious. Witness did all that was possible for her. On examination he discovered that she had recently given birth to a child. The child was missing. The woman died within five minutes after his arrival at the house.

The body of the infant was found under the mattress of the bed where the woman slept. The doctor testified it had been born alive but died from asphyxia. The woman died from postpartum haemorrhage. He added that with proper attendance at the birth it was probable the woman would have lived. The coroner remarked that it was 'a very sad occurrence'. However, he added that if the woman had lived she would have been charged with murder. Another point which makes this report unusual was the reference to the 'person responsible'. While this may have formed a part of other inquests, it was rarely referred to in the press. Yet in this case it was mentioned on more than one occasion. The woman's employer testified 'that she was in the habit of going to cross-road dances in the vicinity during the summer – in the months of May, June and July'. He further added that she had been cautioned about staying out late at night.

Infanticide is associated almost exclusively with women. Men are rarely implicated. Historical evidence from other sources suggests that this was a long established pattern in the prosecution of infanticide cases going back over the centuries.[20] The matter-of-fact style in which infanticide cases were reported completely distanced them from any mention of sex, conception and birth control. By referring to the young woman going to dances in the summer months this report went perilously close to suggesting that she had had casual sexual relations with a man. However, the suggestion that her condition was the result of going to dances removed any suspicion that her employer might be 'responsible'. In addition, the coroner reassures the jury that had her employer known of her condition he would not have allowed her to stay in his employment or in his house. The respectability of the employer is asserted against the moral irresponsibility of the employee.

What can be interpreted from the very 'factual' accounts given by the woman's family, her employer and the doctor? We can only speculate about the role of the journalist in summarising and editing the report in particular ways. It appears that, prompted by fear of losing her job, this young woman had decided to embark on the dangerous course of concealment. This was a difficult decision not only because of the physical risks to one's health, but, in addition, it was a criminal offence. For most of the women who decided to conceal their pregnancy and the birth of their baby, it seems likely they intended to abandon the infant, to passively allow it to die or to actively kill it, usually by means of suffocation or strangulation.

In Dublin, it appears from press reports that babies were frequently abandoned in very public places including trains, trams and even in Woolworths. Of course, this plan necessitated a woman's speedy recovery after the birth and being well enough to leave the house, unseen, carrying the infant's body in a bundle of old clothes or a suitcase. As Hearn's research suggests, domestic servants had little privacy or leisure time. They may, therefore, have had to conceal the infant's body for several days or weeks before they had the opportunity to leave the house and dispose of it. But in large cities the chances of the authorities tracing an unidentified infant, dead or alive, to its mother must have been slight.

There was undoubtedly a class dimension to the infanticide cases reported in the papers. It appears that the women who were prosecuted were either domestic servants or poor women living in rural areas. Again, this can be interpreted in two ways. It is possible to speculate that working-class women were more likely to become pregnant outside marriage. This would certainly be in line with the predominant stereotype of working-class morality.[21] But, on the other hand, it is also possible to speculate that unmarried, middle-class women who found themselves pregnant had more options available to them. For example, placing the baby in a private adoption would probably have been easier. In addition, as a result of class prejudices, a 'respectable' middle-class young lady was less likely to be suspected of any unsavoury activity.

V

In rural areas, there may have been more opportunity for concealing the body of an infant, by burying it in a field or throwing it in a river to be carried down stream, but there also appears to have been a high rate of detection. Based on their local knowledge, the civic guards seem to have played an active role in initiating investigations even before infant bodies were discovered.[22] From the newspaper coverage, it appears that police enquiries began for two reasons. Usually the discovery of a body signalled the start of a search for the mother. However, in several reported cases the investigation began with the mother and culminated in the discovery of an infant's body. Three such cases were reported in the *Examiner* during 1926 (15 April, 27 August, 22 December). All of these cases occurred in rural areas and were initiated by the suspicions of the local civic guards. In each case, the guards, aware that a local woman was pregnant, began investigating when it was apparent that no baby had arrived. In all three cases other family members were implicated. The fact that civic guards became suspicious and began investigating the whereabouts of expected babies suggests that the occurrence of infanticide was widespread.

On 15 April 1926, the *Examiner* carried a report under the headline

'Murder Charge, Brother and Sister on Trial, Co. Cork Infant's Death'. Like the report of the Fermoy inquest, this article also provided a very detailed summary of court proceedings. However, this case was unusual as it involved both male and female family members. The article told how the local civic guards became suspicious when an eighteen-year-old woman returned home from the workhouse without her baby. On making enquiries at the girl's home, the guards were informed that the baby had died and that the woman's twenty-four-year-old brother had buried it in a soapbox. The civic guards accompanied the man to the graveyard but the body could not be located. He was unable to explain why the body and the soapbox had disappeared. The report then related the testimony of witnesses who had found the body of a male infant in a nearby river. However, when the guards arrived to retrieve the body they found that only four tiny bones remained. The attack on the corpse was linked to dogs and otters which had been seen in the area near the body. No post mortem was possible and the cause of death was unknown. The *Examiner* then very briefly summarised the case for the defence made by Mr Reardon. He argued that the initial statement, that the brother had buried the baby in a soapbox, was inadmissible because that statement was made casually before he had been charged or arrested. Reardon is also reported as saying that the young man was of a very nervous disposition, having been in the Free State army for a long time. In the dock the young man now said that the baby had died from exposure on the long journey from the workhouse in Clonakilty back to their home four miles outside of Drimoleague. When the baby died the brother and sister simply threw it into the river. The *Examiner* concludes the report with the simple statement 'The prisoners were found not guilty and discharged'.

But this statement deserves further analysis. Although the report of this case in the *Independent* is far shorter, only forty-three lines, it does supply more details of the defence case. In fact, the article is sub-headed in bold print half way through the report as '**The Defence**'. Naming the male defendant it says: '– – said that on their way from the county home they had to wait four hours for trains in sleet and rain and had afterwards to walk four and a half miles home in bad weather'. The next part of the testimony was indented and bold: '**The child, which was weak, died from exposure on the way, and he threw the body into the river**'.

This style of reporting, especially in a short article which omitted many of the confusing details printed in the *Examiner*, adds some credence to the brother and sister's story. The *Independent* further adds one more interesting fact, the time taken by the jury in reaching their verdict: 'After thirty-five minutes absence the jury found the prisoners not guilty and they were discharged'. Thus, not only did the jury believe the story told by the young woman and her brother, but they arrived at their decision with considerable speed. Like the case of the young domestic servant in Dublin who had hidden her baby's body in a suitcase, the jury refused to find them guilty of murder. What does this suggest about public attitudes to infanticide? Why were juries so reluctant to find women guilty in the face of medical evidence and the testimony of the civic guards?

On 12 March 1926, the *Examiner* reported on the trial of a young domestic servant charged with murdering her seven-week-old baby, whose body had been found in a river in Co. Tipperary. The woman protested that her baby had died peacefully in her arms, but the post mortem revealed that death was due to a fractured skull. In this case, like that in Clonakilty, the woman claimed that she had simply thrown the dead body into the river. In both cases the defendants admitted to throwing the body into the river, almost as if this was a perfectly ordinary thing to do. This may indicate the social acceptance of infant mortality and the low value placed on 'illegitimate' babies. The paper reported the vehemence with which this particular case was prosecuted. The prosecuting barrister is reported as telling the jury that this was not a case of 'concealment' of a birth but the 'wilful murder' of a seven-week-old child. The report quoted him as telling the jury:

> you will find this woman guilty to warn all others that there is such a crime as infanticide punishable, and that the massacre of innocents, which takes place at present in this and other countries must be stopped, and it will be stopped here.

The jury, however, disagreed and returned a verdict of manslaughter. According to the *Independent* of 12 March 1926:

> Mr Justice Johnston said he would accept the verdict, which was, he added, rather unfortunate, as there was no evidence of manslaughter ... Accused was sentenced to three years penal servitude, the judge remarking that if the verdict had been wilful murder he would have had to sentence her to death.

VI

There appears to have been a remarkable reluctance on the part of jurors to convict these young women of murder. One obvious factor which needs to be considered is the severity of punishment imposed on convicted women. In the Irish Free State there was no Infanticide Act until 1949.[23] Thus, prior to that date, women accused of infanticide were charged with murder and hence the death penalty could be invoked. On 4 June 1926, for example, the

Examiner reported that a married woman from Co. Wicklow was charged with infanticide at the Central Criminal Court in Dublin. The newspaper reported the judge as saying that:

> cases of infanticide unfortunately were appearing in that court more frequently than they should. The whole social fabric depended on strict administration of the law.

While the jury found the woman guilty, they made a strong recommendation for mercy. The judge, however, sentenced the woman to death. On the 26 June, the *Examiner* reported that this sentence had been commuted to penal servitude for life, only four days before the execution was to have been carried out. On 10 November 1926, the paper carried a similar report of another woman whose death sentence had been commuted to life imprisonment. The knowledge that a guilty verdict could mean the death penalty may have influenced the verdicts of other juries as:

> Nobody wanted it on their conscience that they had been instrumental in subjecting the distraught and lonely defendant to the ordeal of the Black Cap.[24]

In the two infanticide trials discussed in some detail above, the frustration of the prosecuting barrister is obvious. In both the case involving the brother and sister from Clonakilty and the young domestic servant from Co. Tipperary, the *Examiner* recounted the statements of the prosecution, led in each case by Carrigan. On the 12 March 1926, the *Examiner* reported in the Tipperery case that:

> Mr Carrigan ... said that everyone felt a certain reluctance in prosecuting women such as the prisoner, and charging her with murder; but in this particular case they would have to consider whether it was not which ought to be punished unless the law was to lapse completely, and unless infanticide was to be considered punishable no longer.

Obviously, the jury chose a different solution to this moral dilemma. The post mortem did suggest that the baby had died a violent death. In returning the verdict of manslaughter they did find the woman responsible for her actions but not guilty of premeditated murder. Almost exactly one month later, in the Clonakilty case, Carrigan found himself losing another infanticide trial. Once again, the *Examiner* of 15 April 1925 reported his address to the jury:

> Mr Carrigan, prosecuting, said that it was a sad and painful case, and there was no alternative but to charge the prisoners, brother and sister, with murder. If life was to be protected, if infant life was to have any

security, a case like this could not pass without being subjected to the verdict of a jury on the capital charge.

This time, in the absence of a post mortem, the jury entirely disagreed with Carrigan. His address to the juries in both cases suggested that he was well aware of public sympathy or perhaps public reluctance to acknowledge that infanticide may actually be occurring in Irish society. It is, however, impossible to assess whether juries acquitted women because they did not believe these women capable of committing infanticide or because they acknowledged that young women in desperate circumstances were forced to make difficult decisions.

In Britain it appears that juries drawn from the local community were frequently sympathetic to young women accused of infanticide and 'chivalrous members were notoriously reluctant to return verdicts in infants' cases indicating culpability on the mother's part'.[25] It has been suggested that juries' verdicts reflected not only an acceptance of high infant mortality, but also the low value attached to illegitimate infant life. Moreover, infanticide was 'seen as less serious than other kinds of murder because the baby has no self-awareness and the public at large did not feel a threat to themselves'.[26] Although this also seems to be relevant in Ireland, there were some significant differences. Most notable was the marked decline in infanticide in Britain during the 1920s, which was not apparent in Ireland. By the mid-1920s, it has been claimed that in Britain infanticide was fading as a social issue in the face of more widely available contraceptives, a fall in infant mortality and subsequent changes in the value attached to infant life and more stringent adoption regulations which improved the life chances of children given up for adoption. In the Irish Free State, not only were contraceptives becoming more difficult to obtain, but attitudes to infant life and adoption were still causing serious concern in some quarters.

VII

In 1925, in a series of very lengthy reports, the *Irish Times* addressed the 'problem' of unwanted children and unmarried mothers. These reports were prompted by a commission being held in Dublin which investigated poor law reform and the workhouse system. On 15 July 1925, the *Times* revealed the inadequacies of the fostering and adoption system where hundreds of babies were placed in overcrowded and unsuitable situations. The report publicised the findings of the commission that 110 children were currently being fostered in one Dublin slum. Foster families were paid a lump sum varying between £3 and £20, and even if the baby subsequently died they were under no obligation to return the money. The Dublin Union reported that they had 180 children boarded out to families in the local community. These were overwhelmingly the babies of unmarried women, 161 of whom had gone to the union for their confinement between 1924–25. As the commission continued to take evidence on the conditions of unmarried mothers and their illegitimate children, the *Times* devoted an editorial to the subject on 16 July 1925. Entitled 'Unwanted Children', it referred to 'a nefarious trade in unwanted children practised in Dublin ... evils are rampant in the Irish underworld which call for the pen of a Dickens for their adequate exposure'. The editorial called for the proper adoption of these children into loving homes.

The *Times*' reports reveal the predominant attitudes which then existed towards unmarried mothers. The general emphasis appears to have been on reforming 'fallen' women and punishing those who would not be reformed. Some like Miss Cruise, founder of St Patrick's Guild in Dublin, believed that many of these women could go on to become 'respectable' married women, and they therefore deserved a second chance in life. On 17 July 1925, the *Times* reported her evidence to the commission in which she stated that, in the previous year, 227 babies had been born at St Patrick's Guild. The majority of mothers were domestic servants. The paper quotes her as saying that 'the problem of the unmarried mother is a very big one, but so far we in Ireland have closed our eyes to it'. The reports in the *Times* also reveal the very limited range of options available to unmarried mothers. The work-house and other institutions all believed that mothers and babies should be separated as soon as possible. The mortality rate for boarded out babies was extremely high. In the case of one institution, fifty-four of the eighty-six babies boarded out in Dublin died.[27] Furthermore, the Dublin Union admitted that ninety-four of 274 children boarded out had died.[28] The knowledge that illegitimate babies had such a slim chance of survival may well have influenced the decisions of young women contemplating concealment and, indeed, the jurors who would later hear their cases.

VIII

Newspapers are recognised as offering an important insight into the processes through which nations are created and sustained.[29] Newspapers in their roles as entertainers, educators and reporters of news, also reveal many of the tensions and contradictions which lie beneath the surface of any society. In this the Irish press is no exception. While the 1920s represented an important period of nation-building in the Irish Free State and the press actively participated in defining the identity of the new nation, press reports also suggest some of the hidden problems of Irish society.

In this essay I have used newspapers to analyse an under-researched aspect of Irish history. While clearly the newspaper reports offer limited and partial information, it is possible to piece together certain patterns of police investigations and court prosecutions. Drawing on wider research sources it is possible to supplement the partial accounts available in the press. In so doing, I have suggested why certain women may have featured disproportionately in infanticide investigations and why juries were often reluctant to convict these women. In addition, by using other newspaper reports on the general attitudes to illegitimacy, I have suggested reasons why women might have felt forced into concealing their pregnancies and committing infanticide.

Nevertheless, newspapers are far from being ideal research sources. In Ireland cases of infanticide tended to be reported in very particular ways. The press reports drew on legal and medical discourses to construct their 'factual' accounts of events. Thus, although infanticide was regularly reported it was marked off as an aberration from normal life. By keeping newspaper reports brief and by reporting the events in a summarised, 'matter-of-fact' way, as criminal investigations, infanticide was marginalised from mainstream society. In addition, the press reports of infanticide trials were carefully written to avoid any direct mention of sexual intercourse. The young servant in Fermoy, for instance, was suspected of going to dances in the summer months. That is as far as the *Examiner* went in suggesting a direct link between sex, unwanted pregnancy and infanticide. However, the press reports, perhaps inadvertently, do reveal the diversity of opinion in Irish society – the civic guards, judges, prosecuting barristers, members of the juries, witnesses and families of the accused all propounded different understandings of infanticide.[30] Of course, it is difficult to know how contemporary readers interpreted the brief but regular accounts of infanticide in their daily papers. But it is possible that these reports may have unwittingly alerted some young women to ways of disposing of infant bodies and avoiding detection.

The frequency with which infanticide was reported makes it an aspect of our history which cannot be ignored. However, in addition to helping us understand the past, a study of infanticide may also provide a fuller knowledge of the changing nature of birth control and population control techniques used throughout Irish history.

Irish Women's Emigration to England, 1922–60: The Lengthening of Family Ties

SHARON LAMBERT

I

It is not just the attitudes of the host community which determine how far immigrants are assimilated into that society – immigrants also bring with them values and traditions from their original country. Women coming to England from Southern Ireland after 1922 left a climate of post-colonialism in which Irish cultural identity was emphasised as being distinctly not British, or more specifically, not English.[1] During a period when Irish women's roles were becoming increasingly circumscribed and defined by familial duties, thousands of them left their family homes and emigrated, the majority to England. Using oral evidence from the life histories of forty Irish women who were living in Lancashire between 1922 and 1960, this essay investigates how Irish women coped with the apparent contradictory forces of family duty and leaving home, and Irish patriotism and settling in England.[2] An argument is developed that rather than escaping from increasing family ties and responsibilities, Irish women in England were motivated to keep in close contact with their original homes in Ireland. The cultural climate of newly independent Ireland generally ensured that emigrants to England left with a desire to uphold their Irish identity in the country from which Ireland had only recently gained independence. Indeed, it seems that as an Irish woman's identity was defined by her role within the family she was less likely to sever family ties than to adopt strategies of maintaining them from a distance.

In the first forty years after partition, the new Irish state pursued successive policies which emphasised not only its political but also its economic, spiritual and cultural independence from its colonial past. Gaelic sports, music, dancing and language and the Catholic faith were vigorously promoted as examples of a distinctly Irish national identity. Attempts at economic self-sufficiency during this period can be seen as another example of the Irish state ideologically distancing itself from Britain, its main trading partner. Southern Ireland could not win its economic war with industrialised Britain but material deficits were translated as spiritual superiority. De Valera's famous St Patrick's Day broadcast of 1943 epitomised the idealised rural Ireland which dominated official rhetoric and ignored the reality of economic stagnation and high emigration:

> That Ireland which we dreamed of would be the home of a people who valued material wealth only as a basis of right living, of a people who were satisfied with frugal comfort and devoted their leisure to things of the spirit; a land whose countryside would be bright with cosy homesteads, whose fields and villages would be joyous with sounds of industry, the romping of sturdy children, the contests of athletic youths, the laughter of comely maidens; whose firesides would be the forums of the wisdom of serene old age.[3]

Closely linked to this rural ideal was the symbol of the family which dominated the ideology of Irish society. McCullagh has located the roots of the Irish ideology of the family in the post-famine period.[4] This ideology had lost none of its symbolic force by the twentieth century. For instance, Article 41.1 of the 1937 constitution stated that:

> The State recognises the Family as the natural primary and funda-mental unit group of society, and as a moral institution possessing inalienable and imprescriptible rights, antecedent and superior to all positive law.

Of all the ideologies of independent Ireland, women's lives were most affected by the idealisation of the family and their roles became increasingly circumscribed to caring for the family within the home. Successive govern-ments passed acts which restricted women's involvement in the public sphere: the 1927 Juries Act, for example, virtually excluded women from jury service by making it necessary for them to formally apply; the Conditions of Employment Bill of 1935 regulated the hours of women workers and the industries which were allowed to employ them; a marriage bar forced female civil servants to retire on marriage. Moreover, Article 41.2 of the 1937 constitution institutionalised the ideal of Irish womanhood as serving the family within the home:

> In particular, the State recognises that by her life within the home, woman gives to the State a support without which the common good cannot be achieved.

The State shall, therefore, endeavour to ensure that mothers shall not be obliged by economic necessity to engage in labour to the neglect of their duties in the home.

Thus, by 1937 the ideal of Irish women in the home was being equated with patriotism, necessary for the 'common good' of the state. During this period, when Irish women's roles were becoming increasingly defined by familial duties within the home, hundreds of thousands of Irish women were leaving their family homes and emigrating. Between 1926 and 1951 about 52,000 women left Southern Ireland for the United States and a further 180,000 went to Britain.[5] Another irony is that it was also during this period of post-independence, when official rhetoric was promoting all things Irish and denigrating all things British, that Britain replaced the USA as the main destination of Irish emigrants by 1929. Maura, for example, reluctantly left her home on a small farm in Co. Roscommon to find work in Lancashire in 1945 when she was eighteen. She saw the absurdity of the idealisation of rural Ireland, combined with anti-English rhetoric, when the mass exportation of people across the Irish Sea was continuing:

They taught us to hate England and then they sent us here!
[Maura, b. 1927, Co. Roscommon]

In explaining the high rate of female emigration to Britain in the 1940s and 1950s, O'Carroll has suggested that: 'Essential to this move was a desire to distance themselves from control by family and patriarchal society'.[6] However, given the strength of the family ideal in Irish culture it is likely that a complete rejection of family ties after emigration was, at the very least, difficult for most Irish women. Furthermore, the colonial relationship between Ireland and Britain, which was still very recent, would make it even harder for an Irish woman in England to abandon her family obligations, since her national identity was defined by her role within the family.

II

All the women in this study either offered unprompted information or were asked specifically about their reasons for emigrating from Ireland. Economic reasons were most often cited as the impetus for emigration, especially amongst women from poorer rural backgrounds where labouring on the family farm or domestic service were usually the only local employment alternatives. Small family farm incomes were unable to sustain all offspring as they left school. Indeed, women who worked on the farm expressed an awareness of being a financial burden on the family and a sense of prolonged childhood as they had to ask for money to buy new clothes or go to dances. Only two women, however, said that they emigrated in order to distance themselves from what they perceived to be excessive parental control. One was Maeve, who was born into a wealthy family in Co. Tipperary in 1917. In 1927, her family moved to Dublin and Maeve was educated in private convent boarding schools and University College Dublin where she qualified as a doctor in 1943:

> I wanted to come to England, I didn't want to try for a job in Ireland. Well frankly I wanted to get away from home because my mother was one of those, you never had very much freedom. I never had very much freedom growing up, being the only girl she was strict with me. And I knew that if I stayed in Dublin I would never be able to lead my own life.

Another informant, Patricia, was born in 1925 in Co. Donegal. She left school at fourteen to help her stepmother sew shirts at home. A few years later she went to work in a shirt factory across the border in Derry:

> I went to work in Derry in 1943, the war was on at that time ... Shortly after that me sister Harriet followed. When I first went to Derry I must have been about seventeen and we earned £3 a week. Out of that then we used to give most of it to our father. We used to just, more–or–less, live on bread and syrup and bread and jam. We used to have to give our parents nearly all the money that we earned ... We were about six years in Derry when we decided to [emigrate]. Oh me father was in a terrible state altogether. He thought England was a terrible place to come to. He was quite happy with us coming working in Derry ... We had always wanted to come across to England but me father would never allow us. That particular week–end, on the 23rd March, 1949, we came away to England. Just before we left Derry to go to England we wrote to tell my father that by the time he got the letter we would be in Manchester.

Even after their clandestine move to Manchester, Patricia and her sister continued to send money from their weekly wages to their father in Ireland until they married. This suggests that they had limited, rather than renounced, their familial obligations. The majority of women in this study viewed emigration as a means of assisting rather than escaping from their familial duties, as the following examples demonstrate.

The economic situation of her family and her order in the family were important factors in determining whether or not a woman emigrated. Lena was one of eight children born to a small farmer and his wife in Co. Galway in 1930. She left school at fourteen and worked on the family farm until she emigrated to England at the age of fifteen and a half with the assistance of an agency which arranged employment for her as a childminder in London. Lena was desperately unhappy in this job and left after three months to live and work with her sister in Kent. She was the fifth child of the family and the fifth to emigrate to England. Her early emigrant years were spent travelling between her siblings throughout England and working in various occupations before she trained as a nurse and settled in Morecambe in 1950. Despite expressing feelings of homesickness and unhappiness as a young emigrant (she eventually moved back to Ireland in 1982) Lena saw emigration as a necessary family obligation, since the remittances from older siblings enabled her younger brothers and sisters to receive a secondary education:

> All my family used to send money to my mother. They needed it in this country [Ireland] then. But every family, all the children who went in the '40s and '50s, did the same thing. They went to help the younger children and to educate them. Yeah, we did, we educated them.

Several respondents also noted that their younger brothers or sisters progressed to secondary education, whereas they and their older emigrant siblings did not. Economically assisting their family, rather than themselves, was a common motivation for Irish women's emigration.

The strength of the family ideal in Irish society meant that the behaviour of individual members reflected upon the reputation of the whole family. Indeed, upholding the good name of the family was an important motivation for conforming to socially acceptable behaviour. A strict moral climate prevailed in the post-independence years where sin was exclusively equated with sex.[7] Without exception, respondents to this case study reported that the greatest shame they could have brought upon their families in Ireland was to have had an illegitimate child:

> If a girl had a child and she wasn't married they treated her worse than if she had took a gun and murdered half a dozen people. It was a thing that was never forgotten, and probably wouldn't be to this day ... Their mother and father usually threw them out. If they didn't come over here [England] there was a place called the County Home over there where young expectant mothers went. And I heard people talk that they were treated worse than criminals in it. And then, when the baby was born, the mother and child had to stay in that home until one of her parents and a priest signed her out. And some o' them people was never signed out; they had to stay there for years. [Siobhan, b. 1938, Co. Donegal]

The taboo on sex outside of marriage was so strong that even discussing it was forbidden in most Irish families. It would appear that most girls were not even prepared for the onset of their periods. Only two respondents were told about them, one by her mother and the other by a female cousin.[8] The overwhelming memories of the rest of the women were of being shocked and frightened when their first period occurred and feeling ashamed by the secrecy of the monthly rituals of soaking and washing soiled cloths and towels which had to be kept hidden from male family members. Given this taboo, it is perhaps not surprising that most women reported that they were ignorant of sexual matters during their youth. As Siobhan recalled:

> There was no such thing as teaching the facts o' life. Most parents wouldn't talk about it because they weren't told when they were young and it was an embarrassing situation. You probably got a clip round the earhole if ye asked, ye weren't allowed to ask questions like that. So you weren't told but ye sorta got yer own instinct that it was wrong, you know, to have sex outside of marriage … But the girls that had illegitimate babies, I think they had them out o' ignorance, because they weren't told anything.

Whether because of sexual ignorance or otherwise, many single pregnant Irish women were forced to emigrate rather than bring shame upon their families at home. Some women in this study hid their pregnancies and others left with the assistance of their families. Two of Siobhan's sisters-in-law emigrated to Britain to have illegitimate children and her recollections of their situations show that a diversity of experiences could occur within a single family:

> One o' his sisters she come over here and she was pregnant when she come over. Her parents didn't know and she worked in Oliver's Cafe and then she had this little boy and she put him in Nazareth House [a convent in Lancaster which included a children's home] … Then she met this fella over here and she brought him out of the Nazareth House when he was about four or five. Another sister o' me husband's was working in Scotland and his mother went over to Scotland and left him looking after the younger ones at home. [Siobhan's husband was unmarried at this time and his father had died.] She'd gone over because that one was having a baby in Scotland and she was staying wi' another married sister. She had the baby adopted. But me husband didn't know, his mother didn't tell him. They sorta kept things from the boy. He didn't know until he came over here and I told him.

A pattern of female family members colluding to conceal unmarried women's pregnancies is evident in several of the life histories. Lily, who was born in Athlone in 1929, had lived in Morecambe for two years when she arranged the marriage of her pregnant sister and provided a home for the young couple. Her story is significant because it illustrates that Protestants (she was Baptist) were as keen to hide family indiscretions as Catholics:

> My mother wrote to me and she said: 'I'm sending her over, arrange a wedding!' It was a bit of a rush wedding. They came over here because it might not have been the right thing for people to know at home ... The child was born here but they didn't like it here and they went home. They didn't go back to Athlone ... they got a job outside Wicklow.

The young couple had not wanted to emigrate, or even leave Athlone, but they did so in order to protect the reputations of their families. The circumstances of Lily's own emigration in 1950, when she was twenty-one, also highlight how emigration was often undertaken less for individual than for family needs. At this time, Lily had a good job in a shop and she was very happy living in Athlone. In her life history she revealed that neither she nor her sisters were allowed to date Catholic boys when they were young, but there were comparatively few Protestants in the town and her family were related to a lot of them. She had no intention of emigrating but was forced to do so by her mother when she became friendly with a male cousin. Her mother also wanted Lily to move near to two of her uncles who had lost contact with the family in Athlone:

> I was friendly with a cousin at home. I used to go to his house a lot and we became very friendly. I didn't think there was anything wrong with it but quite suddenly I was told: 'You're not to go over there anymore'. I think my mother saw what was coming and decided it was time I was shipped out. She had two reasons, that was one, and the other one was to find out what her brothers were doing ... I had no notion of emigrating and I had no inclination to be a nurse. But my mother wrote off to the Lancaster Infirmary and I was taken on as a student nurse ... In those days you had to be obedient to what your parents said ... I remember thinking: 'I don't really want to be a nurse. I don't really want to be going anywhere'.

Lily hated nursing and soon after emigrating she left Lancaster Infirmary and moved into her uncle's home in nearby Morecambe where she found work as a shop assistant, a job she had enjoyed in Athlone before she was forced to leave. Claire was another woman who did not want to emigrate, but her mother decided otherwise. She was eighteen and had been working for two years in Northern Ireland when, on a visit home, her mother decided that she should go to live with an aunt in Halifax. As in Lily's situation, it was because her mother wanted her to end a romantic relationship:

> I went home to Clare and my mother didn't want me to go back to Northern Ireland again … I met a young boy there and he was a non-Catholic, and o'course they were all against it in those days. She wouldn't let me back. So she says: 'You can go to Halifax in Yorkshire and you can stay there'. So I went to my auntie's. [Claire, b. 1932, Co. Clare]

Not only could family pressures push emigrants out of Ireland, they could also draw them abroad. Sheila, who was born in Dublin in 1923, spent most of her life caring for relatives in Ireland and England. At the age of nineteen she left her job in a Dublin mill to nurse her dying mother. She then took care of her younger brothers and sisters for five years whilst her father was working in England. When her father returned home she was persuaded, against her wishes, to look after her uncle's family in Lancaster:

> I came to Liverpool in 1947, then I came here to Lancaster. Me uncle was desperate, his wife was dying and there were four small children. I started the whole routine all over again. I nursed me mother until she died and I nursed his wife until she died … He was away in the Merchant Navy so I looked after his wife and then I had those children to look after. I wasn't going to do it at first because I thought well I'd done it once, me brothers and sisters like, you know, and it was a hard job … I didn't really know what to do, you know, but I did feel sorry for him.

The emigrant women in this study left Southern Ireland for various economic or social reasons but, whatever the basic cause was, it usually concerned the emigrant's family as much as herself individually. It has been shown that some women even emigrated involuntarily in order to fulfil their families' expectations. Family networks were also the most important means of arranging and maintaining emigration. It was, however, only in the area of concealing a pregnancy that the familial network became gendered. In other instances women were as likely to have their emigration arranged by, or to go and stay with, male relatives as female. Moreover, most women went to live in areas where they had relatives. It seems therefore that female emigration from Ireland cannot be simply explained as a conscious rejection of family duties, since family involvement and networks were crucial to the emigration process.

III

The importance of familial ties is also demonstrated by the efforts which women made to maintain contact with their Irish homes and families after emigration. Telephones were not easily accessible to working–class people in Ireland or England during the period of this study. Letters, therefore, remained the cheapest and most utilised form of communication between the two countries. The impression gained from this oral history is that Irish women regularly wrote to, and received letters back from, their families in Ireland, apart from some mail restrictions during the Second World War for security reasons. The nature of the letters which passed between women and their relatives in Ireland shows a pattern of transmitting only good news wherever possible:

> Oh you always wrote, always. But you never told the bad things. No, nobody ever does; you just told the good things ... It didn't matter how bad you were, you'd suffer in silence, you'd pretend everything was splendid. Me mother would write great big long letters. And she'd tell you about everybody you knew; where they were; if they were home; the children that were born. She'd tell you about the animals and all the news from there. That was your lifeline. She didn't tell us anything bad. Yet there must've been bad things mustn't there? But she never did tell us them. [Joan, b. 1915, Co. Mayo]

Emigrants could also prioritise news which they knew their families would want to hear. For instance, when Agnes came to Rochdale to train as a nurse in 1945 she was delighted to be able to inform her mother in Roscommon that she was keeping up her religious practices:

> My mother had an awful thing about being allowed to practise your religious duties and we were always called on Holydays of Obligation for Mass. We were on the wards at half-seven so the Mass was usually at half-six and we were called for it. I was very glad to be able to devote one page of a letter to tell my mother that we were called for Mass. [Agnes, b. 1925 in Coventry but returned with her family to Co. Roscommon in 1926]

It was easier to include reassuring information than to exclude news which would alarm the family at home, but one emigrant in this study managed to conceal her life-threatening illness from her parents despite writing to them regularly during her six-month stay in an isolation hospital in 1940. She was only able to conceal this information with the agreement of her brothers and sisters in England:

I was six months on my back in the isolation hospital and it was touch
and go because diphtheria affects your heart. I was so weak. And I kept
writing home, just three lines, and the ward sister would post it for me.
But I never told them that I was in hospital. I told my family not to tell
my mother and father. [Attracta, b. 1915, Co. Sligo]

Written contact was not only selective but it could also be fabricated.
Emigrant letters were not just a source of news but also of entertainment for
the family in Ireland, and they could be embroidered accordingly:

I was always writing letters to my mother and I was always writing
things that made her laugh. Long rubbishy letters, you know, telling
her about the mental hospital patients. Most of it was made up but it
was just to give her a laugh, you know. [Lena, b. 1930, Co. Galway]

Before the telephone became widely available and largely replaced the
emigrant letter, all of the respondents claimed to have kept in regular contact
by mail with their families not just in Ireland, but throughout the world.
However, oral evidence has shown that the contents of emigrants' letters
should not necessarily be accepted as a complete, or even accurate, representation of the everyday lives of emigrants or their families in Ireland. An over-
positive image was often portrayed in letters from both sides of the Irish Sea.
Female emigrants consciously cultivated an optimistic view of their lives
abroad, partly for their own self-esteem and also to alleviate their parents'
anxiety.

Letters were not the only form of postal communication between emigrants and their families in Ireland. By the middle of the twentieth century
the sending of parcels and money was a well-established tradition amongst
Irish emigrants. The importance of emigrants' remittances to the Irish
economy was noted by the Commission on Emigration and other Population
Problems, which conducted a major survey between 1948 and 1954.[9] It seems
that many Irish families relied on money and parcels sent from their
offspring abroad. Maura's experience was typical of many emigrant women.
She worked as a chambermaid in Morecambe and before her marriage sent
most of her wages back to Roscommon:

My generation was great for sending money. I used to send as much as
ever I could. You'd send and do without, you know. I sent it to my
mother. They needed it really because there was four younger than me
still at home. Everybody that went sent it. I remember a woman in
Ireland and if her daughters wrote and they hadn't sent money she
usen't to answer it! She wouldn't answer it unless there was money in

it. You could send it by telegram and they used to be waiting for the telegrams in Ireland. [Maura, b. 1927, Co. Roscommon]

The overall impression gained from the Irish emigration experience is one of families being poorer in Ireland than their more affluent emigrant members abroad. This was, however, not always the case. To cite one example, Molly's family background in Co. Longford was not prosperous. She was one of thirteen children born to a gamekeeper and his wife in 1931, but when she was struggling to raise her own six children in Lancaster her mother sent parcels from Ireland:

Every Christmas, for years and years, I never had to buy anything for Christmas because about a week before every Christmas she sent me a parcel. And there was a turkey, there was butter and there was sauce. There was everything that you could think of, pudding and everything, for Christmas. I never used to have to buy anything. She was so good to me. Always at Christmas I used to wait for this box coming.

Most women in this study reported sending money or parcels to their families in Ireland at least while they were single but some women never sent any and others, like Molly, received gifts from Ireland. Although it is impossible to quantify the extent of remittances which were sent from both sides of the Irish Sea, the overall impression is that it was more normal for emigrants to offer financial support to their families at home. There were, however, exceptions to this rule and some families in Ireland assisted their children abroad. Overall, the transfer of gifts and money across the Irish Sea appears to have been extensive.

The greater proximity of Britain than the previously favoured emigrant destination of the USA, and improved and cheaper sea passages, made visits home more accessible to Irish emigrants in the mid-twentieth century than at any previous time. Irish women in Lancashire were favourably placed on the west coast of England with the two ports of Heysham and Liverpool offering regular sailings to Ireland. Apart from proximity and affordability, social factors also determined whether or not women visited their families in Ireland. It has already been shown that some women were selective in what they wrote to their families and the fear of disclosing a secret also kept some women from travelling home. Attracta, who omitted to inform her parents that she had contracted diphtheria, did not visit them for two years until the signs of her illness were no longer visible. Bernadette, who was born in Co. Mayo in 1915, became pregnant in 1945 when she was unmarried and working in Blackpool. She eventually wrote and told her parents in Co. Mayo that she had an illegitimate son when he was eight months old. Although they were supportive, she did not go home when he was a child for fear of embarrassing the family. Overwhelmingly though, Ireland was the usual holiday destination of the women interviewed and most of them spoke of 'going home' as often as they could afford to. Single working women, especially nurses who did not have to take fixed holidays, were often able to accrue their leave entitlements and have extended summer holidays in Ireland. There was also a labour shortage in post-war Britain and when the National Health Service was founded in 1948 some health authorities used subsidised travel home as an incentive to recruit Irish women into nursing:

> I came to Manchester and for the three years I was training our fare was paid back every six months. It was subsidised under some scheme through the Labour Exchange. I think I had to pay something like 7/6d. But the English girls, which I can understand, were furious about it because they couldn't afford their fares home on the buses and our fares were being paid to go back to Ireland ... So I went back on the subsidised trips every six months. Back home they'd be waiting all the time for good news, and they got good news. [Áine, b. 1929, Co. Cavan]

Factory workers were usually more restricted than nurses in taking their holidays when they pleased but two Irish women in Manchester regularly took longer than their official leave allocation, as their employer made allowances for them:

> From when we went to England me sister and I always went home twice a year at August and Christmas. We worked in a shirt factory in Manchester and Mr Bernstein, our Jewish boss, he used to always call it the 'Irish month' because we'd go for a month and we'd stop six weeks! That went on right up till we got married. [Patricia, b. 1925, Co. Donegal]

Having children, rather than getting married, was the point in women's life-cycles which most affected their ability to visit Ireland. The expense of taking the whole family over appears to be the main reason why some Irish women went home less often after they became mothers:

> When the children was little we didn't go home every year; about every two years, or every three years sometimes. It was as often as I could afford, otherwise I would ha' been there every year. [Siobhan, b. 1938, Co. Donegal]

Noreen was married to a labourer, who like her came from Donegal, and she struggled, but just managed, to afford the trips home for themselves and their seven children:

We used to go home nearly every year, for a week or a fortnight. It was hard. 'Cause it was hard to keep the children clothed never mind anything else! But I worked nearly all me life while I was here. Ye had tae work in with them [the children] as best you could. I done mostly nights 'cause me husband was at home then. [Noreen, b. 1913, Co. Donegal]

The situation was different for women in better-off circumstances, who could spend whole summers in Ireland with their children. Their husbands often stayed working in England for part of the time and joined them later:

Me sister and myself went over to Ireland for the whole summer. The men stopped in Manchester and worked. He would come over for the last two weeks then ... It was lovely for the children to have a good holiday over there and the free life that they had. Me brother and me sister's children and mine they used to be fishing up the rivers catching trout. And making their own fishing rods with the long salley rod with the leaf on the end and the fly. [Patricia, b. 1925, Co. Donegal]

Patricia viewed her children's summers in Ireland as preferable to spending them in urban Manchester. Maeve could also afford to bring her children to Ireland for the whole summer, as she and her husband were both doctors in Liverpool. She shared the Irish Nationalist sympathies of her family but was sensitive to the fact that her children were born into a middle-class family in England. She wanted her children to spend time in Ireland in order to make their own informed decisions as to which culture they identified with:

We'd split our holidays and he'd take them for a month and then he'd come back and I'd go for the next month ... So they grew up knowing Irish people and knowing the culture of Ireland you see. [Maeve, b.1917, Co. Tipperary]

Maeve's three children subsequently adopted Irish identities; her two sons chose to attend Irish universities and one son and a daughter now live and work in the west of Ireland. A desire to acquaint their children with their relations in Ireland and their Irish cultural inheritance was often expressed by mothers, but ironically some could not afford to travel back to Ireland as frequently once they had children.

Women also made visits to Ireland for reasons other than holidays. Caring for old or infirm family members was a significant reason for emigrant women to return, sometimes for lengthy periods. For example, Eileen left her husband in Morecambe and took her young daughter back to Wexford in order to nurse her sick mother:

My mother became ill and I went home when Kathleen was a baby. Bill said: 'Stay as long as you like'. And I did, I didn't come back until Kathleen was five! I used to come back and forth to visit him. [Eileen, b. 1927, Co. Wexford]

Childbirth provided another reason for some women to return to their family in Ireland:

The eldest one was born in Ireland 'cause I went back to have him. I was afraid, you know, so I went back to have him amongst me own. I was more familiar with Ireland, ye know what I mean? And I thought I'd be safer over there, which was all nonsense. [Barbara, b. 1935, Co. Donegal]

My daughters were both born in Ireland and I think it was really important for me that they were born there. They were Irish you see. [Eileen, b. 1927, Co. Wexford]

Patriotism and a desire to be with their family and in familiar surroundings at an apprehensive time were the reasons given for Irish women returning to Ireland to give birth. The death of parents was another life-cycle stage which affected women's pattern of visiting Ireland. Some women continued to visit but expressed regret that things had changed whilst for others, especially if all their brothers and sisters had emigrated, it marked the end of 'going home':

There's nothing there, you know, after my father and mother died, the nostalgia, it was terrible. They were such happy days that we had there and it's all gone; finished! No, I never wanted to go back. [Mary, b. 1917, Co. Mayo]

In conclusion, significant contact was maintained between emigrant women in Lancashire and their families in Ireland. Letters and parcels were frequently sent from both sides of the Irish Sea. Ireland was the favourite, and in most cases the only, holiday destination of emigrants, and significantly most women referred to these visits as 'going home'. The less affluent women in the study expressed a desire to have returned home more often if they had been able to afford it. Some women also returned home to give birth. Life-cycle stages affected the frequency of visits to Ireland, especially mother-hood, when ironically a desire to acquaint children with their Irish families and cultural inheritance was often accompanied by increased financial restraints. Female emigrants also took on the responsibility of caring for family members in Ireland and it seems that they were more likely to return home for this task than Irish men. But it was the death of parents and siblings in Ireland which often signified a change in the pattern of visits.

IV

The experiences of Irish emigrant women in Lancashire between 1922 and 1960 contradict the conclusions of O'Carroll's research on female emigration to America in which she stated: 'Irish women turned their backs on Ireland', and 'the rejection of family life was a major theme in the story of Irish emigrants to the USA'.[10] Conversely, it is argued here that the family often played an extensive role in the female emigration process and some women even emigrated against their own personal wishes in order to enhance the economy or protect the reputation of their family. Furthermore, existing family networks were an important feature of emigrant women's destinations. Although some women undoubtedly used emigration as a means to escape from family ties, there is more evidence to suggest that emigration was often their only means of fulfilling family obligations. Regular contact was frequently maintained between emigrants in Lancashire and their families in Ireland and the overall impression is that emigrant women generally welcomed this contact and often made sacrifices in order to sustain it.

One explanation for the continuance of traditional family ties after emigration can be found in the cultural climate of post-colonial Ireland. Irish identity was strongly promoted and an important measure of Irishness was its distinction from anything English. A woman's perception of Irishness was increasingly associated with her role within the family and the home. All of the women interviewed in this study maintained extensive contact with their families in Ireland and elsewhere after they emigrated. Most of those who had children also expressed a desire to transmit Irish culture to their children. These women had no problems with their national identity: they were Irish emigrant women who happened to live in England. The centrality of the family to Irish women's national identity is most poignantly summed up by the reflections of an Irish woman who was excluded from family life in Ireland. Caroline grew up in a convent with little knowledge of her family background. She emigrated to Lancaster and married an Irishman. Her accent is Irish, she was a champion set dancer and has taught Irish dancing to her own two daughters and other children in a Catholic club in Lancaster. She plays Irish music on the accordion and has frequented Irish clubs since moving to Lancashire. Yet Caroline still has problems with her Irish identity because she cannot identify with a family in Ireland:

> I wouldn't let anybody run Ireland down or nothing like that but Ireland to me doesn't mean as much as probably it would to you and people that were brought up in a family environment, you know ... That's what I missed most, not having a sort of home to go to: roots. Now I didn't

have any roots in Ireland, only Nazareth House, and you wouldn't call them roots really would you? A lot of them say they want to go back to their roots but I've no roots to go back to. And I do miss that you know. I do … I mean you wouldn't really call me Irish, would ye? … You know, the real Irish would talk about their family homes, and what it was like, and always wanting to go back. I mean, I have no such home to talk about. The only home I've got to talk about was the Nazareth House and, to me, we probably missed out on a lot o' the real Ireland … Honest to God, I think it must be lovely to come from a big ould Irish family! [Caroline, b. 1944, Co. Cavan]

Caroline's reflections show the centrality of the Irish family home to emigrant national identity.

The familial contact which was maintained by Irish emigrant women has implications for challenging the accepted notion of the assimilation of Irish women in twentieth-century Britain.[11] Lennon *et al.*'s pioneering oral study of Irish women in Britain found that 'none of the women who emigrated from Ireland considered herself to have assimilated', but they also observed that 'women face greater pressures to adapt to British society than men, because of their family role and responsibilities'.[12] The argument of this essay is that in the years after independence Irish women in England were less likely to assimilate because their 'family role and responsibilities' were affected by post-colonialism. The cultural climate of newly independent Ireland generally ensured that emigrants to England left with a desire to uphold their Irish identity in the country from which Ireland had only recently gained independence. Furthermore, as an Irish woman's identity was defined by her role within the family she was less likely to sever family ties after emigration than to adopt strategies of maintaining them from a distance. Whilst Irish women's comparative invisibility in Britain has been taken to mean that they asserted their Irishness less readily than Irish men, their absence from the male dominated Irish public spheres of clubs, pubs and associations could also be evidence of a continuance of Irish patriarchal culture after emigration. Irish emigrant women were maintaining their Irish identities within their families and, by their extensive links with their family homes in Ireland, they were transmitting an Irish cultural identity to their children.

Women Workers in Dublin and Belfast during the Second World War

MARY MULDOWNEY

I

Recent years have seen the publication of several volumes of oral history which have incorporated questions about the nature of memory, both individual and collective, in a consideration of history and the past. Amongst other issues, they have noted how our recollection of the past is subject to change as our self-image changes and how the diverse nature of human memory can help the formation of a democratic consciousness.[1] The ambiguities inherent in the very expression 'oral history' can cause problems. Oral history is at the same time a means of constructing life histories, of researching the 'facts' essential to historical assessment, of working on the functioning of memory and of understanding the dynamic between the historian and her or his source. The interview as a social relationship, with its own conventions of discourse, represents a contract between the interviewer and the informant. As Tonkin writes:

> Of all the time that the historian considers, not the least important in an oral context is the timing of a particular incarnation of the oral text itself – an incarnation because it fuses the narrator, narrative and audience at this moment of time in a perspective on all those other moments. The narrative becomes a kind of dialogue and the structure contributes to the meaning. If the interviewer's voice is cut from the transcripts the narrator's voice is thus distorted.[2]

Whilst Tonkin's warning is valid and should be heeded, the excerpts from interviews which are used in this essay have been chosen to illustrate the points I am making about specific aspects of my research, and to that extent I believe that the trust implied by the original interview contract has not been broken. As women have committed much less to writing than men, oral histories of women's lives are often the only form of access to many of their experiences.

While not suggesting that only a female historian could share the kind of complicity with her informant which would lead to the narrowing of the distance between interviewer and interviewee, I conducted my interviews in the belief that the more intimate, conversational tone which women adopt when talking to each other was more likely to elicit significant revelations.[3] This approach led to some situations where roles were reversed and the interviewee's interest in my life and circumstances became the dominant focus of the dialogue. Deflecting this interest without impairing the trust created by the sharing of intimate information was sometimes difficult. Many women are not used to speaking publicly and older women, in particular, will have grown up in an environment where women's speech was devalued and their public discourse rarely encouraged:

> Women who do not participate in the male socio–communication sub-culture do not usually want to talk about activities and facts, and they are unused to developing topics without a high degree of collaboration from other women.[4]

Memory is not based on the individual's gender, but varies according to the events of the individual's life, but as a consequence of this, is sexualised. It follows that history has also been divided by a gender division of roles. In order to bypass this division and restore women's equal place in history, we have to ask questions about women's involvement in men's environments. The history of war, for example, will no longer be only a history of soldiers, politicians and military engagements, but also a history of the women who continued to 'keep the home fires burning' and who were successfully co-opted into a more public social role in times of national crisis.

II

Research into the social position of Irish women in both the north and the south reveals many similarities with the social and economic status of women in Britain, Europe and North America.[5] In Southern Ireland, the de Valera government's attitude to women working outside the home was outlined in the 1937 constitution, which firmly stressed the role of women as the nation's homemakers and child bearers. This had particular implications for working-class women, who had always done paid work to supplement the family income but who now had to cope with the extra stresses imposed by the additional expectations of their families and society.

Bourke found that the movement of Irish women, particularly in rural areas, from paid to domestic, non-paid employment was a result of the declining opportunities for women in the labour force.[6] She argues that this movement was not necessarily a retrograde step because the traditional areas of paid work open to women had generally been low paid and low status. Although women who were engaged in full-time domestic activity lost a measure of economic control, there was a certain amount of creativity attached to their role. This finding is supported by Roberts, who, in her study of women in three northern English towns, found that women's dual role as family financial manager and moral guide cannot be underestimated.[7] However, the official Irish view is evident in the census categorisation of women engaged in home duties as 'persons not gainfully employed'. In Northern Ireland, as in Éire, employment policy was based on the assumption that men were the primary breadwinners and women's function was essentially domestic. This led to particular difficulties for working-class women in Belfast during the depression of the 1930s when widespread unemployment created additional difficulties for women, on whom the main responsibility for decisions about the apportioning of family income fell. The linen industry was traditionally one of Belfast's key employers of women, and many families survived because of the income earned by mothers and daughters. However, by the end of the 1930s nearly 11,000 of the industry's women workers had been laid off. Unemployment benefits in Northern and Southern Ireland, as in the UK and Europe, were significantly lower for women than men, emphasising the official perception of women's dependency.[8]

Women did not seek self-fulfilment at the expense of their family because they saw little distinction between their own good and that of their families. This identification of women with their families may have been to their detriment in that they had to deal with increased expectations of their domestic role, while their men may not have been earning enough to allow them to give up paid work altogether. As Catherine, aged ninety-one, a former cleaner and home laundry worker in Dublin remembered:

> The work my husband had, he was a tradesman, and it was a very hard job, the cooperage. You know, making the barrels that the drink was put into, you know. Making those, and all he had was £5. Just imagine, pay rent, pay everything, feed them, dress them, and pay all the bits of bills, gas, electric, that you get, out of that. That was the hardest part of all.

Women of the poorest families suffered most from the combination of increased domestic responsibilities with decreased employment opportunities during the inter-war period. These women had little control over where and how they worked. They needed to be close to home and were not in a position to bargain for better wages.[9] Married women who had to get paid work generally sought jobs as casual labourers and devised their own short-term employment strategies, often by taking on badly paid factory outwork which they could do in their own homes. By the first decades of the twentieth century, children had assumed an equal status in working-class families to that in middle-class homes and consequently married women spent much more time in caring for them. The lengthier period of compulsory schooling also meant that older siblings were no longer available to care for the young children of a family and more domestic responsibility devolved on the mother. Catherine's testimony is illustrative of women's increased sense of maternal responsibility:

Q: You had a skilled job before you got married. Did you ever think of going back to that?

A: Well, no, because I'd be out all day. I wouldn't be in my home look-ing after my family, you know, like they were very young, you had to watch them coming from school. And meet them and bring them home, afraid anything would happen them and that sort of thing, you know.

A report written for the UK government in 1929, *A Study of the Factors which have Operated in the Past and Those which are Operating Now to Determine the Distribution of Women in Industry*, claimed that women's confinement to semi-skilled or unskilled work was entirely natural.[10] It was not deemed necessary that women should acquire employable skills because marriage (which was seen as inevitable) would be accompanied by their withdrawal from paid work. Women were also believed to be intrinsically unsuited to heavy duty or wet work, regardless of the fact that traditional women's work, such as domestic service or work in laundries and with textiles, was all of those things. Despite the expansion of white-collar work in the years between the wars, women were marginalised into 'women's areas', such as sten-ography and repetitive clerical work. Even highly educated women who tried to move out of these sectors were accused of taking men's jobs, regardless of the equality and standard of their qualifications. The Conditions of Employment Act of 1935 conferred on the Irish Minister for Industry and Commerce the power to prohibit the employment of women or to fix the proportion of women to men in any industry. Although Ireland was subsequently blacklisted by the International Labour Organisation, there was only token resistance to the act.[11]

Middle-class women, in the inter-war years and during the Second World War, were rarely employed outside the home, except in a voluntary capacity. In the Irish Free State and Northern Ireland, marriage bars were imposed in many of the professions in the 1920s and 1930s, confining even better-educated women to the home. It is arguable that these women were actually more oppressed by the stress on women's domestic function, as they rarely had the control of the household finances which was an essential component of a working-class woman's responsibilities.

Young women in working-class families traditionally worked to supplement the family income until they had families of their own. However, in the early decades of the twentieth century, at least in Britain and France, these young women experienced a growing autonomy, being allowed to keep and control a significant portion of their wages. They spent their money on clothes and entertainment, in contrast to their mothers, whose earnings, if any, were used for the benefit of the family.[12] When they married, they returned to dependence but also assumed authority in their role as household managers. In Ireland, young women were less likely to be independent of their families. As Nancy, aged seventy-seven, a former mill worker in Belfast recalled:

> My mother died Christmas Eve and my Aunt Marie took us over. You got your pay and you'd give your money in. You didn't open it, you'd have been afeared to open it. You know what I mean? Now don't get me wrong, she was the best, my aunt was the best and my mother, but I mean it wasn't that they were strict but you knew not to do them things.

In addition to this, traditional areas of women's employment contracted during the inter-war period. There was a lower demand for domestic servants, partly because of the higher wages expected for this work after the First World War and partly because the changing nature of housework no longer necessitated the full-time, live-in service which had previously employed so many women. Employment in the textile industry had also declined and while white-collar work expanded, many of these positions required an extra period of time to be spent in schooling. This was resisted by many parents, who looked forward to the wage which was contributed to the family income by their daughters. The attraction of working for one's own family was obvious when compared to the often monotonous work at subsistent wages which was frequently all that was available to women:

> It is no wonder that working class culture adopted the image of the married woman at home as the sign of the health, stability and prosperity of a household. The expression of this idea was less a result of the embourgoisement of the working class than it was a statement about the realities of working class experience.[13]

In the early decades of the twentieth century, women in Europe were still strongly influenced by the belief that childbirth should take place only within marriage. This made sexual intercourse for unmarried women risky, as there was still very restricted access to contraception. The stigma of pregnancy outside marriage was strengthened by the emphasis on social welfare provisions (such as they were) for 'respectable' families. Council houses in Britain and Ireland were made available only to conventional family units. In Ireland, the 1937 constitution entrenched the public perception of women as 'mothers' but did not see men as 'fathers'. The constitutional provisions for women valued them as wives and mothers rather than citizens. This evaluation is reflected in the number of domestic education classes which were available in the 1920s and 1930s. These classes were popular because they maximised the contribution of women who chose domestic work as a way of life.[14] The emphasis of the classes, in both Ireland and Britain, was to strengthen the ideal of 'hearth and home'. In England, social welfare agencies tended to deal directly with working–class mothers and expected them to be 'thrifty' and to stretch household budgets by absorbing middle-class advice on 'economising'. This gender-specific division of family responsibility allowed official policy on poor families to be directed towards educating the mothers to 'improve' themselves, rather than providing supplementary income or nursery facilities for working mothers.

But limited employment opportunities, poor wages and lack of childcare provision were not the only problems women workers faced. Trade union activity amongst working women was never as extensive or as successful as it was amongst men. One reason for this was the different attitude of most women to their work, which they tended to see as temporary. In addition, many employers were resistant to a unionised workforce, because women were seen as cheap, easily manipulated labour, who might be persuaded to demand better pay and conditions if they became organised. This fact was highlighted by Lily, aged eighty-two, a former mill worker in Belfast:

> There was one woman, she was a Union woman and she was taking money for the girls … she was sacked. She went somewhere else. Her forewoman was against it.

Ironically, male trade unionists were just as reluctant to involve women in their activities, not just because they saw women as their wives, mothers and dependants, but also because they feared being replaced by lower-paid women workers. Family pressures also interfered with the ability of single and married women to devote time and money to a union. Some unions were ambivalent about organising women whilst others, like the Amalgamated Engineering Union, actively discouraged the recruitment of women by making it clear to employers that industrial action would be consequent in any attempt to employ women workers. In Ireland, although the number of women in industry grew steadily during the 1930s, they were overwhelmingly concentrated in unskilled or semi-skilled jobs and in the lower paid sectors, such as the textile industry. An essential role in the involvement of women in the trade union movement was played by the Irish Women Workers' Union (IWWU), which focused attention on the problems of women workers and raised women's status in the trade union movement as a whole. The 1930s saw a significant rise in Irish women's trade union membership, but this declined again during the 1940s when unemployment rose in the course of the Second World War. A vital role was however played by women laundry workers, whose strike in Dublin in 1945 secured the provision of a fortnight's annual paid holiday for all workers, both female and male. The self-confidence gained by women actively seeking to improve working conditions is reflected in the following open letter from the Strike Committee to all members of the Oireachtas:

> We have been three months on strike to win a concession which is admitted to be reasonable – a Fortnight Holiday with pay. We have been treated with contempt by the Federated Union of Employers who demand us to return to work before they will consider our claim. This is tyranny. We refuse to submit to tyranny. When our just claims have been justly met, we will return to work. The Constitution of the Éire Government promises equal rights to all citizens. But the Government have not protected our rights in this matter. They have tolerated the Employers' refusal to recognise our right to strike. Every worker is entitled to:
>
> > Adequate Leisure
> > A Just Wage
> > Respect for Personal Dignity
>
> We call upon the Government and all members of the Oireachtas to assist us to secure these rights.[15]

Despite small successes, like that won by the laundry workers of 1945, the middle-class ideal of the two-parent family with gender-specific roles was propagated in official policies throughout inter-war Europe. That women subscribed so widely to their relegation to a primarily domestic function was as much a means of negotiating power as it was a retreat from the public sphere. Women could earn respect in their role as household managers and arbiters of family and neighbourhood standards, a respect from which they were excluded in the world of work. In the Free State, the Fianna Fáil government concentrated its social policy on helping widows and children. The focus on women as non-earning dependants was also reflected in the measures undertaken by the Northern Irish and British governments:

As far as it touched home life, the aim of government policy was to help the very poor or 'disadvantaged' to survive, in other words to support those who could not subsist as a man's dependent, such as the widow or the unmarried mother. The official emphasis was less on mothers themselves than their children. No policy offered married women any encouragement to work, even though a rising proportion of women either wanted or were compelled to do so.[16]

III

Histories of the Irish Free State during the 'Emergency' are lacking in accounts of women's activities from 1939 to 1945. Women are similarly absent from the majority of accounts of Northern Ireland during the Second World War. In Britain (including Northern Ireland), the government desperately needed women to conduct war work but was hampered by a reluctance to compel women (particularly married women) to leave their 'traditional' place in the home. However, many oral histories contradict the widely accepted affinity of women and peace and it is obvious in twentieth-century wars that this image has been useful as a propaganda weapon by Western governments. But the same governments have also worked hard to achieve a balance between maintaining this image and at the same time enlisting the 'weaker sex' in both the armed forces and in war work:[17]

> It would be naïve to suppose that, because they took little or no part in public affairs, women did not share the ideology which justified the conflict in which they found themselves directly or indirectly involved. Also, the fact that war was often an exciting opportunity for a young woman to escape the tedium imposed upon her by social convention must not be forgotten.[18]

Nicholson's collection of women's accounts of their war work in Britain, *What did you do in the war, Mummy?*, contains many references to the liberation experienced by young women.[19] As Pauline recalled:

> Before the war, I had simply expected to get married. It was the norm ... When I removed that pinny from my body I removed it from my mind as well.[20]

It was possible for young women whose working lives had been strictly controlled by their fathers or family circumstances to find new roles for themselves with the justification of the country's necessity to support them.

Peggy, who was an auxiliary nurse with the Auxiliary Territorial Service (ATS) was able to use the war to fulfil her own ambition:

> I'd always wanted to be a nurse but my father didn't want me to do that and in those days you did what your father said ... I took the opportunity to join the Civil Nursing reserve.[21]

Nursing allowed women to get close to the action without arousing any misgivings about their suitability as combatants. In Ireland, nursing was a profession to which women must pay to enter and this forced many working-class women to go to Britain for training. As Sheila, aged eighty-six, a former clerical worker in the Navy, Army and Air Force office in Belfast highlighted:

> People hadn't the money then to pay for education. A lot of girls left and went to England to nurse. Because you had to pay to get into the hospitals here to do nursing.

A nurse in Dublin who became engaged to be married in 1944, reminisced about how she went to an English hospital for two years where she worked in an advanced burns unit, rather than settle for less demanding work:

> in those days you didn't work after you were married unless you did private nursing, you see there were no jobs for married women, so I said I'm going off for a year, I can't bear to be hanging around ... I went off to England to a RAF hospital to do plastic surgery.

Male attitudes, reflected in official policy, were not changed by women's involvement in the services or in war work. It has been argued that, in the Second World War, neither the Nazi mother making munitions for her son nor America's 'Rosie the Riveter' made permanent changes to women's economic status or to the public's basic beliefs about women's 'nature'.[22] In their deliberations about the mobilisation of women for war work in Britain, neither the Women's Consultative Committee nor the Ministry of Labour which they advised seemed very concerned that women would abandon their families for war work. They assumed that everyone shared their basic respect for the conventional role of women in the home and this coloured their attitude to the provision of child care:

> [the Ministry of Labour] is only concerned to suggest the provision of nursery care where the employment of married women with young children is necessary to satisfy the demands of industry in wartime, bearing in mind that it is not the Ministry's policy to encourage such employment except where it is the only means of filling labour demands.[23]

Significantly, the same views were expressed by Louie Bennett, secretary of the IWWU, as the union's annual report for 1940 stated:

> We are often told that woman's place is the home. We agree that it is her special sphere. But war and social injustice are both enemies of the home. Women and children are their victims as well as men. It is in order to defend the home and the family that women must now take a larger part in public life and politics.[24]

Although the British Ministry of Labour did manage to increase the number of nurseries from fourteen in 1940 to 1,345 in 1943, its preference for minders in the home (perhaps as surrogate mothers?) acted as a major constraint on wartime child care policy.[25] Little consideration was given to the fact that women still did most of the domestic work, in addition to child-minding. As the oral testimony of Rose, aged seventy-six, a former Woolworths counter girl in Belfast, illustrates:

> Wednesday was your half day then, you got a half day on Wednesday and Wednesday was cleaning day and scrubbing day. You started upstairs and came down ... boys didn't do very much then. Men didn't do very much ... You had to work and you had to keep house, you know, and as I say, your parents were waiting on the money.

Male co-workers were generally resistant to the influx of women to war industries, particularly in engineering areas, from which women had traditionally been excluded. One of the concessions made to women who were called up for work in wartime, in addition to their continued domestic responsibilities, was the introduction of part-time and shift work. This enabled women to carry on their war work with decreased interruption of their domestic arrangements. The fact that the women themselves lost the little leisure time they had was not considered. Offering part-time work to women alone reinforced the stereotypical view of women as casual workers who merely supplemented the family income. But for some widowed women, part-time work was a matter of survival. Catherine remembers working as a part-time cleaner when her husband died:

> So I said, well, I've six young children, now what do I do? Well, he said, you can come into work, he said, at six every morning. I used to leave here at half past five ... I got home by about half nine to see that the children got out to school, you know.

Part-time and shift work had an added advantage for employers in reducing their wage bills and insurance costs while increasing productivity. In the early 1940s an interesting reflection of this was seen in Ireland, where subscription rules for the Federated Union of Employers (FUE) stated: 'For the purposes of this bye-law, two female employees shall be reckoned as one employee'.[26] The reason given was two-fold: small businesses employed a high number of female workers and those women did work which was significantly different from their male counterparts. In any case, the owners of small businesses could not afford to pay subscriptions commensurate with the number of women employed and had opted to pay subscriptions based on their rates of pay instead. As women were paid so much less than men, even in the same job, employers' subscriptions to the FUE were significantly reduced and membership was made more attractive.

Emigration of Irish workers to Britain rose significantly during the Second World War. The Irish economy was deeply affected by the shortage of raw materials for industry and as many as 50,000 Irishmen had joined the British forces by the end of the war. Large numbers of Irish women workers joined munitions works, factories and hospitals and made a considerable contribution to the British war effort. The numbers varied in the course of the war, from a total of 3,272 women (from various occupational groupings) in 1941 to a peak of 19,003 in 1943, falling to 10,609 in 1945.[27] There was industrial discontent in Ireland as a result of high unemployment, and the Wages Standstill Order was introduced under emergency powers in May 1941, which also outlawed strikes for higher wages. Whilst the specific impact of this legislation on women's employment remains unknown, they would certainly have been affected in their domestic role by the depression in living standards and the increase in the cost of living during the war years. The Irish Housewives' Association, for example, was motivated by the scarcity of basic goods and the levels of poverty and malnutrition among children in Dublin to lobby the government to introduce rationing. It organised a petition of the government in May 1941 calling for the institution of a rationing system of essential commodities, in which prices would be strictly controlled. The IWWU made many representations to Eamon de Valera, as premier of the Irish Free State, for relief for working-class families hit by unemployment and low wages.

Similar hardship was experienced in Belfast. Although the middle classes lived in relative affluence during the war, many working-class areas of the city suffered high levels of unemployment, low wages, high rents, overcrowding, poverty and ill health.[28] Northern Ireland's health service was very poor by the standards of mainland Britain, as were social welfare services in general, although they compared fairly well to those in Southern Ireland. In the oral reminiscences of Susan, aged eighty-three, who was a medical social worker in Belfast and Dublin, she remembers the problems of finding accommodation for a married woman, disowned by her husband and family who claimed that her new-born baby was not his:

I think we went round to three different lots of relations and not one of them would take her and I knew they wouldn't take her back at the hospital. It wasn't a shelter or anything like that and there wasn't anyplace that she could go to ... she had no money or anything ... I managed to get her a bed in the Union hostel. It was very hard to get anyone in to the hostel, the Union, they wouldn't take them unless they absolutely had to, but I rang and explained she had an eight-day old baby and so I took her to the Union and they took her in.

All accounts of women's work during the Second World War, whether from Ireland or Britain, agree that women contributed in all manner of ways to their country's war effort. The most essential way was in carrying on their household work despite the shortages and difficult conditions. Women had to cope with rationing, price and wage controls, scarcity of basic commodities and finding nutritional substitutes to keep their families healthy. In belligerent countries, women had to cope with missing husbands and family members, often bringing up children in dreadful conditions. During wartime, however, such difficulties were seen as a sort of patriotic sacrifice. An interesting variation of the concept of patriotism was the 'beauty is duty' propaganda, particularly in Britain where women were exhorted to beautify themselves for the sake of morale. The Northern Irish government, unlike its London counterpart, did not commission propaganda directly, but Ministry of Information leaflets were widely disseminated, as were UK magazines and papers carrying this message. Both the *Belfast Telegraph* and the *Irish News*, as representatives of both sides of the sectarian divide, also promoted the concept. Patriotism in Southern Ireland adopted a different form, as the policy of neutrality was identified with the urge towards securing the recently-won independence. During the 'Emergency', about 250,000 men became involved in defence roles of one kind or another. Irish women had to cope with severe shortages and Dublin women in particular were faced with the anxiety about bombing raids after the 'mistaken' bombing of the North Strand in 1941.[29] Many of the same women would have been living in sub-standard housing (a survey of the tenements of Dublin in 1938 found that 60 per cent of tenements and cottages were unfit for human habitation).[30] Others experienced the problems caused by moving from the inner city to new housing estates in Crumlin and Drimnagh, which were still without many amenities in the early 1940s.[31] As Catherine recalled:

And I had no washing machine, the washing all had to be done in the big sink bath, and a scrubbing board which I still have, for washing ... and I'd do the clothes in that ... I'd have to heat the water.

In their analysis of oral history interviews with labour and political activists, both Unionist and Republican, in Belfast in the 1930s, Munck and Rolston emphasise that the experience of unemployment and low-paid, casual employment was not confined solely to men. The additional difficulties of making everyday decisions about paying the rent and buying food and clothes, when there was not enough money to cover basic expenses, were disproportionately allotted to women:

> Being left holding the baby at home was problem enough. Having to keep down paid employment while being the only person deemed able to look after the children was even worse ... The arrangement of male supremacy and female inferiority was not confined to the home. It took in many aspects of working class life as well; at work, in terms of unequal wages and the male bias of the trade unions ... Outside of work, the most obvious sign of the arrangement was that it was women who had the much greater amount of worry in trying to make ends meet, attempting to help the family and by extension, the community, to survive, even in the most basic material sense of the word.[32]

In spite of these difficulties, the war made little concrete difference to the perception of women's role in society. They were mobilised for the war effort by the belligerent governments but in such a way that their domestic role was not radically altered. The 'Emergency' does not seem to have impinged significantly on the consciousness of the Dublin women I have interviewed and this is understandable both in terms of Éire's neutrality and the censorship of war reports, which was used to bolster that policy in the south. In Northern Ireland and in Belfast in particular, however, there were significant consequences of involvement. As Jean, aged eighty-seven, a former Belfast shop owner highlighted:

> very often we went to bed without undressing because we knew they were coming. We dreaded the light nights, we dreaded them because that was their best time.

The question of political and sectarian division was an added dimension in the experience of Northern Irish women which must be borne in mind when they tell their war stories. It is particularly important in the case of Belfast, which suffered violent sectarian upheaval in the 1930s. The women I have interviewed to date claim not to recall specific incidents of sectarian division, but their recollections focused on their immediate family and neighbourhood circles. It seems that they had little experience of interaction with other communities, even with co-religionists. Moya Woodside, a diarist for the Mass-Observation survey in the 1940s recounts an illuminating story based on her experience as a welfare worker:

Spent most of the morning trying to find lodgings for a temporarily homeless Catholic girl, who had left her employment on account of illness and was without relatives or friends ... I telephoned three other hostels (Salvation Army, Girls' Help Society and something else) but all of them, on hearing the girl was a Catholic found they didn't have any beds ... Eventually, we got on the track of a Catholic social worker, who, we were assured, would find some lodgings for the girl in *the right religious surroundings*. One forgets how wide the gulf between Catholics and Protestant is here until something like this happens.[33]

Blake, in *Northern Ireland in the Second World War* (which was commissioned by the British government as the 'official' history of the war) identified various areas in which the war impinged on everyday civilian life. These included blackout regulations, rationing of food, restriction of coal and fuel consumption, restrictions on travel, the introduction of identity cards, the necessity to register with local authorities and censorship. Northern Ireland seems not to have been as adversely affected by food rationing as the rest of the United Kingdom but restrictions on coal and fuel had a marked affect on civilians, and women in particular, who developed their own strategies for coping with the difficulties. Sheila recalled the bus runs from the North to the Free State for shopping without strict rationing:

They used to run trips every Wednesday across the border and you could get butter, tea, sugar, whatever you wanted, as long as you were prepared to hide it and didn't have it taken from you. ... They had ladies there for body searches.

Despite urging by the Northern Irish government to introduce conscription, the Westminster government believed there was too much danger of resistance amongst the Nationalist community. They were also concerned about prompting a violent reaction from the IRA. As a result, conscription into the armed forces or the labour force was never introduced in Northern Ireland.

Northern Ireland, however, seems to have benefited from increased employment as a result of war production, but even in the best years unemployment persisted. Workers in Belfast were better off than other areas because both Harland and Wolff and Short and Harland urgently needed to complete orders for ships, aircraft and munitions:

it would seem indeed, that a substantial body of workers, especially women, in Northern Ireland, whose labour had become redundant in textile manufacture, was drawn into the engineering industry. In fact, during the Second World War, more people were employed in ship-building, aircraft manufacture and engineering than at any other time in the history of Northern Ireland.[35]

Women who worked for the government benefited from better conditions than would have been possible before the war. As Sheila, one of my informants, remembered:

> When I left I was getting, from when I started at 10s a week, you got a penny out of that to go home on the tram for your dinner, Shank's Mare the rest, and then when I left, £1 a week and I went into the NAAFI [Navy, Army and Air Force Institute] and got over £7 a week. No wonder you'd want to change.

Despite the overall increase in employment levels and the improvement in living standards, Belfast suffered continued industrial disruption. Some of the trouble was due to dislocation after the blitz, but a large part of the trouble was due to social tension arising from class and sectarian suspicion.[36] Doherty describes the affect on the local community of the destruction of the York Street Flax Spinning Company in the bombing raid on the night of 15–16 April 1941, which resulted in the deaths of thirty-five people and the demolition of more than sixty homes:

> For generations the mill was the sole means of support for the people of the district. During the Depression years of the 1920s and 1930s it was the women in the mill who supported their families when the men could not find work. The York Street spinning factory was the largest of its kind in the world and its destruction led to many economic problems in an already deprived and run down area. The war as yet had not brought full employment to Northern Ireland and the mill was one of the few factories which was working at full capacity ... With its passing went the familiar early morning scene of dozens of girls and women, some of them wearing men's boots, moving along through the narrow streets with arms linked and singing at the tops of their voices the well known mill songs or parodies based on the popular songs of the day.[37]

His account evokes the strength of the working women of Belfast and their characteristic humour and resilience. The bombing raid of 4–5 May 1941 was equally destructive and a 'powerful surge developed to get away from Belfast'.[38] Belfast's civil defence services were eroded by a shortage of personnel and industrial production was reduced to 25 per cent of pre-blitz levels, a situation which lasted for some weeks.[39] Industrial relations were affected because many workers felt that management was apathetic towards air raid precautions. Meetings were held in the autumn of 1941 demanding greater provision for workers in factories near the docks, particularly for those expected to do night shifts. After the bombing raids, there had been a significant dispersal of production out of the Belfast city area to less vulnerable sites in the suburbs. As Sheila recalled:

> Our office was blitzed ... and we went away, we got offices in Ballymena and from Ballymena we got a place in Bangor. There were more than me travelled from home ... We went by train and the bus met us at the railway station.

These moves generated potentially divisive questions related to wage levels, work schedules, transport costs, allowance for time spent travelling and accommodation. The implementation of a dilution policy, the introduction of unskilled workers into areas previously reserved for highly skilled operatives, particularly in the engineering industry, became much more difficult as disheartened workers were reluctant to co-operate. In Belfast the highly skilled engineering workers in the ship-building industry, in particular, were all Protestant and resistant to any change which might admit Catholic workers. There was also bitterness about the perceived management indifference to worker safety when bombing raids were still a danger.

The expansion of female employment in Northern Ireland was much less dramatic than in other parts of the United Kingdom. The total number of female insured workers in the six counties increased from 111,900 in 1939 to a wartime peak of 118,600 in 1943.[40] The nature of their work did change, however, with many women moving from pre-war employment in the linen and textile industries to engineering, munitions and agriculture, including 7,500 women who transferred to work in mainland Britain. Another outlet for female employment is referred to by Doherty:

> To meet the demand for accommodation, a new and enterprising type of woman appeared on the scene. These were the landladies, some of whom were locals, but most came from the country and acquired large houses on the main roads and converted them into boarding houses for the migrant workers.[41]

But whatever work women performed during the war, domestic or industrial, it made little material difference to the perception of their role in society. Women were mobilised for the war effort, but this was done in such a way that their domestic role was not radically altered.

Blake's insistence that Northern Ireland showed a united front in the face of a common enemy demonstrates a wilful disregard of the tensions that were very much a part of public and private experience during the Second World War. These were evident in the industrial unrest which dogged war production even at the height of the war effort. In the south, there was a high level of strike activity in the early stages of the Emergency which led to the introduction of the Trade Union Bill and the Wages Standstill Order in 1941. There was a period of working-class militancy in opposition to these measures, which culminated in a demonstration in Dublin by an estimated 20,000 people.[42] On 22 June 1941, members of fifty-three trade unions from all over the Free State marched from Parnell Square to College Green in Dublin, where Jim Larkin addressed the meeting and symbolically burned a copy of the Trade Union Bill. A campaign against the terms of the bill was conducted in the following months but the bill was enacted in 1942 with only minor amendments, with the affect that trade unions had to apply for a licence to negotiate, thereby eliminating many of the smaller groups or subsidiaries of UK unions who could not afford the licence fee and the upkeep of an office registered in the Free State.

The experience of the two parts of Ireland differed widely after the war and the people of the north benefited materially from the strengthening of the Union and an equal share in the British social welfare system. The Labour government which came into power in 1945 was aware of Northern Ireland's strategic importance in the course of the war and this influenced their post-war administration of social policy. The recommendations of the Beveridge Report in terms of housing, education and social welfare were all applied to Northern Ireland in the immediate post-war period, and mainly funded by the Exchequer in London, thereby opening up a significant gap in living standards between Northern Ireland and the Free State.[43] In the south, social policy was strongly influenced by Catholic social teaching based on *Quadragesimo Anno*, a papal encyclical published in 1931, which advocated the organisation of society into vocational groups or corporations, in which the role of the state would be to facilitate the co-operation of employers and workers but in a subsidiary role. The 'Commission on Vocational Organisation' was set up in 1939 to seek the views of key social groups on the direction Irish society should take and while most of its recommendations were never enacted, the Catholic ethos which it embodied continued to influence government policy for many decades, thereby entrenching the precarious position of women workers.

IV

History is a construct … Any point of entry is possible and all choices are arbitrary. Still, there are definitive moments, moments we use as references, because they break our sense of continuity, they change the direction of time. We can look at these events and we can say that after them things were never the same again. They provide beginnings for us, and endings too.[44]

A world war would seem to be one of those cataclysmic occurrences that fix events in our memories. People unconsciously reshape their memories in accordance with who they have become and their 'honest' recollections of former times are coloured by their experiences between the past they are describing and the present. This has been very evident in the recollections of some of the women I have interviewed, although it is not always easy to identify exactly which events were influential in terms of altered perception.[45]

Male attitudes to women's work, exemplified in the social policies which were developed by all the belligerent allied nations, did not change because of women's role in war work and they were exactly the same as that of the neutral Southern Irish government. While many women shared these attitudes, many more did not, but they were left with little choice in terms of establishing themselves outside the home. Both the Northern and Southern Irish governments seem to have been united in their determination that women's work should remain unrecognised economically.

Oral history's value to the interpretation and understanding of social history is indisputable. However, Passerini points out that:

> The naïve claim of oral history to simply give voice to those who had been silenced by history is almost derisory. Fighting silence is not enough, 'silence' is not an appropriate term for the task to come: what is to be fought is not only silence but distortions or 'false memory'. The problem is that even 'tradition' is not enough. The very idea of tradition has been questioned and put out of date by the developments of capitalism, in which traditions become aesthetic objects for consumption and mass tourism.[46]

In the age of mass communication, memory and the language by which it is transmitted are subject to faster alteration by more rapid input of new information than at any other time in our history and this poses many dangers to the maintenance of a democratic consciousness. Democracy can survive only if it embraces diversity and plurality. Oral historians can participate in different memories, in the awareness that hopes, fears and projections for the future can shape people's memories of the past. We must be careful to ensure that the potential of mass communication technology to create an homogenous, if not necessarily totalitarian future, does not lead to the 'forgetting' or obscuring of the invaluable diversity of remembered experiences.

Oral historians need to ask informed questions about the use of language in life stories if we are to understand and interpret the words that we record.

However, our commitment to greater critical awareness of the techniques of oral history should not lead us to be so caught up in the analysis of what the narrators are saying that we lose sight of their intrinsic contribution to the process of understanding history. The long-term value of oral history will be the expression it can give to our abiding interest in and sympathy with other lives in other times and places. That most of these people will not have been heard before is an added bonus, both to the researcher and to developing our knowledge of the past.

The Decline of Breast-Feeding in Twentieth-Century Ireland

CAITRÍONA CLEAR

I

The Republic of Ireland has, at present, one of the lowest rates of breast-feeding in Europe.[1] The incongruity of a decline in such a natural, apparently traditional practice in a country not noted (at least up to the 1970s) for rapid change in matters to do with childbearing and childrearing, has been remarked upon.[2] Breast-feeding a baby is still seen as a departure from the norm in Ireland today.[3]

Breast-feeding has been in serious decline all over the western world over the past century.[4] Several reasons have been advanced for the progressive neglect of this unmatched natural resource, such as the need of vested business and agricultural interests to offload milk surpluses; the takeover of childbirth and infant care by medical 'experts' and their promotion of a method of breast-feeding which was neither comfortable nor conducive to a good milk supply and cultural changes which made this use of women's bodies somehow unacceptable.[5] In Ireland a comprehensive, countrywide maternity scheme was introduced in 1953, and this decade saw the definitive move of the place of birth from the mother's home to a hospital or nursing home.[6] However, it seems that breast-feeding was already in decline by this time and that there were reasons other than the hospitalisation of childbirth for the rise in bottle-feeding.

II

It is not exactly clear when the breast began to be replaced by the bottle. Curtin and Varley, reviewing the anthropological literature, suggest that it had died out in some rural areas by the 1930s.[7] Scheper-Hughes interprets the failure to breast-feed in the Kerry community she anthropologised in the 1960s as part of the Irish pathology of cold and unfeeling childrearing.[8] Russell, in the Gaeltacht community he studied in the 1970s, also noted that breast-feeding was uncommon. As a sixty-five-year-old female informant told him: 'Breast-feeding isn't good for the little ones, you know', and Russell was inclined to reach the same conclusion as Scheper-Hughes.[9] However, neither Russell nor Scheper-Hughes are able to explain why this physical distancing of mother from child did not extend to an aggressive and proactive 'management' of the child into early toilet-training. Children, they note with some bewilderment, were often left in nappies until they were ready to go to school.[10] If adherence to bottle-feeding was mainly due to the desire to control and to manage the child, to eschew contact with 'polluting' bodily fluids and to avoid over-involvement with the body of the child, then surely early toilet-training would have accompanied it.

Statistical and other evidence which we have – incomplete though it undeniably is – suggests that while bottle-feeding was creeping in from the 1930s, breast-feeding had by no means died out. Indeed, many babies seem to have been both breast-fed and bottle-fed, sometimes simultaneously. For instance, a survey in Cork city in 1930–31 revealed that of a sample of births, over 61 per cent of babies received some breast-milk; 25.4 per cent were 'breast-fed only' and 35.6 per cent were 'breast and artificially fed', by six months. The rest, 39 per cent, were artificially fed only. In Co. Kildare in the same year, 40.9 per cent of babies were 'breast-fed only', 36.84 per cent were 'breast and artificially fed', and 22.37 per cent were 'artificially fed only'.[11] These are only two regions, admittedly, but in the absence of any other information for this period we can note that in the more rural area over three-quarters of the babies had some breast-milk, compared to three-fifths in Cork city. From these examples, simultaneous breast and bottle-feeding appears to have been quite common. Though not immediately relevant to this study, as it refers to Belfast, Deeny's survey of infant mortality in that city in 1940 explained that the designation 'breast-feeding' covered even mothers who gave a bottle as well as the breast, 'as nowadays so many receive supplements'.[12] Perhaps breast-feeding mothers often mixed breast and bottle-feeding in a way which current breast-feeding advocates lead us to believe is impossible.

The magazine *Woman's Life* had a 'Happy Irish Babies' column in the 1930s, which solicited photographs and dietary details of babies throughout the country, and about half of the babies whose photos were sent in 1936–39 had been or were being breast-fed for periods ranging from three months to a year.[13] Was this a reflection of the situation in the general population? Were *Woman's Life* readers more inclined to worry about babies' health and therefore more inclined to breast-feed *or* to bottle-feed from anxiety about intake, growth curves and so on? Humphreys found that breast-feeding, or nursing as he calls it, was almost universal among artisan mothers in Dublin in the 1920s and 1930s and that it was still 'common practice' in the 1940s, and mothers were very aware of its importance.[14]

My own research reveals no clear geographical or class pattern among those who breast-fed or did not breast-feed, but there was definitely a greater incidence of it in the first two decades after independence. To cite a few examples: Delia R.*'s mother, an artisan's wife in Limerick, breast-fed all her children for at least three months in the 1920s and 1930s; Tom and Joan K.*, born on medium to large farms in Mayo and Wexford, respectively, in the 1920s, were breast-fed as were all their siblings; T.J. McD.* and his three brothers, born on a seventy-acre Cavan farm in the late 1930s, were breast-fed for a few months, then put on milk 'straight from the cow'; Jane S.*, a farmer's wife in Cavan, breast-fed all her children, born in the 1930s, for a few months; Anna A.*, from a small holding in Sligo, and all her brothers and sisters, born in the 1940s, were also breast-fed. Wheels could turn from one generation to another: Madge C.*'s mother, in a middle-class area of Dublin city in the 1930s had not breast-fed, but Madge, a teacher, who married in 1960, breast-fed her three children. Delia R.*'s mother had breast-fed, but Delia's two sisters (one rural, one urban) who married in the late 1940s and early 1950s, bottle-fed their large families. Maureen O'R.*'s mother did not breast-feed, but Maureen herself tried with her first child in 1962, getting little or no encouragement from her mother. Josephine E.* and Lily G.*, both living on small farms in Mayo in the 1950s, at least attempted breast-feeding, as did Mary Ellen D.* on a large midlands farm in the same decade.[15] But breast-feeding had become so unusual by the 1960s that it was possible for somebody born in 1960 into a milieu heavily populated with children, never to see or hear of a breast-fed baby until the practice began to be revived by the generation who had babies in the mid-1970s.[16]

The number of beliefs and stories about nursing mothers in the folk tradition would indicate that in Ireland, as elsewhere, for centuries breast-feeding was the normal method of infant rearing. One of the great advantages of the narrator's garden, in the exuberant hymn to domesticity, 'Táimse 'gus Máire go sásta 'nár n-aigní' (Máire and I are well-satisfied), is the profusion of fruits and berries to make 'Subh is misleáin don báb is don banaltra'/(Jam and sweet things for the baby and the nursing mother).[17] When Méiní Dunlevy, the Blasket Island nurse/handywoman, brought her new baby back to the island from her mother's house on the mainland in 1897, she brought a new teat and milk bottle with her, which suggests that the baby was at least partly bottle-fed. Moreover, the fact that the bottle is remembered in the lore of

Note: an asterisk denotes that the name is a pseudonym. Brief details about people cited in the text are given in the Appendix.

the island suggests that it was unusual.[18] There are indications from some rural areas that bottle-feeding had crept in by the 1930s. Indeed, elderly people at this time did not allow the decline in breast-feeding to go unremarked: 'When I was a boy there was no talk of bottles to rear children', John McAuliffe from north Cork told the Irish Folklore Commission in 1933, going on to relate an archetypal story about a mother, dead in child-birth, who came back to nurse her child.[19] Liam Ó Caoimh, a pensioner from Dungarvan in Co. Waterford, opined that:

> Na leanaí atá siad ag tógaint anois níl phioc den dúchas na máthar ná an t-athar ionta mar níl siad ag ól bainne na máthar. 'Sé bainne na bó atháid ag ól agus dá chomhartha sin go bé béic an laoigh atá ag a bhformhór.
>
> [The babies that are being reared now they haven't a scrap of their mother or father's heritage [dúchas] because they're not drinking their mother's milk, they're drinking cow's milk, and so it's the cry of the calf that most of them have].[20]

William Downey, a contributor to *No Shoes In Summer*, remembered an eccentric neighbouring woman's running commentary at the cinema in Portarlington in the 1930s:

> Will you look at the lovely baby, a fine child God bless it! Must be six months old. Mary help us, will you look at that pram! I declare I never seen the like of that. Don't them women have it easy, when you think of us. God help us. Look, look, she's given it one of them bottles, well God forgive you. You hussy, why don't you feed the child right, there's enough of you in it, as anyone can see.[21]

Arensberg and Kimball also quote the remarks of an old farmer in Clare comparing his son's wife with his own wife, in the presence of both:

> Here is a woman that has no more milk of her own. They shouldn't allow a woman like that to breed because a man should always keep his wife in the milk. The old woman, God bless her, raised every child on the didi [breast].[22]

The anthropologists were surprised at the old man's frank references, and in mixed company, to fecundity and bodily functions. For our purposes it can be noted that such insensitive criticism, if indulged in by many older people, male or female, cannot but have inculcated in younger women a negative attitude towards breast-feeding and an association of it with coercive patriarchal authority.

A survey in Cork city and suburbs in 1952–53 by Curtin provides more information about the extent of breast-feeding.[23] Curtin, in a survey of 1,007 infants born in this period, found that over a third of infants received no breast-milk at all, and that less than half – 46.6 per cent – of two-week-old babies were being breast-fed and just over a quarter at two months. A comparable figure for British eight-week-old babies in 1946 was 57 per cent. In Cork, only 9 per cent of babies were still being breast-fed at six months. Curtin found that babies born at home were less likely to be breast-fed than babies born in nursing homes or hospitals, which would appear to contradict some modern breast-feeding advocates' beliefs about a link between institutionalisation and artificial feeding.[24] In the National Maternity Hospital in Holles Street, Dublin, where staff insisted upon mothers breast-feeding, a survey in 1951 found that 51 per cent were still relying on breast-feeding alone 'a few weeks' after leaving hospital and a further 20 per cent were breast-feeding with a supplement. These figures compare very favourably with Curtin's findings for Cork.[25] In Portiuncula Hospital in Ballinasloe the nursing sisters, according to Mary Ellen D.*, 'made us all breast-feed', while the Medical Missionaries of Mary in Lourdes Hospital in Drogheda also actively encouraged breast-feeding.[26]

Throughout the 1930s and 1940s health authorities explicitly stated the importance of breast-feeding almost annually in the reports of the Department of Local Government and Public Health. Breast-feeding also featured in articles written by doctors in medical journals in that great era of debate about a national health system, the 1940s.[27] Part of the task of the public health nurse, following on from the Public Health Act of 1945, was to promote breast-feeding.[28] Doctors and midwives had their own theories about why natural feeding failed. Obstetrician Dr Alex Spain believed that women did not get enough rest immediately after birth to enable them to establish breast-feeding; Dr James Deeny, pioneer of public health in independent Ireland in the 1940s, recommended leaving babies in bed with their mothers for the lying-in period, not only to encourage breast-feeding but also to counteract infection. Deeny cited Dublin's Coombe Hospital as an example of where this was common practice, having the highest breast-feeding rates and the lowest rates of infection among infants.[29] In Holles Street, in the 1940s and 1950s, it was against hospital rules for a baby to receive a bottle-feed (except, one imagines, in extremis).[30] Dr Charles Coyle, the obstetric tutor in this hospital in the 1940s and later its Master, published an article on breast-feeding in 1945. He did not believe in the kind of nipple preparation recommended by Truby King[31] and still being urged in some publications up to the 1950s: 'The use of a nail-brush, hard or soft, on the nipples, we absolutely condemn'. Nor did he believe in disinfecting the nipples and the hands before and after every feed; ordinary cleanliness, with perhaps a bit more care than usual, was all that was needed. Mothers should not worry about 'emptying the breast' (another Truby King obsession); those who advocated it were influenced by agricultural practice and the milking of a cow was after all 'a wholly unnatural and artificial process'. The most important thing was a peaceful and calm atmosphere in the days immediately after birth.

However, Dr Coyle, in common with nearly all of his contemporaries, believed in regularity of feeding; babies over six pounds should, he believed, be fed four-hourly, babies under six pounds, three-hourly.[32] When Máire Mullarney had her first baby in Holles Street Hospital in the late 1940s, she tried to follow this advice, and was also influenced by a friend, a female doctor, who constantly warned her of the dangers of over-feeding. By six weeks her little daughter had not gained on her birth weight, so a bottle supplement was introduced.[33] Feeding on demand, whenever the baby requires, is in most cases essential for the establishment of a milk supply as the breasts make milk in response to the baby's sucking.[34] Olive A.*, who believed 'if you can breast-feed, it's marvellous', tried feeding her first baby in the early 1950s, as encouraged by the nuns in the Bons Secours in Cork:

> I tried breast-feeding with one, and she had lovely rosy cheeks ... and in six weeks she had hollow cheeks, skin like a sheet. And she was screaming her head off. And I wasn't too well myself with it all. And the next one, then, I gave it 12 days, and she was screaming too, so, bottles after that.

It is easy to see how breast-feeding would fail, under a regime of strict regularity, unless the mother had a powerful supply of milk and the baby was placid and an efficient feeder.[35]

Medical 'experts' were becoming more and more powerful in this period. In 1927 the *Irish Nurses' Union Gazette* expressed a view prevalent all over the western world:

> Our teaching should fit the mother to manage her affairs alone, and not be obliged to turn to her neighbours and to kind-hearted old women who are sure to find the doctor's treatment too difficult to carry out and who will replace it with those old women's remedies which can be so dangerous.[36]

Needless to say, the ideal mother would not manage her affairs 'alone', she would also rely on medical advice. There might well have been harmful folk beliefs about maternal and infant health and much room for improvement in many aspects of the way people lived, but there was also the expertise of generations about breast-feeding, an expertise which was irrevocably lost in this period. Meanwhile, it seems that modern breast-feeding advocates are right when they point out that medical authorities, including some trained midwives, who prized textbooks over lived experience[37] (although not all did this[38]) were simultaneously insisting on breast-feeding whilst making it difficult for women to breast-feed. The decline of this method of infant feeding in twentieth-century Ireland cannot, however, be laid entirely at their door; there were other reasons for it.

One very important reason why women on farms began to substitute bottles for breasts around the 1940s and 1950s had to do with help, or the lack of it. The numbers of single women leaving the land accelerated after 1936, and the horizontally-extended family was dying out. This change in family structure seems to have been welcomed by young married women at the time, many of whom objected to a sister or a sister-in-law living with them much more than they would have objected to a mother or mother-in-law.[39] However, women's flight from the land meant that there was less able-bodied help available for women's work on the farm. This work involved not only the care of the house and its inhabitants, but also the making of butter and the care of poultry, the feeding of farmyard livestock, and, given that only 12 per cent of rural dwellings had an indoor water supply in 1961,[40] the drawing and disposing of water several times a day, to say nothing of the disposal of household waste. The availability of electricity and water on tap seems, if anything, to have made bottle-feeding easier. Ann Kennedy, the very modern farmer's wife who wrote a diary for *The Irish Times* in the 1950s, described a six a.m. feed for her month-old baby where the bottle, taken from the fridge, was heated in an electric bottle-warmer.[41] Successful breast-feeding demands that a woman can sit down with the baby several times a day. This might have been possible if there were other able-bodied, trust-worthy women present who could have done some of the heavy women's farm work. Josephine E.*, in Mayo in the 1950s, seems to have experienced such difficulties. She breast-fed her first child, but thereafter: 'I had to be inside and outside, and I had my mother, so I couldn't'. Her mother was an invalid, someone who could easily give a bottle to a baby, but who could not haul buckets and do other heavy work. Lily G.* also had to work inside and outside while her husband, like Josephine's, was employed locally:

> I breast-fed the first one for quite a while, the second one then, was a lad, and of course he wasn't as easy … I had to start giving him a bottle as well as breast-feeding, I did mix, then. I fed them all for nearly a month.

Lily's view that a boy was harder to satisfy than a girl is one that is still current.

Fathers could also give bottles, and many women, particularly in the 1950s, seem to have welcomed this opportunity for the father to get involved in baby care and do something for their wives. When Mary Ellen D.* brought her ninth and last baby home from hospital, she only had to give him one bottle-feed a day, as his brothers and sisters competed for the privilege of feeding him when they could and his father got up during the night. Curtin, in the survey referred to above, also found that the larger the family, the more chance there was of the new baby being bottle-fed.[42] Giving a bottle is an easy and pleasant job which can be done by, as pointed out above, a feeble grandparent or even a quite young child, neither of whom would be able to take over the woman's jobs either inside or outside of the home.

Moving away from farms, the reasons women gave for weaning or for bottle-feeding in the first place varied. Most of those who spoke to me weaned early because of inability to maintain a milk supply, but a startlingly large proportion in Curtin's survey, over a fifth, 'did not believe in breast-feeding'. Also, 17.5 per cent had 'abnormal breasts and nipples' (probably inverted nipples) and there were a number of other almost equally-weighted reasons – mother in poor health, insufficient breast milk, debility or illness of the child, prospect of paid work or heavy domestic commitments. Prematurity was also cited as a factor.[43] The smaller the baby the more it needs the protection of its mother's milk, but perhaps because of incubators and the greater trend towards in-hospital care of premature babies, there was less chance of establishing breast-feeding as premature babies cannot suck very well and are often fed by tube. However, even here and with hospital-isation in general, expressed milk could be used, given the right amount of encouragement. For example, when Joan K.*'s first baby suffered an injury at birth and was kept in hospital for some time, Joan expressed milk and brought it into Holles Street Hospital to him. As far as weaning was concerned, nearly 70 per cent of those who weaned early did so because of insufficient breast milk, 'but only in a few cases was failure of lactation confirmed by test-weighing'. Curtin concluded that a negative attitude to breast-feeding was probably the single most important factor predisposing women to bottle-feed. He recommended the provision of education and information, and wisely advised against imbuing mothers with a sense of failure for not breast-feeding.

It is easy to see how propaganda which sternly emphasised breast-feeding as the mother's duty would have been counterproductive, annoying and irritating for women who had little choice about pregnancy in the first place. Indeed, opting to bottle-feed might well have been one way of retain-ing some measure of control over one's body. Olive A.* was highly indignant with a nun in the Bon Secours in Cork who said that cow's milk was only fit for calves:

> But then, it may have been she or some other one who said she hated midwifery because mothers don't need nursing. I mean, did you ever in all your life!

Here, the link between breast-feeding and an unacceptably austere attitude to mothers' comfort, is made explicit. The irony is that full breast-feeding without supplements can (though it does not inevitably) suppress ovulation, so women might have had longer intervals between babies by feeding for at least nine months.[44] Josephine E.* says that this is one reason why many of her neighbours in Mayo went on with breast-feeding:

> They used to have a [belief], that when you were feeding a baby you couldn't get pregnant, and twas more or less a safety thing, and there were a lot trying it … Some of them the creatureens they used be feeding a baby and they wouldn't even get to feel the [new] baby [kicking], do you know what I mean?

If people suspected, then, that breast-feeding might suppress ovulation, and still did not practise it, one can only conclude that the desire not to breast-feed was stronger than the desire to avoid pregnancy. As far as I know breast-feeding was never promoted in Ireland in this period as a natural method of spacing births, but then, neither was anything else. Catholic medical theology was not altogether clear about the point at which a couple could morally decide that they had completed their family and go on to avoid conception, even by natural means.[45] Indeed, a book explaining Catholic-approved methods of birth control was banned by the Irish censors in 1941.[46] Spacing births was simply not an issue.

Nowhere did I encounter the view that breast-feeding was somehow immodest. However, it is unlikely that such a view would have been expressed to me by the people I interviewed, when it became clear that I had breast-fed my own babies.[47] Certainly the official Catholic position as expressed in Catholic publications and by prominent Catholics was all in favour of breast-feeding. *The Irish Messenger of the Sacred Heart*, for example, a widely read Catholic periodical, carried a highly technical and frank article about care of the nipples in a 1947 issue.[48] Nuns as midwives were among the most fervent advocates of breast-feeding. Maura Laverty, however, suggests that a kind of false modesty could ruin healthy and happy breast-feeding. In her novel, *Lift Up Your Gates*, published in 1946, a young middle-class mother, Eileen Harte, delights in breast-feeding her little boy, contrasting it to her own mother's furtive and over-modest way of feeding Eileen's little brother under a voluminous shawl. Laverty was a deeply spiritual and idealistic writer, well within the bounds of orthodox Catholicism, with nothing but praise for priests and nuns. In spite of this, some of her books were banned as indecent in the 1940s because of her frankness about bodily matters and her sympathy for sexual transgressors.[49] Breast-feeding might not have been considered immodest, but it might have been popularly associated with the earthiness/

rurality, 'ignorance' and poverty which many Irish people were desperately trying to discard in the 1940s and 1950s.

III

Palmer mentions that in parts of southern Germany and Finland in the nineteenth century, breast-feeding was traditionally regarded as a lazy and self-indulgent practice and that bottle-feeding rates were very high.[50] These were rural regions with much in common with rural Ireland, where the women's contribution to the family economy was vital. Why did Irish farm women, like their counterparts in other rural economies, not simply tie on their babies and let them feed at will as they went about their work?[51] This would, I submit, have been aesthetically unacceptable to most Irish women, particularly from the 1940s. It was not just that the powerful influences of emigration and mass media were meeting little or no resistance in people's outer appearance, tastes and leisure pursuits, to the immense concern of some observers at this time. It was also that more and more Irish girls and women were turning their backs on 'assisting relative' status on the farm or the life of a 'stay-at-home' in the town. There was a modest increase in jobs for females in the towns and more consumer goods to be purchased, and there was a strong perception (accurate or not) that young people were postponing marriage in order to enjoy this freedom.[52] The self-sacrifice and hard work of fathers and of mothers stood out starkly. Women of the house, their moral bargaining power increased by the rising tide of public concern about population decline, were becoming more insistent on whatever comforts they could glean from lives of unceasing hard work. These comforts could have been as 'big' as the co-operative, companionate spouse, freely selected and the house serviced with water and electricity (or likely to be so in the future) and free of other female relatives, or as 'small' as the occasional visit to the hairdresser, or outing of any kind.[53] Cutting down on family size does not seem to have been an option until the 1960s,[54] but giving birth away from home represented comfort of a sort, with lying-in periods of ten days to a fortnight. Part of the attraction of the hospital or nursing home was that everything was done for the mother.[55]

Though medical and midwifery authorities advocated breast-feeding, the kind of advice they gave to breast-feeding mothers at this time, which stressed regularity of feeds and warned against overfeeding, must have resulted for many women in a poor milk supply and early bottle-feeding. However, people often disregard medical advice, or adapt it for their own use. Many mothers, for example, bottle-fed babies on demand, contrary to medical advice. What is surprising about Ireland in the 1940s and 1950s is that the popular lore of breast-feeding, passed on from one woman to another for generations, did not emerge in competition with medical lore. One can only conclude that the majority of Irish mothers turned consciously and firmly away from breast-feeding in these years. By doing so they were not only defying the authority of medical experts, but also discarding the advice and expertise of their elders. In the overwhelmingly Catholic population, most of them had little choice about pregnancy. The method of infant feeding was one area of their reproductive lives over which they could, and did, exercise control. This meant that they were put to the trouble of washing and cleaning bottles, usually made of glass, and teats and often making up formulas several times a day. It meant that feeding time did not necessarily involve the mother sitting down to relax with her baby. But it also meant that she could be doing other things while the baby was fed by somebody else, or by a propped bottle, and that she had one less physical tie to house and family.

For instance, Mary Ellen D.* weaned one of her babies at six weeks because she wanted to attend the wedding of a close friend in Dublin. She was a hard-working woman who, at this stage of her marriage with a small family, got out about once a year to a social event of any kind. Ethel R.*'s mother, who worked hard in the house, was active in the Irish Countrywomen's Association and got out to meetings and other committees quite often; she bottle-fed her four girls, born from the mid-1940s, and Ethel's father was quite handy with bottle-feeding. Therefore, it seems that breast-feeding came to be seen not only as a drain on precious resources of nutrition and energy, but as a way of secluding and isolating the mother in the house. Such isolation was unacceptable to the women who started their families from the mid-1940s. This is why modern breast-feeding mothers are often told 'Aren't you great' or asked 'Are you mad?' by these women who became mothers from the 1940s. In 1973, a very practical Irish-published book of babycare advice could envisage no other way of breast-feeding besides stripping to the waist and either brazening it out in company or slipping up to 'the cold bedroom like a chambermaid with a secret vice'.[56] Traditional lore about preserving bodily privacy while feeding a baby was long gone, and an expertise adapted to modern conditions and modern clothes, though promoted by breast-feeding advocates, had still not reached even somebody as obviously well-informed as the author.

Appendix: Details about contributors cited in the article: all names are pseudonyms

Madge C. was born in Dublin city in 1933. Her father was an insurance salesman. She trained as a teacher and married in 1960.

Tom and Joan K.: Tom was born c. 1924 on a sixteen acre farm in Mayo, with five brothers and two sisters and his mother was widowed early; Joan was born c. 1924 with nine siblings on a large farm in Wexford. They married in 1951 and lived all their married life in Dublin city. Tom was a bus driver until he retired, while Joan was an office worker before she married. They had five children born between 1952 and 1960.

Anna A. was born in Co. Sligo in 1940 on a farm of about ten to twelve acres, which belonged to a grand-aunt and was worked by her parents and her grand-aunt. She had three sisters and two brothers.

Olive A. was born c. 1929 in Cork city. She was an office worker before her marriage, while her husband had a business. They married in 1951 and had six children. She trained as an elocution teacher in the late 1960s.

Jane S. was born in 1906. She worked at home on the farm, until she married a farmer in 1928 and had eight children. She ran a successful poultry business in the 1950s.

Maureen O'R. was born in 1937 in a 'working-class family', the eldest of eight children in a sizeable Cork town. Her father was a casual labourer, while her mother had a small source of income.

Josephine E. was born 'on a very small farm' in Mayo in 1928. She had one brother who died of TB in 1947. She worked in the local town during the early 1940s and then emigrated to England, where she married in 1957. She returned in 1959 to look after her mother and ran a small farm, whilst her husband did building work locally. They had four children and lived in a house which had no water or electricity until 1970.

Mary Ellen D. was born in 1928 on a big farm in Roscommon. She had one sister and worked on the home farm until her marriage, in 1951, to a big farmer from Westmeath. They had nine children.

Lily G. was born in Mayo in 1923. She taught in England, but returned in 1948 and married in 1950. She inherited a small farm whilst her husband worked locally. They had seven children.

Ethel R. was born in 1944 in a Cork town. She had three sisters and her father was a bank manager. She was active in the Irish Countrywomen's Association, as was her mother.

T.J. McD. was born c. 1935–40 in Cavan on a low-lying seventy acre farm. He had three brothers and his mother was widowed in 1944. He ran the family farm.

Delia R. was born in 1921 in Limerick city. She was the fourth eldest (third surviving) of nine children whose father was an artisan with a small business. Her mother was a farmer's daughter.

Afterword:
A Feminine Occupation for a Female Audience?:
A Future for Irish Women's History

ALAN HAYES

I

> There has long been an involvement by women in writing history ...
> But there were decades of history-teaching where women's history
> played no part. Then in the 1970s women's history arrived, partly as a
> search for roots on the part of the second-wave women's movement
> who wanted to find out where they got lost and what had happened,
> and methodologically, because the tools of social history, particularly
> economic history, began to be widely used at that time and these were
> the best tools for researching women's history.[1]

Thus said Margaret MacCurtain, pioneer of the history of women in Ireland,
in an interview published in 1994. MacCurtain has long been a facilitator for
a wide range of historical themes and topics and, amongst her numerous
publications, she was co-editor, with Donnchadh Ó Corrain, of the first
collection on modern Irish women's history, *Women in Irish Society: The
Historical Dimension*, published by Arlen House in 1978 – a collection which
this current work, and indeed most works on Irish women's history, have
been influenced by. Indeed, she considers this work to be her most
significant, stating that 'its essays ... are an expression of the vitality of the
intellectual and creative energy of the 1970s'.[2] That work consisted of essays
by young dynamic female and male scholars who have played an important
role in Irish academic writing since, albeit some have not developed the
gendered aspects of their research since this first development.

For a consideration of the growth of women's history since that important first major development which arose from the second-wave feminist

movement, and an examination of the current state of the profession in Ireland, it is necessary to explore developments over recent decades and examine relevant debates on the integration of women's history into the mainstream in an international context.

II

Since the 1960s women's history has emerged internationally as a specialist subject, offered in a huge number of educational establishments either as an optional or compulsory subject for undergraduates, and as an increasingly chosen option for post-graduate research. It has developed alongside 'traditional' history, which presents itself as neutral but actually isn't, since many aspects of the historical past are absent or misrepresented, including that of gender. The pursuit of women's history attempts to give back some of this neutrality to mainstream history, by working towards achieving equity in the curriculum and in historical writing, by helping to make history more meaningful for all readers and by giving them a more balanced perspective when exploring historical events and themes.

In Ireland we are still at an early stage in the development of women's history in third-level institutions, let alone tackling its introduction into second-level history courses (apart from the few token examples). Most institutions now offer courses at undergraduate level on the history of women. Unfortunately, they are often marginalised as optional courses and can be regarded by many students as being directed mainly towards female students, and indeed appear to be largely taken by women. Likewise, women's history courses offered within the discipline of women's studies are overwhelmingly taken by female students. The presentation of these courses is largely based on the research and personal interest of mainly female members of staff. This dependence is a fragile foundation which can lead to the termination of the course if the lecturer is no longer available. While this is true of many options which rely on specific focused research by a particular academic, should the history of half the population be seen as 'optional'?

III

In a debate on the integration of women's history into mainstream history courses in late 1997, mainly concerning the history of the United States, a number of interesting views were exchanged over the H-Women (History Women) e-mail discussion list. A correspondent on the list brought forward an experience she had had while teaching a course in 'World Civilization'.

After assigning some outside reading which dealt with women for this mainstream course, she met with some antagonism:

> I find that many students feel as if I have some agenda because I attempt to integrate women's history. I understand that this may have something to do with the rural/traditional background of my students, but I would like to have feedback from those who have had similar experiences with students who are reluctant to learn women's role in history.[3]

One student commented that 'your teacher must be a woman' because the teacher had disseminated material relating to women. The responses which this request received crossed many divides and many reported hostility from both male and female students from different walks of life to the integration of women's history into mainstream history courses. E-mail responses from students claimed that lecturers in courses which integrated themes of sexuality, gender and family were either 'PC', 'revisionist', 'dykes' or 'feminists' ('which they saw as a terrible thing!'). Another lecturer was told that she had a clear 'agenda', which is true of all teaching and not necessarily bad, although in this example it was clearly meant to be a criticism, and not an acknowledgement of another's differing politics. One response referred to a male colleague, who was considered 'enlightened' because he lectured about gender relations, while a female colleague was assumed to be speaking from either bias or self-interest when lecturing in this area. Another response suggested that being open from the start and directly stating that the aim of the course was the best option, for example in this case, 'to explore the interdependence and differing perspectives of all peoples in society' necessitates an examination of women as well as minority groups and white men. This is a prime example of a way forward which we could explore in Irish history, in the continuing development of women's history and in the integration of new specialisms into mainstream history teaching, research and publishing.

IV

The process of writing women back into history challenges the validity of past centuries of history writing and necessitates a thorough reworking and re-evaluation of 'knowledge' as it stands at present. Women's history is more than writing about the 'great women' of history (much like mainstream history is more than the 'great men' approach) and it must also avoid stereotyping and trivialisation. We will be regularly rewriting the historical record as new evidence is uncovered and analysed (and then re-analysed) and all our perceptions will constantly need to be re-evaluated. Thus all scholars, both female and male, will need to be aware of new developments which will alter traditionally held beliefs. The first major development in women's history in Ireland, *Women in Irish Society: The Historical Dimension*, threw down challenges to Irish academia, many of which have been taken on board. A large amount of gender-related research has been carried out in Ireland since the 1970s and published both nationally and internationally. The one challenge which has not fully been met has been the participation of men in the writing of Irish women's history. Apart from a few examples, there has been no substantial effort from male historians to incorporate the experiences of women into their writing and research. The challenge from MacCurtain and Ó Corrain to all scholars, both male and female, to examine gender and explore its implications, still needs to be addressed. The women's history community also needs to accept male participation in this field, even if that participation may not be written from a feminist political perspective. Indeed, women's history written by women is not necessarily written from that particular political agenda either. Histories of women written by men can be either feminist or not, it shouldn't matter what the author's political bias is as long as the work is of an acceptable standard.

The history of women and of gender must be integrated into all aspects of historical teaching, research and publishing in order to more accurately represent the past. Much evidence has already been discovered and there is much more to find[4] – what is needed is the understanding and interest of the entire historical community, both female and male, to acknowledge that the history of half the human race is a worthwhile endeavour and integral to our continuing quests to understand the past. As Helen Concannon stated:

> To understand any nation we must understand its women. But in the case of Ireland, the necessity is particularly great. It is always as a woman that her lovers have thought of her.[5]

Notes

CHAPTER ONE

1 Kuno Meyer (ed. and trans.), *Hail Brigit: An Old-Irish Poem on the Hill of Alenn* (Dublin, 1912); P.L. Henry (ed. and trans.), *Dánta Ban: Poems of Irish Women, Early and Modern* (Cork, 1991), pp. 46–9.
2 Rudolf Thurneysen, D.A. Binchy *et al.*, *Studies in Early Irish Law* (Dublin, 1936); Donnchadh Ó Corráin, 'Women in Early Irish Society' in Margaret MacCurtain and Ó Corráin (eds), *Women in Irish Society: The Historical Dimension* (Westport, CT, 1980), pp. 1–10; Lisa M. Bitel, *Land of Women: Tales of Sex and Gender from Early Ireland* (NY, 1996).
3 Kim McCone, 'Brigit in the Seventh Century: A Saint with Three Lives?', *Peritia*, 1 (1982), pp. 107–45; Richard Sharpe, 'Vitae S. Brigitae: The Oldest Texts', *Peritia*, 1 (1982), pp. 81–106. Cf. the Leinster genealogies which claim Leinster on behalf of Brigit's bishop Aed mac Colmáin, d. 638: M.A. O'Brien (ed.), *Corpus Genealogiarum Hiberniae* (Dublin, 1962), p. 339.
4 Kim McCone, *Pagan Past and Christian Present in Early Irish Literature* (Maynooth, 1990), pp. 162–3.
5 Whitley Stokes (ed. and trans.), *Lives of the Saints from the Book of Lismore* (Oxford, 1890), pp. 51, 198; John Ryan, *Irish Monasticism: Origins and Early Development* (Dublin, 1931), pp. 134–6, where he speaks of Brigit as 'perhaps the greatest woman of whom Irish history tells', p. 134; Peter Beresford Ellis, *Celtic Women: Women in Celtic Society and Literature* (London, 1995), p. 149. Between the devout and the goofy, the scholarship on Brigit is considerable. See, for example, Dorothy Bray, 'The Image of St Brigit in the Early Irish Church', *ÉC*, 24 (1984), pp. 209–15; Bray, 'Secunda Brigida: Saint Ita of Killeedy and Brigidine Tradition' in Cyril J. Byrne *et al.* (eds), *Celtic Languages and Celtic Peoples* (Halifax, 1989), pp. 27–38; Sean Connolly, 'The Authorship and Manuscript Tradition of Vita I S. Brigitae', *Manuscripta*, 16 (1972), pp. 67–82; Mario Esposito, 'On the Earliest Latin Life of St Brigid of Kildare', *Proceedings of the Royal Irish Academy*, 30c (1912), pp. 307–26; Esposito, '"Cogitosus": Notes on Latin Learning and Literature in Medieval Ireland', *Hermathena*, 20 (1926–30), pp. 251–7; Esposito, 'On the Early Lives of St Brigid of Kildare', *Hermathena*, 24 (1935), pp. 120–65; James F. Kenney, *The Sources for the Early History of Ireland: I. Ecclesiastical* (reprinted Dublin, 1994), pp. 356–64, see also pp. 267–78; McCone, 'Brigit'; Felim Ó Briain, 'Brigitana', *ZCP*, 6 (1977), pp. 112–37; Séamus Ó Catháin, 'Hearth-Prayers and Other Traditions of Brigit: Celtic Goddess and Holy Woman', *Journal of the Royal Society of Antiquaries of Ireland*, 122 (1992), pp. 12–34; Donnchadh Ó hAodha, 'The Early Lives of St Brigit', *JKAS*, 15 (1971–76), pp. 397–405; Pádraig Ó Riain, 'Sainte Brigitte: Paradigme de l'Abbesse Celtique?' in M. Rouche and J. Heuclin (eds), *La Femme au Moyen-age* (Ville de Maubeuge, 1990), pp. 27–32; Sharpe, 'Vitae S. Brigitae: The Oldest Texts'.
6 Dáibhí Ó Cróinín, *Early Medieval Ireland, 400–1200* (London, 1995), pp. 154–62; F.J. Byrne, *Irish Kings and High-Kings* (London, 1973), pp. 130–64, esp. pp. 133, 151–4.

7 Ludwig Bieler (ed. and trans.), *Patrician Texts in the Book of Armagh* (Dublin, 1979), pp. 190–1.

8 McCone, 'Brigit', pp. 141–4.

9 Cogitosus writes *caput pene omnium Hiberniensiam ecclesiarum*: J.P. Migne, *Patrologia Latina* (Paris, 1844–64), vol. 72, cols. 777–8; S. Connolly and J.M. Picard (trans.), 'Cogitosus: Life of Saint Brigit', *JRSAI*, 117 (1987), p. 11; cf. the ninth-century *Félire Oenguso* where Brigit is called 'cenn cáid caillech n-Érenn', 'chaste head of all the nuns of Ireland', Whitley Stokes (ed. and trans.), *Félire Óenguso Céli Dé* (reprinted Dublin, 1984), p. 58.

10 Ibid.

11 Migne, *Patrologia Latina*, pp. 72, 777–80.

12 Ibid., pp. 72, 784.

13 Ibid., pp. 782–3.

14 Ibid., pp. 72, 786–7.

15 Bieler, *Patrician Texts in the Book of Armagh*, pp. 90, 108–13, 148.

16 Migne, *Patrologia Latina*, pp. 72, 781.

17 Roland M. Smith (ed. and trans.), 'The Senbriathra Fithail and Related Texts', *Revue Celtique*, 45 (1928), p. 53; Kuno Meyer (ed. and trans.), *The Instructions of King Cormac Mac Airt* (Dublin, 1909), pp. 28–34; Hermann Wasserschleben (ed.), *Die irische Kanonen-sammlung* (Leipzig, 1885), p. 187.

18 Migne, *Patrologia Latina*, p. 781.

19 Pádraig Ó Riain, *Corpus Genealogiarum Sanctorum Hiberniae* (Dublin, 1985), p. 115. For dating the list: Ó Riain, xxiii; Kenney, *The Sources for the Early History of Ireland*, p. 361.

20 Migne, *Patrologia Latina*, pp. 72, 788–9.

21 The monastic annals regularly list the obits of abbesses, abbots, bishops and other officers of Kildare. See, for example, Seán Mac Airt and Gearóid MacNiocaill (eds), *The Annals of Ulster (to A.D. 1131)* (Dublin, 1983), for the years 520, 524, 639, 696, 698, 709, 725, 732, et passim.

22 Aubrey Gwynn and R. Neville Hadcock, *Medieval Religious Houses: Ireland (With an Appendix to Early Sites)* (London, 1970), pp. 311, 320.

23 In Cogitosus, hospitality/generosity miracles bracket four other episodes: a woman spared birth-pangs; a man for whom the saint changed a stone into salt; a blind man cured and a dumb girl restored to speech: Migne, *Patrologia Latina*, pp. 72, 780–1, omitting the birth-pang incident, for which see *AASS*, 1 February, 136.12. Cf. Vita Prima. *AASS*, 1 February, pp. 120–1: a one-handed man and male lepers cured; a nun and two paralytic virgins healed; two blind Britons (male) healed; two women's cows found. See also Sean Connolly (trans.), 'Vita Prima Sanctae Brigitae', *JRSAI*, 119 (1989), pp. 18–19. In the ninth-century *Bethu Brigte*: women's calf found; calf and cure granted to male leper; nun healed of ague; chronically sick man healed; two paralytic virgins healed; male Britons healed. Donnchadh Ó hAodha (ed. and trans.), *Bethu Brigte* (Dublin, 1978), pp. 7–9.

24 McCone, 'Brigit', pp. 139–44; Sharpe, 'Vitae S. Brigitae', pp. 105–6.

25 *AASS*, 1 February, p. 121; Connolly, 'Vita Prima', p. 20.

26 The secular laws on this question tend to favour the accused, see *CIH*, 232, 856, 914; Fergus Kelly, *Guide to Early Irish Law* (Dublin, 1987), p. 108.

27 *AASS*, 1 February, pp. 122–3; Connolly, 'Vita Prima', p. 23.

28 *AASS*, 1 February, p. 125; Connolly, 'Vita Prima', p. 29.

29 In a thematically-related episode, a crowd asks Brigit the significance of a mysterious lightning bolt. She defers its interpretation to Patrick, who tells her before the assembled: 'You and I know equally well. Reveal this mystery to them', *AASS*, 1 February, p. 126; Connolly, 'Vita Prima', p. 30.

30 Ibid.

31 AASS, 1 February, pp. 126–8.

32 Ibid., p. 131.

33 JoAnn Radner (ed. and trans.), *Fragmentary Annals of Ireland* (Dublin, 1978), p. 70.

34 *AASS*, 1 February, p. 134.

35 Ó hAodha, 'The Early Lives of St Brigit', esp. pp. 7–8, 10–12, 21–25, et passim.

36 Ibid., pp. 6, 24.

37 Ibid., pp. 15, 31–2.

38 Henry, *Dánta Ban*, pp. 50–1; *AASS*, 1 February, p. 120.

39 Whitley Stokes (ed.), *Three Irish Glossaries* (London, 1862), p. 8.

40 Elizabeth Gray, *Cath Maige Tuired* (Naas, 1982), CIH, 377, 1654; all cited in McCone, *Pagan Past and Christian Present*, pp. 162–3, et passim.

41 Gerald of Wales, *The History and Topography of Ireland*, trans. by John J. O'Meara (London, 1982), sec. 68–9.

42 Charles Plummer (ed.), *Vitae Sanctorum Hiberniae* (Oxford, 1910), Vol. I, cxxxvi, No. 3; Proinsias McCana, *Celtic Mythology* (reprinted Feltham, Middlesex, 1986), pp. 32–4; Nerys Patterson, *Cattle-Lords and Clansmen: The Social Structure of Early Ireland* (Notre Dame, 1994), pp. 129–30.

43 See Bray, 'Image of St Brigit'.

44 Bitel, *Land of Women*, esp. pp. 26–7, 204–6.

CHAPTER TWO

1 Some of the most famous of the nunneries in the early medieval period in Ireland were Kildare founded by St Brigid; Killeevy, Co. Armagh, founded by St Moninna or Darerca; Killeedy, Co. Limerick, founded by St Ité. For brief details see A. Gwynn and R.N. Hadcock, *Medieval Religious Houses: Ireland* (Harlow, 1970), pp. 319–21, 392, and for some discussion see Lisa Bitel, *Land of Women: Tales of Sex and Gender from Early Ireland* (Ithaca and London, 1996), pp. 167–203.

2 Gwynn and Hadcock, *Medieval Religious Houses*, provides an invaluable starting point for any research into medieval monastic history. For post-conquest nuns see pp. 307–26.

3 R. Gilchrist, 'Community and Self: Perception and use of space in medieval monasteries', *Scottish Archaeology Review*, Vol. 6 (1989), p. 55.

4 P.J. Dunning, 'The Arroasian Order in Medieval Ireland', *Irish Historical Studies*, Vol. 4, No. 16 (1945), pp. 297–315.

5 M. Sheehy (ed.), *Pontifica Hibernica: Medieval Papal Chancery Documents concerning Ireland, 640–1261* (Dublin, 1962), Vol. II, p. 137.

6 *Sext. Decret.* lib. III tit. XVI.

7 James Brundage and Elizabeth M. Makowski, 'Enclosure of Nuns: The decretal *Periculoso* and its commentators', *Journal of Medieval History*, Vol. 20 (1994), p. 145.

8 Ibid.

9 P. Johnson, *Equal in Monastic Profession: Religious Women in Medieval France* (Chicago, 1991), pp. 112–30.

10 J. McNamara, *Sisters in Arms: Catholic Nuns through two Millenia* (Cambridge, MA and London, 1996), p. 362.

11 Public Record Office of Northern Ireland (PRONI), *Registers of the Archbishops of Armagh*, 'Register of John Swayne', f. 26v, and transcript, Trinity College Dublin (TCD), MS 577/4, pp. 85–7.

12 Ibid., ff. 106–106v, 120v; for transcript see TCD, MS 577/4, 379–84; 420–1; Calendared by D.A. Chart, *The register of John Swayne, archbishop of Armagh and primate of Ireland, 1418–1439* (Belfast, 1935), pp. 51–2. The entries to either side of the two undated entries give the approximate dates according to Chart.

13 H.J. Lawlor, 'Calendar of the Register of Archbishop Sweteman', *Proceedings of the Royal Irish Academy*, C, Vol. 29 (1911–12), p. 242.

14 … contra regularem earundem observanciam …, N.B. White (ed.), *Irish Monastic and Episcopal Deeds* (Dublin, 1936), p. 179.

15 For a general account of Kilculliheen, see W.P. Burke, 'The nunnery of Kilculliheen', *Journal of the Waterford and South East of Ireland Archaeological Society*, Vol. 8 (1902), pp. 9–17 and for a summary and translated extracts from the bishop's judgment against her see, John Mulhulland, 'The trial of Alice Butler, Abbess of Kilculiheen', *Decies, Old Waterford Society*, Vol. 25 (January 1984), pp. 45–6.

16 H.S. Sweetman and G.F. Hancock, *Calendar of Documents relating to Ireland* (London, 1875–86), Vol. II, p. 436; Vol. III, pp. 109, 177, 184; Vol. IV, p. 177 and on the connections between male houses and the nunneries dependent on Clonard see J. Brady, 'The nunnery of Clonard', *Ríocht na Mídhe*, Vol. 2, No. 2 (1960), pp. 4–7.

17 National Archives of Ireland, 'Calendar of Justices Itinerant Rolls, Roll No. 5, 53 Hen III', RC 7\1, p. 463.

18 National Archives of Ireland, 'Calendar of Common Bench Rolls, Dublin, Roll No. 7. 9 Ed I', RC 7\2, p. 95.

19 National Archives of Ireland, 'Calendar of Justices Itinerant Roll H 29 Ed I. Roll No. 57', RC 7\8, pp. 261–2.

20 In 1367, see *Calendar of Inquisitions Post Mortem and other analogous documents preserved in the Public Records Office – Miscellaneous* (London, 1904), No. 636, p. 236.

21 See among many others, J. Hamburger, 'Art, Enclosure and the Curia Monialium: Prolegomena in the Guise of a postscript', *Gesta*, Vol. 31 (1992), pp. 108–10.

22 Brundage and Makowski, 'Enclosure of Nuns', pp. 148, 154.

23 J. Mills, *Calendar of Justiciary Rolls 1295–1307* (Dublin, 1905–14), p. 79.

24 Kilcreevanty is in Co. Galway; M. Griffith (ed.), *Calendar of the Justiciary Rolls or the proceedings of the Court of the Justiciar of Ireland. I–VII Edward II*, prepared under the direction of H. Wood and A.E. Langman (Dublin, 1957), pp. 113–14.

25 From Patent Roll 20 Ed III, calendared in E. Tresham, *Rotulorum Patentium et Clausorum Cancellarie Hibernicae Calendarium* (Dublin, 1828), p. 51.

26 Co. Louth.

27 L.P. Murray and Aubrey Gwynn, 'Archbishop Cromer's register', *Louth Archaeological Society Journal*, Vol. 8 (1933–6), pp. 177–8.

28 Lina Eckenstein, *Women under Monasticism: Chapters on Saint-Lore and Convent Life 500–1500* (Cambridge, 1896), p. 425.

29 E. Curtis (ed.), *Calendar of Ormond Deeds 1172–1603* (Dublin, 1932–43), Vol. III, p. 297.

30 Public Record Office of Northern Ireland (PRONI), 'Prene's Register', ff. 17v–20, and transcript, Dublin, TCD, MS 557/6, pp. 414–9.

31 For the evidence for the foundation of the priory of St John the Baptist in Cork see Mills, *Calendar*, p. 154 (8 July 1297) and *Calendar of Documents of Ireland*, Vol. IV, pp. 363–5 (19 April 1301).

32 *Calendar of Documents of Ireland*, Vol. IV, p. 365, and Mills, *Calendar*, pp. 154–5.

33 *State Papers: Henry VIII* (London, 1832–52), Vol. III, p. 130.

34 John Nellan, 'A commentary on the nobility and gentry of Thomond, c. 1567, from Oxford, Bodlein, Carte MS 55', transcribed by K.W. Nicholls, *Irish Genealogist*, Vol. 4, No. 2 (1968), pp. 70–1.

35 J.T. Gilbert (ed.), *Chartularies of St Mary's Abbey, Dublin* (London, 1884), Vol. I, pp. 165–70; also see for discussion A.J. Otway-Ruthven, 'Parochial development in the rural deanery in Skreen', *Journal of the Royal Society of Antiquarians of Ireland*, Vol. 94 (1964), p. 119 and Kelly, p. 52.

36 Theiner, op. cit., p. 86; and *Pontifica Hibernica*, p. 317.

37 Rowena Archer, '"How ladies … who live on their manors ought to manage their households and estates": Women as Landholders and Administrators in the Later Middle Ages' in P.J.P. Goldberg (ed.), *Woman is a worthy wight: Women in Medieval English Society*

1200–1500 (Gloucester, 1992), pp. 149–81.

38 National Archives of Ireland, 'Calendar of Common Bench Rolls, Dublin, Roll Nos 47 and 48, 28 Ed I', RC 7/7, pp. 8, 56, 105, 131, 141–3.

39 M. Archdall, *Monasticon Hibernicum or an history of the Abbies, Priorie and other religious houses in Ireland* (London, 1786), pp. 217–18 quoting the Chief Rememberencer.

40 Kathleen Cooke, 'The English nuns and the Dissolution' in John Blair and Brian Golding (eds), *The Cloister and the World: Essays in Medieval History in Honour of Barbara Harvey* (Oxford, 1996), pp. 286–301.

41 B. Bradshaw, *The Dissolution of the religious orders in Ireland under Henry VIII* (Cambridge, 1974), p. 113.

42 H. Gallwey, 'The Cusack family in Counties Meath and Dublin', *The Irish Genealogist*, Vol. 5 (1974–9), pp. 311, 591–3.

43 She and Anne Weldon were still in receipt of their pensions in the early 1560s, see Rawl. A. '237 Miscellaneous papers relating to Ireland' in C. McNeill, 'Report on recent acquisitions in the Bodlein Library', *Analecta Hibernica*, Vol. 1 (1930), p. 70.

44 National Archives of Ireland, 'Deeds and wills extracted from Inquisitions, Exchequer series', Vol. II, Eliz 1–James 1, Co. Dublin, RC 10/2, pp. 444–6.

CHAPTER THREE

1 John Wesley (1703–91) founded the Methodist Society in 1739 as an evangelical movement within the Church of England. By 1791 the society had 100,000 members. In Ireland, membership grew from 2,801 in 1767 to 19,292 in 1800. Methodism was strongest in urban areas and among English-speaking Protestants, but had less appeal for those at the top and bottom levels of society and for Catholics. Growth was most pronounced in Ulster, particularly in the area around Lough Erne and in the 'linen triangle' south of Belfast. See David Hempton, 'Methodism in Irish society, 1770–1830', *Transactions of the Royal Historical Society*, 5th series, Vol. 26 (1986), pp. 117–42.

2 John Wesley, 'On family religion' in Thomas Jackson (ed.), *Works*, Vol. VII (London, 1872), pp. 76–86, esp. 79.

3 Ibid., p. 86. For a discussion of Wesley's views on the family, see Robert C. Monk, *John Wesley: his puritan heritage* (London, 1966), pp. 180–92.

4 Henry Abelove, 'The sexual politics of early Wesleyan Methodism' in J. Obelkevich, L. Roper and R. Samuel (eds), *Disciplines of faith: studies in religion, politics and patriarchy* (London, 1987), pp. 86–99, 92–3; Gail Malmgreen, 'Domestic discords: women and the family in East Cheshire Methodism, 1750–1830', ibid., pp. 55–70, 61.

5 C.H. Crookshank, *History of Methodism in Ireland*, Vol. I (Belfast, 1885), p. 22.

6 Olwen Hufton, *The prospect before her: a history of women in Western Europe, 1500–1800* (London, 1995), p. 357.

7 Max Weber, *Sociology of Religion* (London, 1966).

8 Hufton, *The prospect before her*, p. 415.

9 Ibid., pp. 415–16. For a discussion of the reasons for Methodism's success, see David Hempton and Myrtle Hill, 'Women and Protestant minorities in eighteenth-century Ireland' in Margaret MacCurtain and Mary O'Dowd (eds), *Women in early modern Ireland* (Dublin, 1991), pp. 197–211, and Hempton, 'Methodism in Irish society', pp. 119–25, 128–33.

10 E.K. Brown, 'Women of Mr Wesley's Methodism', *Studies in Women and Religion*, Vol. II (New York, 1983), quoted in Hempton and Hill, 'Women and Protestant minorities', p. 197; Malmgreen, 'Domestic discords', pp. 57–8; David Hempton, *Methodism and politics in British society, 1750–1850* (London, 1984), p. 13.

11 Crookshank, *History*; Crookshank, *Memorable women of Irish Methodism in the last century*

(London, 1882); Hempton and Hill, 'Women and Protestant minorities'; Hempton and Hill, *Evangelical Protestantism in Ulster society, 1740–1890* (London, 1992), pp. 129–42.

12 John Walsh, 'Methodism and the mob in the eighteenth century' in G. J. Cuming and Derek Baker (eds), *Popular belief and practice* (Cambridge, 1972), pp. 213–27, 224; Hempton and Hill, *Evangelical Protestantism*, p. 137.

13 Crookshank, *Memorable women*, p. 135.

14 Crookshank, *History*, Vol. I, p. 216; Vol. II, p. 11.

15 Ibid., p. 329.

16 Ibid., pp. 263, 277.

17 Ibid., pp. 255, 293.

18 Hempton, *Methodism and politics*, p. 119; Hempton and Hill, *Evangelical Protestantism*, p. 8. According to Hempton and Hill 'in England Wesley saw himself as having a special, but not exclusive ministry to the poor, and frequently made barbed criticisms of the worldliness of the English Church and its gentry patrons'. In Ireland, however, efforts to make converts among the poor had much less success. Obstacles included the peasantry's loyalty to Catholicism, the opposition of the Catholic priesthood and the language barrier – although Irish-speaking itinerant preachers were deployed in an effort to overcome this difficulty.

19 Crookshank, *History*, Vol. I, p. 293.

20 Ibid., p. 255.

21 Ibid., p. 203.

22 For example, both Edward and William Smyth followed their wives into the society. The third example cited above was also converted (Crookshank, *History*, Vol. I, pp. 203, 256, 302).

23 Crookshank, *Memorable women*, pp. 8–9.

24 Crookshank, *History*, Vol. I, pp. 192, 216.

25 Ibid., p. 211.

26 Ibid., pp. 287, 362.

27 Ibid., pp. 290–1.

28 Ibid., p. 229.

29 John Wesley, *Christian correspondence: a collection of letters written by the late Rev. John Wesley, and several Methodist preachers in connexion with him, to the late Mrs Eliza Bennis, with her answers* (Dublin, 1842). Eliza Bennis to John Wesley, Limerick, 8 July 1770, pp. 34–7, 36 (hereafter referred to as EB to JW).

30 Wesley, *Christian correspondence*, JW to EB, Limerick, 15 May 1771, p. 43. For other examples of Wesley's reliance on EB, see ibid., JW to EB, Yarm, 13 June 1770, pp. 33–4; JW to EB, Ashby, 27 July 1770, pp. 37–8; JW to EB, Colchester, 3 November 1772, pp. 65–6; also Crookshank, *History*, Vol. I, pp. 237, 250, 253, 264.

31 Crookshank, *History*, Vol. I, p. 354; John James McGregor, *Memoir of Miss Alice Cambridge ... compiled from her papers and the communications of friends* (Dublin, 1832), p. 38. Alice Cambridge was born in 1762 in Bandon, Co. Cork and joined the Methodist Society in about 1780. She spoke at meetings all over Ireland, becoming one of the most famous Methodist female preachers. Ill-health forced her to retire in 1823 and she died in 1829.

32 McGregor, *Memoir of Miss Alice Cambridge*, p. 39.

33 MS 4810, Wicklow Papers, National Library of Ireland (NLI); Mrs Blachford's career is described in Crookshank, *Memorable women*, pp. 140–7.

34 Crookshank, *Memorable women*, pp. 152–9. On the role of women in eighteenth-century philanthropy, see Rosemary Raughter, 'A natural tenderness: the reality and the ideal of eighteenth-century female charity' in Mary O'Dowd and Maryann Valiulis (eds), *Women and Irish history: essays in honour of Margaret MacCurtain* (Dublin, 1997), pp. 71–88.

35 For details of the social background of these individuals, see Crookshank, *Memorable*

women, pp. 105, 117, 140, 152–3.

36 Ibid., p. 121.

37 Ibid., p. 462.

38 Ibid., p. 256.

39 Ibid., p. 142. Details of the social relationships of these families can be found in MSS 3575, 4810, 4814, Wicklow Papers, NLI and in MS 18,430, diary of Lady Anne Jocelyn, NLI, passim.

40 Crookshank, *History*, Vol. I, pp. 180, 235; Hempton, 'Methodism in Irish society', p. 117.

41 Crookshank, *History*, Vol. I, pp. 263, 293.

42 Crookshank, *Memorable women*, pp. 137–8, 142; Crookshank, *History*, Vol. I, p. 303. On Mrs Smyth's contacts with local women, see Crookshank, ibid., pp. 307, 360. On the Smyths and Margaret Davidson, see Crookshank, ibid., pp. 300–2.

43 McGregor, *Memoir of Miss Alice Cambridge*, pp. 15–17.

44 Crookshank, *Memorable women*, pp. 37, 60.

45 See Dorothea Johnson, *Memoirs* (Cavan, 1818). Dorothea was fifty-two when she married John Johnson.

46 The circuit or round was the district assigned to an itinerant preacher. Ireland was divided by the 1752 Methodist Conference into six circuits (Crookshank, *History*, Vol. I, pp. 92–3). Ministers, therefore, were frequently absent from home for long periods: according to Crookshank in *Memorable women*, p. 15, a married preacher 'could seldom be with his family, more than three days in six weeks'.

47 The first Irish Methodist Conference in 1752 resolved that '£10 a year was to be allowed for the support of each preacher's wife, with something additional for children' (Crookshank, *History*, Vol. I, p. 92). However, some congregations found this expense too onerous. In 1771 Eliza Bennis complained to John Wesley that the congregation in Limerick was 'rather cast down by having another married preacher, with a young family sent to us, before we can recruit our finances … Could we not have a single preacher at least every other year, till we are out of debt?'

48 Wesley, *Christian correspondence*, EB to JW, Limerick, 15 October 1771, p. 50.

49 Crookshank, *History*, Vol. I, p. 307.

50 Crookshank, *Memorable women*, pp. 94–8.

51 Crookshank, *History*, Vol. I, p. 342.

52 Crookshank, *Memorable women*, pp. 75–9, 84.

53 Crookshank, *History*, Vol. I, p. 218.

54 Ibid., p. 61.

55 Ibid., p. 217.

56 Ibid.

57 Walsh, 'Methodism and the mob', p. 221, notes 'many instances of sexual assault or indecent behaviour to women' in the accounts of mob violence against Methodists.

58 For further discussion of the reasons for anti-Methodist violence, see Walsh, 'Methodism and the mob', pp. 213–27; on dissension within the family, see Malmgreen, 'Domestic discords', pp. 64–5.

59 Crookshank, *History*, Vol. I, p. 238.

60 Ibid., p. 437. On Miss Acton, see ibid., p. 428. Mrs Moore was probably Mrs Henry Moore, wife of a Methodist preacher.

61 For a discussion of Wesley's views on marriage and celibacy, see Abelove, *The sexual politics of early Wesleyan Methodism*, pp. 86–9.

62 McGregor, *Memoir of Miss Alice Cambridge*, p. 24.

63 Johnson, *Memoirs*, p. 15.

64 Ibid., p. 41.

65 For details of Alice Cambridge's tours, see McGregor, *Memoir of Miss Alice Cambridge*, pp. 38, 52–3, 55, 57, 59, 62, 64, 70, 72–3, 74, 76, 84, 86.

66 Wesley, *Christian correspondence*, EB to Mr -, Limerick, 18 October 1756, p. 285.
67 Ibid., pp. 287–8.
68 Malmgreen, 'Domestic discords', p. 60.
69 McGregor, *Memoir of Miss Alice Cambridge*, pp. 7, 9.
70 Crookshank, *Memorable women*, p. 37.
71 Crookshank, *History*, Vol. I, p. 289; Crookshank, *Memorable women*, pp. 101–2.
72 In 1802, for instance, the Irish Methodist Conference expressed disapproval of female preaching. Other factors inhibiting women's influence included the ordination of Methodist preachers from 1816 and the formalisation of structures of church government. See Hempton and Hill, 'Women and Protestant minorities', pp. 202–3; and Malmgreen, 'Domestic discords', pp. 66–7.

CHAPTER FOUR

1 This article is a synopsis of a more in-depth study which I am conducting into Frances Anne, Theresa and Edith Londonderry. I would like to thank the Institute of Irish Studies of The Queen's University of Belfast and the trustees of the Eoin O'Mahony Bursary for financial assistance in conducting this research.
2 For commentary on the Londonderrys' financial position, see John Bateman, *The great landowners of Great Britain and Ireland* (Leicester, 1971 reprint of first edn, 1876) and W.D. Rubinstein, *Men of property. The very wealthy in Britain since the industrial revolution* (London, 1981).
3 The family controlled two parliamentary seats in Co. Down and two in Co. Durham.
4 On the role of upper-class women in politics, see P.J. Jupp, 'The roles of royal and aristocratic women in British politics, c. 1782–1832' in Mary O'Dowd and Sabine Wichert (eds), *Chattel, servant or citizen* (Belfast, 1995), pp. 103–13 and Karl van den Steinen, 'The discovery of women in eighteenth century political life' in Barbara Kanner (ed.), *The women of England from Anglo-Saxon times to the present* (London, 1980), pp. 229–58.
5 Memoirs of Frances Anne, 3rd Marchioness of Londonderry, 27 December 1848 (hereafter Memoirs of Frances Anne), Public Record Office of Northern Ireland (PRONI), D3030/RR/1 and typescript copy D3084/C/A/1, pp. 3, 13.
6 Ibid., p. 6. For instance, in 1819 the gross rental of Frances Anne's Durham estate was £11,136 16s 8d and in the first six months of 1822 her collieries at Rainton and Penshaw earned £61,364 2s 11d (Durham County Record Office, D/Lo/E/489 and D/Lo/B/249).
7 Memoirs of Frances Anne, p. 7.
8 Ibid., p. 14.
9 H. Montgomery Hyde, *The Londonderrys. A family portrait* (London, 1979), p. 25.
10 This occurred after the suicide of his half-brother, Lord Castlereagh (1769–1822). Charles was re-offered this post twenty years later, but refused to accept the position.
11 Unsourced newspaper cutting, included in PRONI, D2846/3/24/1.
12 Christopher Simon Sykes, *Private palaces. Life in the great London houses* (London, 1985), p. 242.
13 Edith Londonderry, *Letters from Benjamin Disraeli to Frances Anne* (London, 1938), p. 172.
14 For instance, J.M. Bourne, *Patronage and society in nineteenth century England* (London, 1986), p. 53 refers to Disraeli as 'truly an outsider and his career owed much to aristocratic patronage'.
15 Londonderry, *Letters*, p. 3.
16 Ibid., pp. xv–xvi.
17 Leonore Davidoff, *The best circles* (London, 1973), p. 73.

18 G.E. Buckle, *The life of Benjamin Disraeli* (London, 1916), Vol. IV, p. 382.
19 Londonderry, *Letters*, p. 79.
20 M.G. Wiebe, J.B. Connacher, John Matthews and Mary Millar (eds), *Benjamin Disraeli letters: 1842–7* (Buffalo and London, 1989), Vol. IV, p. 266.
21 Londonderry, *Letters*, p. 41.
22 Ibid., p. 31.
23 Robert Blake, *Disraeli* (London, 1966), p. 155.
24 Benjamin Disraeli, *Sybil* (London, 1927 reprint of first edn 1845), p. 312.
25 Londonderry, *Letters*, pp. 11–12.
26 Ibid., p. 143.
27 For example, Disraeli tried, unsuccessfully, to prevent Frances Anne's son Adolphus (1825–64) from losing his parliamentary seat for Durham in 1852. In 1854 Adolphus succeeded his brother Henry as MP for N. Durham. For details on the electoral fortunes of the Londonderry family, see Alan Heesom, *Durham City and its MPs, 1678–1992* (Durham, 1992).
28 See PRONI D3030/JJ/13A.
29 Londonderry, *Letters*, p. 187.
30 Ibid., p. 259.
31 Buckle, *The life of Benjamin Disraeli*, p. 304.
32 Memoirs of Frances Anne, p. 1.
33 Londonderry, *Letters*, p. 193.
34 Frederick, fourth Marquess of Londonderry (1805–72), MP for N. Durham 1847–54, thereafter a member of the House of Lords.
35 Henry, fifth Marquess of Londonderry (1821–84).
36 Political notes of Theresa Londonderry, 10 August 1915 (PRONI, D3084/C/B/1/3) and diary extract, 5 December 1918 (PRONI, D3084/C/B/1/14).
37 Ibid., (PRONI, D3084/C/B/3/1), 10 August 1915.
38 Mark Bence-Jones, *Twilight of the Ascendancy* (London, 1937), p. 159; Edith, seventh Marchioness of Londonderry, *Retrospect* (London, 1938), p. 173. For instance, the agreement of April 1911 to organise Unionist propaganda was named the Londonderry House Agreement, as this was where the majority of negotiations had taken place.
39 Margot Asquith, *An autobiography* (London, 1920), p. 191.
40 E.F. Benson cited in Brian Masters, *Wynyard Park* (Teeside, 1973), p. 58.
41 Anne de Courcy, *Circe. The life of Edith, Marchioness of Londonderry* (London, 1992), p. 36.
42 Edmund Gosse to Theresa Londonderry, 12 May 1910 (PRONI, D2846/2/26).
43 Edward Carson to Theresa Londonderry, c. 1913 (PRONI, D2846/1/1/157) and H. Montgomery Hyde, *Carson. The life of Sir Edward Carson, Lord Carson of Duncairn* (London, 1953), p. 125.
44 Ian Colvin, *The life of Lord Carson* (London, 1936), Vol. II, p. 443.
45 Notes of H. Montgomery Hyde on a conversation with Mrs St George Robinson, sister of Edward Carson, 22 July 1950 (PRONI, D3084/H/3/9).
46 Montgomery Hyde, *Carson*, p. 297. Theresa felt that if Carson had been properly approached, he would have accepted the leadership of the Conservative Party in 1911.
47 See, for example, PRONI, D3084/C/B/2/33.
48 This petition was presented to the Commons by Mr Ross, Unionist MP for Londonderry city, 1892–95. Ulster women's signatories numbered 19,632. Nancy Kinghan, *United we stood. The story of the Ulster Women's Unionist Council* (Belfast, 1973), p. 8.
49 UWUC minute book, 29 January 1919 (PRONI, D1098/1/3). Theresa retained this position until a few months before her death in 1919.
50 UWUC Executive Committee minute book, 30 January 1911 (PRONI, D1098/1/1).
51 *UWUC Year Book* (Belfast, 1920).

52 Theresa Londonderry's political notes, 25 November 1915 (PRONI, D3084/C/B/2/56).
53 Ibid., 24 May 1917 (PRONI, D3084/C/B/2/86–91).
54 Ibid., 22 February 1919 (PRONI, D3084/C/B/2/163).
55 Ronald McNeill, *Ulster's stand for union* (London, 1922), p. 112.
56 UWUC minute book, 29 January 1919 (PRONI, D1098/1/3).
57 For details on Edith's early life, see Edith Londonderry, *Henry Chaplin. A memoir* (London, 1926).
58 Londonderry, *Retrospect*, p. 72.
59 See PRONI, D3084/C/B/3/2.
60 Edith actively supported the women's suffrage movement and was a firm believer in women's capabilities. She was awarded a military DBE for establishing the Women's Legion, the first woman to be honoured in this way.
61 Edith Londonderry to Theresa Londonderry, 16 February 1915 (PRONI, D3084/C/E/2/13).
62 See PRONI, D3099/3/13/1–153 and D3099/3/15/1–91.
63 Samuel Hoare to Edith Londonderry, 22 April 1936 (PRONI, D3099/3/15/54).
64 de Courcy, *Circe*, p. 168.
65 *UWUC Annual Report*, 1922 (PRONI, D 2688/1/9). Women appointed under the Ulster scheme were to act as telephonists, telegraphists, nurses, cooks, policewomen and searchers to deal with women suspected of carrying arms or documents.
66 Montgomery Hyde, *The Londonderrys*, p. 159.
67 David Marquand, *Ramsay MacDonald* (London, 1977), p. 693.
68 A.J.P. Taylor (ed.), *Lloyd George. A diary by Francis Stevenson* (London, 1971), pp. 254, 302.
69 de Courcy, *Circe*, p. 231.
70 Ramsay MacDonald to Edith Londonderry, 12 September 1930 (PRONI, D3084/C/D/4/53).
71 Charles Londonderry to Edith Londonderry, 14 April 1932 (PRONI, D3804/CE/29).
72 *Liverpool Post and Echo*, review of H. Montgomery Hyde, *The Londonderrys*, 13 September 1979.
73 H. Montgomery Hyde to Lady Mairi Bury (PRONI, D3084/C/F/6/180).
74 Lord Londonderry explained his motivation for visiting Germany at this time in *Ourselves and Germany* (London, 1938). For information on other aristocrats trying to improve Anglo-German relations, see David Cannadine, *The decline and fall of the British aristocracy* (London and New Haven, 1994), pp. 549–50.
75 Death duties were introduced in 1889 and increased in 1894. The aristocracy, however, were more severely affected in 1919 when duties of up to 40% were introduced on estates worth over £2m. On the changing fortunes of the aristocracy, see Cannadine, *The decline and fall*. The Londonderrys had to pay over £110,000 in death duties following the death of the seventh Marquess in 1949 (*Belfast Telegraph*, 18 June 1949).
76 H. Montgomery Hyde, *Londonderry House and its pictures* (London, 1937), p. vi.
77 Londonderry, *Retrospect*, pp. 251–3.
78 Ibid., p. 11.

CHAPTER FIVE

1 Mary Poovey, *Uneven Developments: The Ideological Work of Gender in Mid-Victorian England* (Chicago, 1988), pp. 164–6. Poovey's discussion of Nightingale becoming more symbol than reality and her analysis of the uses of the 'nightingale image' are both interesting and helpful. She examines the ways in which Nightingale became a symbol of nineteenth-century womanhood. By analysing an obituary written by Harriet Martineau

when Nightingale was thought to have died of a fever in the Crimea, Poovey shows that this image had little relation to the woman herself. Martineau drew on information about the work of the nurses, but implied that Nightingale had single-handedly walked the corridors of the wards tending the sick, caring for orphaned children and comforting the soldiers. Poovey believes that this account ignores both the presence of other nurses and the fact that Nightingale was not only 'a housewifely woman', to use Martineau's description, but also a rigorous administrator. Poovey argues that Nightingale could make use of domestic imagery when it suited her purposes, but could also stress her public work when that was necessary. The earliest published source on the sisters in the Crimean War is Austen Carroll, *Leaves from the Annals of the Sisters of Mercy* (Silver Spring, MD, c. 1881, 4 vols.). This work contains no footnotes and Carroll does not always attribute letters or excerpts from diaries to particular authors, but incorporates them in the text with phrases such as 'one Sister wrote home that' or 'one account says'. See also Evelyn Bolster, *The Sisters of Mercy in the Crimean War* (Cork, 1964); articles in L. Verne and Bonnie Bullough (eds), *Florence Nightingale and Her Era: A Collection of Recent Scholarship* (New York, 1990); Sr Mary McAuley Gillgannon, 'The Sisters of Mercy as Crimean War Nurses' (unpublished PhD thesis, University of Notre Dame, 1961); Sr Mary Aloysius [Doyle], *Memories of the Crimea* (London, 1897). Doyle was one of the sisters from Ireland led by Francis Bridgeman. Her work contains many letters and its preface indicates that it was published to tell a part of the well-known story of the Crimean War which had not yet been heard by a wide audience.

2 Cecil Woodham-Smith, *Florence Nightingale, 1820–1910* (New York, 1951), pp. 1–7.
3 Ibid., p. 9.
4 Alison A. Anderson, 'Florence Nightingale: Constructing a Vocation', *Anglican Theological Review*, Vol. 78, No. 3 (Summer 1996), pp. 408, 411.
5 Christopher D. Olson, 'Historical Nursing Leader: Florence Nightingale', downloaded from the InterNurse homepage.
6 Charleville and Bermondsey Sisters in the Crimean War, pp. 120–1. This is a bound volume of photocopies of microfilmed documents, including extracts from the Bermondsey annals, an anonymous life of Mary Clare Moore and the Crimean War diary of Sr Mary Joseph Croke of Charleville, Ireland; Mother M. Evangelist Fallon, *Life of Mother Mary Francis Bridgeman, 1813–1888* (Silver Spring, Maryland), pp. 1–2; Sr Mary Lucy McDonald RSM, *By Her Fruits: Sr. Mary Joseph Lynch Sister of Mercy* (Royal Oak, MI, 1981); Joanne G. Widerquist, 'Dearest Rev. Mother', in L. Verne and Bonnie Bullough (eds), *Florence Nightingale and her era*, pp. 288–9.
7 Marie Jeanne d'Arc Hughes RSM, 'Crimean Diary of Mother M. Francis Bridgeman: War Companion of Florence Nightingale, 1854–1856' (unpublished MA thesis, Catholic University of America), pp. 136–7.
8 Mary Ellen Doona, 'Sister Mary Joseph Croke: Another Voice From the Crimean War, 1854–1856', *Nursing History Review*, Vol. 3 (1995), pp. 25, 29.
9 Michael Hurst, 'Crimean War' in J. Wieczynski (ed.), *The Modern Encyclopedia of Russian and Soviet History* (Gulf Breeze, FL, 1976), pp. 104–5.
10 Ibid., p. 105.
11 Ibid., p. 113.
12 Fanny Taylor, *Eastern Hospitals and English Nurses: The Narrative of Twelve Months Experience in The Hospitals of Koulali and Scutari by a Lady Volunteer* (London, 1856).
13 Ibid., pp. 6–7.
14 Ibid., pp. 8–10. Many of the accounts written by Sisters of Mercy do not distinguish between lay women and Anglican sisters, so it is possible that some of those whom they describe as ladies were not upper-class lay women like Florence Nightingale, Mary Stanley and Fanny Taylor, but nuns. It is interesting that, although the Sisters of Mercy do not distinguish between different denominations of 'Protestants', they do see the

Anglican sisters and the upper-class lay women as ladies and, therefore, distinct from both themselves and hired nurses.

15 Ibid., pp. 13–14.

16 Mary Joseph Lynch, *An Account of the Mission of the Sisters of Mercy in the Hospitals of the East* (Silver Spring, MD), p. 243.

17 Taylor, *Eastern Hospitals and English Nurses*, pp. 175–7.

18 Anderson, 'Florence Nightingale', pp. 1–4.

19 Mary Francis Bridgeman, *An Account of the Mission of the Sisters of Mercy in the Military Hospitals of the East 1854–1856* (Archives of the Religious Sisters of Mercy, Silver Spring, Maryland), pp. 6–8.

20 Anon., 'Life of Mother M. Clare Moore', in *Charleville and Bermondsey Sisters in the Crimean War*, p. 125.

21 Sue M. Goldie (ed.), *'I Have Done My Duty': Florence Nightingale in the Crimean War 1854–1856* (Iowa City, 1987), pp. 55–6.

22 Ibid., pp. 60–1.

23 Ibid., p. 64.

24 Ibid., pp. 89–90.

25 Ibid., p. 141.

26 Lynch, *An Account of the Mission of the Sisters of Mercy*, pp. 244–53.

27 Ibid.

28 Bridgeman, *An Account of the Mission of the Sisters of Mercy*, pp. 6–8.

29 Lynch, *An Account of the Mission of the Sisters of Mercy*, pp. 318–24.

30 Ibid.

31 Ibid.

32 Some of the Irish sisters from the second group and some historians imply that Moore was too conciliatory in her relationship with Nightingale. There are implications in other accounts that Moore might even have neglected her own and her patients' spiritual needs in her attempts to please Nightingale. However, her biographer stressed that she fulfilled her nursing and religious responsibilities in an exemplary manner and always remained obedient to her ecclesiastical superiors.

33 Poovey, *Uneven Developments*, p. 173.

34 Ibid., pp. 174–5.

35 Ibid., p. 176.

36 In the case of Nightingale, Lynch felt that she was too conscious of her own social position.

37 Lynch, *An Account of the Mission of the Sisters of Mercy*, pp. 377–81. Lynch clearly accepts distinctions based on class or on social status, but it is important to remember that she also reports charges of proselytising by the sisters as discussed earlier. If some believed that the sisters' religion interfered with their work as nurses, it would be important to assert their willingness to be co-operative and flexible. Therefore, by describing a good working relationship between other nurses and the sisters, Lynch indirectly refutes the charges of 'religious interference' by demonstrating that the sisters were not anti-Protestant.

38 Bridgeman, *An Account of the Mission of the Sisters of Mercy*, pp. 15–17. Bridgeman's account was dictated to Sr Mary Joseph Lynch, who at times reported Bridgeman's words and at times described what Bridgeman did or said. This is an instance of the latter, so we do not have Bridgeman's feelings on class directly. This passage also reveals the ways in which religion and class are intertwined. One wonders whether Bridgeman objected to eating with the second class passengers because most were Protestant, or because they were working class. Rather than determining which might have been more objectionable to her, it is important to note that both factors played a role.

39 Carroll, *Leaves from the Annals of the Sisters of Mercy*.

40 See especially Bonnie Smith, *Ladies of The Leisure Class: The Bourgeoisie of Northern France in the Nineteenth Century* (Princeton, 1981) and Ann F. la Berge, 'Medicalization

and Moralization: the Creches of Nineteenth-Century Paris', *Journal of Social History* (Fall, 1991), Vol. 25, No. 1, pp. 65–87.

41 Poovey, *Uneven Developments*, pp. 181–2.

42 Taylor, *Eastern Hospitals and English Nurses*, pp. 161–3.

43 Carroll, *Leaves from the Annals of the Sisters of Mercy*, pp. 181–2.

44 The sensational case of Pierce Connelly vs. Cornelia Connelly had been resolved shortly before the sisters left for the Crimea, and the anti-Catholic feelings it provoked must have been fresh in their memories. Mrs Connelly had founded the Society of the Holy Child Jesus after her husband Pierce had been ordained to the Catholic priesthood. He then decided that he no longer wanted to be a priest and sued Cornelia for restoration of conjugal rights. She won the case after an appeal despite Pierce's assertions that she was being held in a convent against her will, and that by living in one, Cornelia was essentially living in a brothel. Mr Henry Drummond, MP for West Surrey and a friend of Pierce's, made proposals for inspection of convents at this time: 'These female religious houses are, in point of fact, either prisons or brothels; indeed, with greater truth one might say they are both'. For an account of Cornelia Connelly's life by a member of the society, see Catherine Gomperts SHCJ, *The Life of Cornelia Connelly 1809–1879: Foundress of the Society of the Holy Child Jesus* (London, 1922). For accounts of Pierce's attempts to control Cornelia and the Society, including his suit, see Gomperts, passim; Positio, *Documentary Study for the Canonization Process of the Servant of God, Cornelia Connelly (nee Peacock) 1809–1879* (Rome, 1983), pp. 302, 306, 307–8 (for the quotation from Drummond), pp. 322, 327.

45 Bernard I. Cohen, 'Florence Nightingale', *Scientific American*, 250 (March, 1984), pp. 128–37.

46 Downloaded from the InterNurse homepage, which contains an article about Nightingale and links to other sites related to her work, as well as this recording.

47 Taylor, *Eastern Hospitals and English Nurses*, pp. 98–9.

CHAPTER SIX

1 Maria Luddy, 'Isabella M. S. Tod (1836–96)' in M. Cullen and M. Luddy (eds), *Women, Power and Consciousness in Nineteenth-Century Ireland* (Dublin, 1995), p. 198.

2 Ibid.

3 J.R. Fisher, *The Ulster Liberal Unionist Association: A Sketch of its History* (Belfast, 1914), p. 19.

4 G. Lucy, *The Great Convention: The Ulster Unionist Convention of 1892* (Lurgan, 1995), pp. 42–3.

5 G. Greenlee, 'Ulster Liberalism, Constructive Unionism and the Issue of Home Rule' (unpublished DPhil thesis, University of Ulster, 1996), p. 99.

6 For one of the few discussions on the role played by women in the Unionist movement before the third home rule crisis, see D. Urquhart, 'The Political Role of Women in North East Ulster, 1890–1940' (unpublished PhD thesis, the Queen's University of Belfast, 1996).

7 R. McNeill, *Ulster's Stand for Union* (London, 1912), p. 12.

8 *The Northern Whig (TNW)*, 1 May 1886.

9 *Belfast News-Letter (BNL)*, 9 December 1896.

10 Ibid.

11 Luddy, 'Isabella Tod', p. 199.

12 Margaret Byers, Tod's friend, fellow women's activist and Liberal Unionist, was also a member of the Elmwood congregation. See A. Jordan, *Margaret Byers: Pioneer of Women's Education and Founder of Victoria College, Belfast* (Belfast, 1993).

13 Tod was one of only 5% of those involved in charitable institutions who served on four or more committees. See A. Jordan, 'Voluntary Societies in Victorian and Edwardian Belfast' (unpublished PhD thesis, The Queen's University of Belfast, 1989), ii, p. 632.

14 *TNW*, 21 March 1880.

15 *The Weekly Northern Whig* (*WNW*), 29 March 1886.

16 Tod sent a private pamphlet to all Ulster's MPs in 1884 in an attempt to raise their awareness of women's issues entitled, *Women and the New Franchise Bill: A Letter to an Ulster Member of Parliament* (Belfast, 1884).

17 I.M.S. Tod to Lord Ava, 12 September 1868 (Public Record Office of Northern Ireland [PRONI], D. 1071 H/B/T, Box 3). I would like to thank Dr A.P.W. Malcolmson for granting permission to view this collection.

18 See *TNW*, 13 December 1886 for Russell's speech at the National Society for Women's Suffrage meeting in Belfast on 12 December. Tod and Haslett also made addresses.

19 See B.M. Walker, *Ulster Politics: The Formative Years* (Belfast, 1989) and F. Wright, *Two Lands on One Soil: Ulster Politics before Home Rule* (Dublin, 1996).

20 P. Gibbon, *The Origins of Ulster Unionism: The Formation of Popular Protestant Politics and Ideology in Nineteenth-Century Ireland* (Manchester, 1975), p. 109.

21 The Conservatives took eighteen seats and the Nationalists took the remaining two.

22 The Conservatives took sixteen seats and the Nationalists seventeen.

23 *TNW*, 27 February 1886.

24 Ibid., 5 February 1886.

25 Minutes of the Political Sub-Committee of the Ulster Reform Club, 26 February 1886 (Club Minute Book of 4 May 1880–18 March 1892, Ulster Reform Club, Belfast).

26 *TNW*, 21 March 1886.

27 Ibid.

28 Ibid., 13 April 1886.

29 Ibid., 27 April 1886.

30 I.M.S. Tod to James Bryce, 13 June 1892 (Bodleian Library, Oxford, MSS 213 ff. 171–4) cited by Greenlee, 'Ulster Liberalism, Constructive Unionism', p. 99.

31 Isabella Tod, 'The Present Duty of Women in Ireland', *TNW*, 9 April 1892.

32 *TNW*, 1 May 1886.

33 Tod, 'The Present Duty of Women'.

34 Ibid.

35 L.P. Curtis, *Anglo-Saxons and Celts* (Bridgeport, 1969).

36 Tod, 'The Present Duty of Women'.

37 Ibid.

38 *TNW*, 1 May 1886.

39 Ibid., 17 June 1892.

40 J. Harrison, *The Scot in Ulster: A Sketch of the Scottish Population of Ulster* (Edinburgh and London, 1888).

41 Davitt made the accusation during a heated exchange with Tod at a debate on the Irish question called by the National Political Union in London. See *TNW*, 11 June 1886.

42 Tod, 'The Present Duty of Women'.

43 J.R.B. McMinn, 'Presbyterianism and Politics, 1871–1906', *Studia Hibernica*, No. 21 (1981), pp. 127–46.

44 I.M.S. Tod to the Marquis of Dufferin and Ava, 13 July 1896 (PRONI, D. 1071 H/B/T, Box 3). Pirrie was made an Irish Privy Councillor in 1897.

45 Luddy, 'Isabella Tod', p. 198.

46 B. Caine, *Victorian Feminists* (Oxford, 1992), pp. 144–5. Amongst the other leading feminists who became Conservatives or Liberal Unionists post-1886 were Emily Davies, Frances Power Cobbe, Helen Blackburn, Lilias Ashworth Hallet and Millicent Fawcett.

47 C. Shannon, 'The Ulster Liberal Unionists and Local Government Reform, 1885–98',

Irish Historical Studies, Vol. xxx, No. 32 (September 1973), pp. 407–23.

48 *TNW*, 1 May 1886.
49 The *Whig* thought that Tod made 'a singularly able plea' on Courtney's behalf at an election rally in Torpoint, *TNW*, 21 June 1886.
50 *BNL*, 14 May 1886.
51 *WNW*, 26 May and 2 June 1888. See also *TNW*, 6 April 1892 for the most complete membership list.
52 The Primrose League, established in 1883, had half a million members in Great Britain and Ireland by 1887. M. Pugh, *The Tories and the People, 1880–1935* (Oxford, 1985), p. 25. In 1886, the league had 1,060 Irish members. See *TNW*, 7 May 1888.
53 Mrs Jaffe, the wife of Otto Jaffe, Belfast's only Jewish Lord Mayor, and Miss Byers also later sat on the central association.
54 M. Pugh, 'The Limits of Liberalism: Liberalism and Women's Suffrage, 1867–1914', in E.F. Biagini (ed.), *Citizenship and Community: Liberals, Radicals and Collective Identities in the British Isles, 1865–1931* (Cambridge, 1996), p. 48.
55 *WNW*, 2 June 1888.
56 *BNL*, 9 December 1896 and *The Witness*, 11 December 1896.
57 *WNW*, 24 June 1892.
58 Tod's house was evidently used as a centre for constituency business, as Arnold-Forster's wife remarked, 'We go to an afternoon gathering at Miss Tod's today where Oakley [Hugh Oakley Arnold Forster] and Lord Wolmer [Liberal Unionist chief whip] will speak'. Mary Arnold-Forster to Jane Martha Forster, 31 March 1891 (Trinity College, Dublin 5000–1, 163a).
59 *TNW*, 7 April 1893.
60 Ibid.
61 D. Urquhart, 'The Female of the Species is more deadlier than the male'? The Ulster Women's Unionist Council, 1911–1940' in J. Holmes and Urquhart (eds), *Coming into the Light: The Work, Politics and Religion of Women in Ulster, 1840–1940* (Belfast, 1994).
62 *BNL*, 9 December 1896.
63 *TNW*, 12 December 1896.
64 William Currie, *WNW*, 3 July 1886.
65 *TNW*, 12 December 1896.
66 Urquhart, 'The Female of the Species', pp. 93–123.
67 *The Present Position of the Home Rule Question: A Statement Issued to the Public by the Executive Committee of the Liberal Unionist Association* (London, 1890).

CHAPTER SEVEN

1 William Booth, *In Darkest England and the Way Out* (London, 1880), p. 283.
2 Salvationist is a term used for work done or published by a member of the army which expresses the ethos of the organisation.
3 For a more detailed examination, see Gráinne M. Blair, '"Equal Sinners": Irish Women Utilising the Salvation Army Rescue Network for Britain and Ireland in the Nineteenth Century' in Margaret Kelleher and James H. Murphy (eds), *Gender Perspectives in Nineteenth-Century Ireland: Public and Private Spheres* (Dublin, 1997), pp. 179–92.
4 Gráinne M. Blair, 'Josephine Butler and Catherine Booth, Political Alliances: The Importance of the Maiden Tribute Agitation and the Eliza Armstrong Case to the Salvation Army in the Nineteenth Century' in *In From The Shadows: The UL Women's Studies Collection*, Vol. II (1996), pp. 55–65.
5 Gráinne M. Blair, 'The Work that Angels Might Envy: Some Aspects of Salvation Army Rescue Work with Irish Women in the Nineteenth Century' in *Pages*, Vol. III (1996),

pp. 97–111.

6 Booth, *In Darkest England*, p. 47.

7 Catherine Bramwell-Booth, *Catherine Booth* (London, 1970), p. 194; Leonore Davidoff and Catherine Hall, *Family Fortunes: Men and Women of the English Middle Class, 1780–1850* (London, 1987); Christine Ward, 'The Social Sources of the Salvation Army, 1865–1890' (unpub. MPhil thesis, University of London, 1970), p. 29.

8 Ward, 'The Social Sources of the Salvation Army'; Gillian Ball, 'Practical Religion: A Study of the Salvation Army's Social Services for Women, 1884–1914' (unpub. PhD thesis, University of Leicester, 1987).

9 Information on Irish women utilising the Salvation Army rescue network was extracted from unpublished records held in the salvationists' London headquarters. Each case history was recorded by an officer and provides extensive details on the woman's life.

10 Salvation Army Final Reports, Country Book I, 1887–1890.

11 Ibid.

12 Ibid.

13 William Booth, 'What is the Salvation Army' in *Contemporary Review*, Vol. XLII (1882), p. 175.

14 William Booth, *Orders and Regulations of the Salvation Army Part 1* (London, 1878), p. 6.

15 Stuart Mews, 'The General and the Bishops: Alternative Responses to Dechristianisation' in T.R. Gourvish and Alan O'Day (eds), *Problems in Focus: Later Victorian Britain, 1867–1900* (London, 1988), pp. 209–29.

16 Blair, 'Equal Sinners', pp. 187–8; *The War Cry*, 25 May 1882; Frederick Coutts, *No Discharge in this War* (London, 1975), pp. 90–1; Adelaide Cox, *Hotchpotch* (London, 1937), p. 59; K.S. Inglis, 'The Salvation Army' in *Churches and the Working Classes in Victorian England* (London, 1963), p. 192; Frank Prochaska, *Women and Philanthropy in Nineteenth-Century England* (London, 1980), pp. 192–3; *The Times*, 9 September 1879, p. 8; 15 October 1881, p. 10 and 13 January 1883, p. 10. See also Christine Dinnis, 'Organisation and Religious Experience in the Salvation Army 1878–1949' (unpub. MPhil thesis, University of Sussex, 1976), pp. 42–9.

17 Londonderry was the name normally used by Unionists, whilst Nationalists usually referred to the city as Derry. Salvationists used both terms. Colours were the flags given to each corps.

18 Ibid.

19 *The War Cry*, 4 September 1886, p. 4.

20 Ibid.

21 Ibid., 15 May 1880, p. 1.

22 *The Deliverer*, 15 September 1889, p. 27.

23 A citadel is a hall used for worship and as a base for corps operations; *The War Cry*, 13 July 1901, p. 12.

24 *The War Cry*, 13 July 1901, p. 12.

25 Ibid., 4 September 1886, p. 4.

26 Ibid., 12 June 1880, p. 4.

27 Ibid., 4 September 1886, p. 4.

28 Ibid., 13 July 1901, p. 12.

29 In these institutions, most children were brought up as Protestants.

30 Joseph Robbins, *The Lost Children: A Study of Charity Children in Ireland, 1700–1900* (Dublin, 1980), pp. 17–48.

31 Ibid.; Jacinta Prunty, 'Margaret Louisa Aylward' in Mary Cullen and Maria Luddy (eds), *Women, Power and Consciousness in Nineteenth-Century Ireland* (Dublin, 1995), p. 65; Desmond Bowen, *Souperism: Myth or Reality, A Study in Souperism* (Cork, 1987) and Desmond Bowen, *Paul Cardinal Cullen and the Shaping of Modern Irish Catholicism*

(Dublin, 1983).
32 *All the World*, September 1902, p. 471.
33 Katherine Butler, 'Dublin's Hallelujah Lassies' in *Dublin Historical Record*, Vol. XLII, No. 4 (September 1989), pp. 128–46.
34 *The Deliverer*, 15 September 1889, p. 27.
35 *The Local Officer*, June 1898.
36 Ibid.
37 Public battles between religious charity organisations were common in nineteenth-century Dublin and were not confined to the salvationists. It was easy to produce large numbers of people on the streets at this time because of lack of employment and overcrowded conditions in the tenements near the main thoroughfares (Prunty, 'Margaret Louisa Aylward').
38 *The War Cry*, 13 July 1901, p. 12.
39 *All the World*, February 1914, pp. 119–22.
40 Ibid., September 1902, p. 472.
41 Ibid.
42 *The War Cry*, 4 September 1886, p. 4.
43 Ibid., p. 471.
44 Other religions also expressed a preference for their own welfare agencies.

CHAPTER EIGHT

1 This meeting is reported in the *Irish Worker*, 9 September 1911.
2 Eloquent and passionate, Larkin had appeared on the Irish labour scene in 1906 when a British dockworkers' union from Liverpool sent him to organise Belfast's dockers. Forging Protestant Unionists and Catholic Nationalists of Belfast into a single union, orange and green together, Larkin led them to a shattering victory which stunned all of Ireland. After that brilliant success he emerged as the dominant leader of the Irish working class. The most comprehensive biography of Jim Larkin is Emmet Larkin, *James Larkin: Irish Labour Leader* (Cambridge, 1965).
3 Larkin was a syndicalist, as far as he had any coherent or systematic political philosophy. Syndicalism advocated the revolutionary change of society, but differed from other schools of socialism, especially Marxism, in the belief that this revolution should be accomplished by the industrial proletariat acting, not through their political parties, but directly through their unions and by means of the general strike to capture the political state. They would then establish a regime of freely co-operative communities.
4 *Irish Worker*, 9 September 1911.
5 Ibid., 22 July 1911.
6 See Emmet O'Connor, *A Labour History of Ireland 1824–1960* (Dublin, 1992), chapters 4 and 5.
7 Desmond Ryan claims that the Irish Textile Workers' Union was affiliated to the IWWU, but this is not how Connolly represents the affiliation in the *Irish Worker*. He argues that it is a branch of his ITGWU. See Desmond Ryan (ed.), *The Worker's Republic: A Selection from the Writings of James Connolly* (Dublin, 1951), p. 106.
8 *Irish Worker*, 28 October 1911.
9 Ibid., 12 August 1911.
10 The IWWU records are contained in the archival collections of the Irish Labour History Society in Dublin. The file on Delia Larkin contains only two pieces of correspondence from 1918 regarding her unsuccessful attempt to re-join the IWWU. The only significant history of the IWWU to date is Mary Jones, *These Obstreperous Lassies: A History of the IWWU* (Dublin, 1988), which covers the early years very broadly in the first chapters.

11 *Irish Worker*, 9 September 1911.
12 Ibid., 16 December 1911.
13 See Nancy Cott, *The Grounding of Modern Feminism* (New Haven, 1987).
14 It is interesting to note that Larkin, herself, did not marry until well into her forties and never surrendered her own surname.
15 *Irish Worker*, 8 March 1913.
16 Ibid., 23 September 1911.
17 Ibid., 7 October 1911.
18 She established exercise classes for members of the IWWU at Liberty Hall.
19 *Irish Worker*, 4 November 1911.
20 Ibid., 4 January 1913.
21 Ibid., 8 March 1913.
22 Ibid.
23 Ibid.
24 Ibid.
25 Ibid.
26 Ibid.
27 The notable exception being Henry Cardinal Manning, Archbishop of Westminster and mediator of the London Dock Strike in 1897. He was known as labour's friend and an advocate of the urban poor. He had no equivalent amongst the Irish bishops.
28 *Irish Worker*, 8 March 1913.
29 See ibid., 10 February 1912 for Delia Larkin's discussion of the wage system.
30 Ibid., 8 March 1913.

CHAPTER NINE

1 Throughout this article I use the word 'madness' rather than the favoured language of the time (lunacy, insanity) or of today (mental illness).The word 'madness' has a long history and recognises the stigma attached to dysfunction in the domain of the mind, important for a study interested less in symptoms and classification (as in a medical model) than in the social context.
2 Elaine Showalter, *The Female Malady* (London, 1987), p. 8.
3 Puerperal mania was believed to be caused by septic poisoning during childbirth; ovarian madness by 'inflammation' of the ovaries; insanity of lactation was brought on by prolonged breastfeeding and climacteric melancholia by menopause. According to these (dubious) medical theories, women's unstable reproductive systems made them vulnerable to madness.
4 W.H. Hallaran, *Practical Observations on the Causes and Cure of Insanity* (Cork, 1818), p. 50.
5 J.C. Bucknill and D.H. Tuke, *A Manual of Psychological Medicine* (New York, 1874), p. 347.
6 Louis Althusser, 'Ideology and ideological state apparatuses (notes towards an investigation)' in *Lenin and Philosophy and other essays*, translated by Ben Brewster (New York, 1971), p. 62.
7 'Annual Reports of Enniscorthy Lunatic Asylum, 1916–1925'. Annual reports and casebooks are held in St Senan's Mental Hospital (formerly Enniscorthy Lunatic Asylum).
8 Showalter, *The Female Malady*, p. 4.
9 Casebook, PN (Patient Number) 4019, 3721, 3310. In order to protect anonymity, the names of all inmates have been changed.
10 Casebook, PN 3972.
11 C.M. McGovern, 'The myths of social control and custodial oppression: Patterns of

psychiatric medicine in late nineteenth-century institutions', *Journal of Social History*, Vol. 20 (Fall, 1986), pp. 3–23.

12 Casebook, PN 4290.

13 Casebook, PN 4221.

14 Casebook, PN 3529.

15 Bucknill and Tuke, *A Manual of Psychological Medicine*, p. 347.

16 For example, the Land Acts of 1881, 1885, 1891, 1903.

17 M.E. Daly, 'Women in the Irish Free State, 1922–1939: The Interaction between economics and ideology', *Journal of Women's History*, Vol. 6, No. 4 (1995), pp. 38–64.

18 Rita M. Rhodes, *Women and the Family in Post-Famine Ireland: Status and Opportunity in a Patriarchal Society* (New York, 1992), pp. 18–32.

19 J.J. Lee, 'Women and the church since the famine' in M. MacCurtain and D. O'Corrain (eds), *Women in Irish Society: The Historical Dimension* (Dublin, 1978), p. 40.

20 Dympna McLoughlin, 'Women and Sexuality in nineteenth-century Ireland', *Irish Journal of Psychology*, Vol. 15, (1994), pp. 266–75.

21 Casebook, PN 3872.

22 Casebook, PN 4177.

23 Casebook, PN 4041.

24 Casebook, PN 3765.

25 Casebook, PN 4122.

26 Letter found in casebook attached to file 4122.

27 McLoughlin, 'Women and Sexuality', p. 273.

28 Casebook, PN 3431.

29 Casebook, PN 4078.

30 Casebook, PN 3774.

31 Compiled from annual reports of Enniscorthy Lunatic Asylum, 1916–1925.

32 Casebook, PN 3990.

33 K.H. Connell, 'Catholicism and Marriage in the century after the Famine', *Irish Peasant Society* (Oxford, 1968), pp. 113–61.

34 Casebook, PN 3576.

35 Casebook, PN 3924.

36 Casebook, PN 3938.

37 Casebook, PN 3721.

38 Casebook, PN 3672.

39 Casebook, PN 4142, 3650, 3462, 3978.

40 Casebook, PN 4107.

41 Casebook, PN 4041.

42 Casebook, PN 4019.

43 Casebook, PN 3810.

44 Casebook, PN 4305.

45 Casebook, PN 3818.

46 Editorial, *Journal of Mental Science*, Vol. liii, No. 120 (1858) p. 164.

47 D.H. Tuke, *Reform in the Treatment of the Insane* (London, 1892), p. 153.

48 Phyllis Chesler, *Women and Madness* (New York, 1972).

49 Annual Report of Enniscorthy Asylum, 1917.

50 Edward Boyd-Barrett, 'Modern Psychotherapy and our asylums', *Studies*, Vol. 12 (1924), p. 29.

51 Annual Memoranda of Inspection of Enniscorthy Asylum, 1919, 1924 and 1925.

52 Ibid., 1924.

53 Casebook, PN 3622.

54 Casebook, PN 4122.

55 Casebook, PN 3763.

56 Annual Memoranda of Inspection of Enniscorthy Asylum, 1925.
57 Annual Reports of Enniscorthy Asylum, 1916–1925.
58 Annual Memoranda of Inspection of Enniscorthy Asylum, 1925.
59 *Dublin Journal of Medical Science*, Vol. 120 (1858), pp. 178–9. Hyoscymus was a sedative.
60 Casebook, PN 4298.
61 Casebook, PN 3763.
62 Letter found in casebook PN 4218.
63 Casebook, PN 4305.
64 Casebook, PN 3446.
65 Joseph Robins, *Fools and Mad: A History of the Insane in Ireland* (Dublin, 1986); M. Finnane, *Insanity and the Insane in Post-Famine Ireland* (Dublin, 1986). These two monograph studies of madness in Ireland seriously address issues of gender. See also articles by Elizabeth Malcolm, 'Women and Madness in Ireland, 1600–1850' in M. MacCurtain and M. O'Dowd (eds), *Women in Early Modern Ireland* (Dublin and Edinburgh, 1991); Oonagh Walsh, 'A Lightness of Mind' in M. Kelleher and J. Murphy (eds), *Gender Perspectives in Nineteenth-Century Ireland* (Dublin, 1996); Pauline Prior, 'Women, Mental Disorder and Crime in Nineteenth-Century Ireland' in A. Byrne and M. Leonard (eds), *Women and Irish Society: A Sociological Reader* (Belfast, 1997). There are, as yet, no gender-centred studies of Irish men's madness.

CHAPTER TEN

1 Martin Conboy, 'Communities and Constructs: National Identity in the British Press' in Susanne Stern-Gillet *et al.* (eds), *Culture and Identity* (Katowice, Poland, 1996), p. 197.
2 Margaret Ward, *The Missing Sex: Putting Women into Irish History* (Dublin, 1991).
3 Terence Brown, *Ireland: A Social and Cultural History* (London, 1987), p. 45.
4 Louise Ryan, 'The Shingle and Short Dresses: the demonisation of the "modern girl" in the Irish Free State'. Conference paper presented to Irish Encounters Conference, Bath College of Higher Education, July 1996.
5 Maryann Gianella Valiulis, 'Power, Gender and Identity in the Irish Free State' in J. Hoff and M. Coulter (eds) *Irishwomen's Voices: Past and Present* (New York, 1995), p. 128.
6 See Mary Clancy, 'Aspects of Women's Contribution to the Oireachtas Debates in the Irish Free State' in Maria Luddy and Cliona Murphy (eds), *Women Surviving* (Dublin, 1989); Frances Gardiner, 'Political Interest and Participation of Irish Women 1922–1992' in Ailbhe Smyth (ed.), *Irish Women's Studies Reader* (Dublin, 1993).
7 See Conboy, 'Communities and Constructs'.
8 Louise Ryan, 'The Massacre of Innocence: Infanticide in the Irish Free State' in *Irish Studies Review*, No. 14 (1996), pp. 17–20.
9 The discovery of an infant's body on a Kerry beach and the subsequent police investigation made national headlines, creating a storm of controversy involving the media, the judiciary, local families and women's groups.
10 Lionel Rose, *The Massacre of the Innocents: Infanticide in Britian, 1800–1939* (London, 1986), p. 35.
11 Ibid., p. 38.
12 Ian Jackson, *The Provincial Press and the Community* (Manchester, 1971).
13 *The Cork Examiner*, 17 October 1925. In his study of infanticide in Britain, Lionel Rose also suggests that single women were more likely to be investigated than married women.
14 Rose.
15 Mona Hearn, *Below Stairs: Domestic Service Remembered* (Dublin, 1993).
16 Ibid., p. 9.
17 Ibid., p. 97.

18 Ibid., p. 98.
19 Jury verdicts in infanticide cases are very interesting and worthy of further analysis.
20 Maria Piers, *Infanticide* (New York, 1978); Peter Hoffer and N. Hull, *Murdering Mothers: Infanticide in England and New England 1558–1803* (New York, 1984); Rose, *The Massacre of the Innocents*.
21 See Hearn, *Below Stairs*; Rose.
22 See Ryan, 'Massacre of Innocence'.
23 An Infanticide Act was introduced in England and Wales in 1922, which recognised infanticide as being separate from murder. However, it did not apply in Northern or Southern Ireland.
24 See Rose, p. 74.
25 Ibid., p. 59.
26 Ibid., p. 73.
27 *Irish Times*, 17 July 1925.
28 Ibid., 15 July 1925. Infant mortality was generally high in the Irish Free State. In 1926, 120 out of every 1,000 babies, in urban areas, died in their first year. See J.J. Lee, *Ireland: 1912–1985* (London, 1989), p. 124.
29 Benedict Anderson, *Imagined Communities* (London, 1991); Homi Bhabha, 'Narrating the Nation' in John Hutchinson and Anthony Smith (eds), *Nationalism* (Oxford, 1994); Conboy, 'Communities and Constructs'.
30 See Ryan, 'Massacre of Innocence'.

CHAPTER ELEVEN

1 From 1 January 1801, Ireland became part of the United Kingdom. Ireland's partition in 1922 resulted in six counties of the province of Ulster being named Northern Ireland and remaining in the United Kingdom. The other twenty-six counties of Ireland received dominion status and were named the Irish Free State. In 1937 the Irish parliament changed the Free State's name to Éire (Ireland) and in 1949 these twenty-six counties became the Irish Republic. Although it has never been an official name, Southern Ireland is commonly used to refer to the twenty-six counties which are now independent from Britain. It is used in this essay because it provides a convenient name for the geographical area in any time period and thus avoids the possibility of confusion from constantly changing the collective name of the twenty-six counties when referring to different years. The women studied here all emigrated from Southern Ireland.
2 This essay is based on aspects of the author's recently completed PhD thesis, which was funded by research studentships from Lancaster University and the ESRC. The traditional themes of research into the Irish in Britain, such as political history, labour and trade union history and studies of conflicts, have resulted in Irish women being rendered invisible despite them usually equalling and often outnumbering Irish men in Britain. Oral life-histories were used in this research to address new themes which were relevant to Irish emigrant women's lives. The main themes of the thesis were family, religion and sexuality. These themes were largely devised by emigrant women themselves, since they evolved from the priority which they were accorded in the life-history narratives. In order to respect the privacy of the respondents, they are only identified by first name pseudonyms, their year of birth and either their county or town of birth. The names of close relatives have also been changed.
3 *Irish Press*, 18 March 1943, p. 1. Quoted in Terence Brown, *Ireland: A Social and Cultural History 1922–1985* (London, 1985).
4 Ciaran McCullagh, 'A Tie That Blinds: Family and Ideology in Ireland', *The Economic and Social Review*, Vol. 22, No. 3 (April 1991), pp. 199–211.

5   Pauric Travers, 'Emigration and Gender: The Case of Ireland, 1922–60' in Mary O'Dowd and Sabine Wichert (eds), *Chattel, Servant or Citizen: Women's Status in Church, State and Society* (Belfast, 1995), p. 190.

6   Ide O'Carroll, *Models for Movers: Irish Women's Emigration to America* (Dublin, 1990), p. 12. Although in this instance she was discussing Irish emigrants to Britain, O'Carroll's source of evidence for her book is Irish women in America.

7   See J.J. Lee, *Ireland 1912–1985: Politics and Society* (Cambridge, 1989), pp. 158–9, for details of how far Irish censorship legislation and Roman Catholic Church pronouncements were concerned with sexual immorality.

8   Barbara, b. 1935, Co. Donegal and Siobhan, b. 1938, Co. Donegal.

9   *Reports of the Commission on Emigration and other Population Problems 1948–1954* (Dublin, 1956), [Pr. 2541] Para. 313.

10 O'Carroll, *Models for Movers*, p. 145.

11 This assumption is identified by Mary Lennon, Marie McAdam and Joanne O'Brien, *Across the Water: Irish Women's Lives in Britain* (London, 1988), p. 15.

12 Ibid., pp. 15–16.

CHAPTER TWELVE

1   David Lowenthal, *The Past is a Foreign Country* (Cambridge, 1994); Luisa Passerini (ed.), *Memory and Totalitarianism: International Yearbook of Oral History and Life Stories*, Vol. 1 (Oxford, 1992).

2   Elizabeth Tonkin, *Narrating our Pasts: The Social Construction of Oral History* (Cambridge, 1992).

3   To date I have interviewed fifteen women in their 70s, 80s and 90s, eight from Dublin and seven from Belfast, who were engaged in paid employment during the years of the Second World War. The women were introduced to me through personal contacts, mainly with people who are involved in local senior citizen groups and through information received from fellow trade union activists. The interviews were relatively informal. I did not use a questionnaire but tried to cover some common areas with each woman: family background, education, details of employment conditions and more general questions relating to women's response to emergency or wartime conditions, depending on the interview's location. Some interviews have lasted as long as five hours (in several sessions), while others have not lasted more than an hour. Each transcript is submitted to the interviewee for approval before I obtain permission to use the material.

4   Kristina Minister, 'A Feminist Frame for the Oral History Interview', in S.B. Gluck and D. Patai (eds), *Women's Words: The Feminist Practice of Oral History*, p. 32.

5   References to 'Ireland' in this text include Northern Ireland and Éire, unless otherwise stated.

6   Joanna Bourke, *Husbandry to Housewifery: Women, Economic Change and Housework in Ireland, 1890–1914* (Oxford, 1993).

7   Elizabeth Roberts, *A Woman's Place: An Oral History of Working-Class Women 1890–1940* (Oxford, 1984) and *Women and Families: An Oral History 1940–1970* (Oxford, 1995).

8   John Blake, *Northern Ireland in the Second World War* (Belfast, 1956), p. 538.

9   Louise A. Tilly and Joan W. Scott, *Women, Work and Family* (London, 1978).

10 See Penny Summerfield, *Women Workers in the Second World War* (London, 1984), p.10.

11 Resistance to the power endowed by the act to restrict the employment of women was spearheaded by the Irish Women Workers' Union (IWWU). The IWWU made representation to the Minister for Industry and Commerce, Seán Lemass, arguing that some industries were better suited to women than men and that the exclusion of women from some jobs would necessitate raising taxes to support women, such as spinsters and

widows, who were not provided for by a male breadwinner. The IWWU also conducted a public campaign, but the predominantly male Congress of Trade Unions and the Labour Party refused to support their demands. The International Labour Organisation's black-listing of Ireland followed communications by Irish and international women's societies, who protested to the Conference on the Status of Women organised by the League of Nations in Geneva in 1935.

12 Bourke, *Husbandry to Housewifery*.
13 Tilly and Scott, *Women, Work and Family*.
14 Bourke, *Husbandry to Housewifery*.
15 Irish Women Workers' Union Archive, courtesy of the Irish Labour History Museum.
16 Diana Gittins, 'Marital Status, Work and Kinship, 1850–1930' in *Labour and Love*, pp. 249–67.
17 Summerfield, *Women Workers*.
18 Eva Figes (ed.), *Women's Letters in Wartime, 1450–1945* (London, 1993), p. 12.
19 Mavis Nicholson (ed.), *What Did You Do in the War, Mummy? Women in World War II* (London, 1995).
20 Pauline Crabbe, a housewife before the war, later awarded an OBE for her work with the National Council for the Unmarried Mother and her Child, in Nicholson, ibid., p. 26.
21 Peggy Cotterill, auxiliary nurse in the Auxiliary Territorial Services, in Nicholson, ibid., p. 81.
22 Leila Rupp, *Mobilizing Women for War: German and American Propaganda, 1939–1945* (Princeton, 1978).
23 Miss Mary Smieton, Assistant Secretary in the Factory and Welfare Department of the Ministry of Labour, Circular MOL, 128/50, 3 June 1941, in Summerfield, *Women Workers*, p. 68.
24 Irish Women Workers' Union, *Report to the Annual Convention 1939*. Courtesy of the Irish Labour History Museum.
25 Summerfield, *Women Workers*, pp. 93–5.
26 Rona Fitzgerald, 'The First 50 Years' in Basil Chubb (ed.), *FIE – Federation of Irish Employers, 1942–1992* (Dublin, 1992), p. 7.
27 *The Economist*, 5 October 1946, pp. 547–548.
28 Paul Bew, Peter Gibbon and Henry Patterson, *The State in Northern Ireland, 1921–1972: Political Forces and Social Class* (Manchester, 1979), p. 102.
29 The North Strand in Dublin, a working-class area just north of the very poor inner city Mountjoy and Rotunda wards, is quite near the coast, perhaps supporting the claim by the German government that the bombing was an accident due to pilot error about this location.
30 T.W.T. Dillon, 'Slum Clearance: Past and Present', *Studies*, Vol. 24, No. 133, p. 19.
31 Ibid.
32 Ronnie Munck and Bill Rolston, *Belfast in the Thirties: An Oral History* (Belfast, 1987), pp. 79–80.
33 Diary of Moya Woodside, Mass-Observation, 5462, 23 August 1941.
34 John Blake, *Northern Ireland in the Second World War* (Belfast 1956), p. 396.
35 David Harkness, *Northern Ireland Since 1920* (Dublin, 1983).
36 Richard Doherty, *Irish men and women in the Second World War* (Dublin, 1999), pp. 101–2.
37 Blake, *Northern Ireland in the Second World War*, p. 239.
38 Brian Barton, *The Blitz: Belfast in the War Years* (Belfast, 1989).
39 K.S. Isles and N. Cuthbert, *An Economic Survey of Northern Ireland* (Belfast, 1957).
40 Doherty, *Irish men and women*, p. 110.
41 Donal Ó Drisceoil, *Censorship in Ireland, 1939–1945: Neutrality, Politics and Society* (Cork, 1996), p. 246.
42 Sir William Beveridge chaired a civil service commission set up in 1941 to look at post-

war reconstruction and future social policy. The Beveridge report was published in December 1942.

43 Margaret Atwood, *The Robber Bride* (London, 1994), p. 4.
44 In two cases, the interviewee was accompanied by a second woman, in one case her daughter, and in the other, her sister. Both of these women had lived with, or close to, the interviewees for most of their lives and been observers of the domestic and working arrangements which were being recalled. In the first case, the mother, who had been widowed at a relatively early age, remembered the difficulty of coping with paid work, which was essential to the family's survival, and her domestic responsibilities. She told a story of self-sacrifice for the sake of her family, who now support her, both emotionally and financially, in her old age. Her daughter totally concurred with the essence of the history, but it became clear to me in the course of the interview as her daughter clarified several points of information, that she, while only twelve at the time of her father's death, had played an indispensable role in the care of the family, and she was still living with and caring for her mother, although now past retirement age herself. Neither woman seemed aware of how the role adopted by the young girl, as her mother's unacknowledged substitute and support, had continued through their lives, so that the family myth of the undoubtedly heroic mother had never taken account of the younger woman's contribution. In the second case, the interviewee was the older sister who had married young and brought up her children while continuing in paid employment on a casual basis whenever the family income needed a supplement. As her children grew up, they contributed to the family income and in her late eighties she was living in a comfortable council house, with a pension which was supplemented regularly by her children. The sister, who had never married, had come to live with her when her husband died. She had spent most of her life as an unpaid companion and help to her mother's sister, and consequently, in her old age, she had only a minimal pension and no home of her own. Both sisters had worked in the linen mills from leaving school at fourteen until their twenties, but their perspective on that work was very different. The older sister remembered the work as hard but as something that belonged to another era which no longer had any relevance to her. The younger sister was very bitter about the conditions they had endured and recalled a particular practice as an illustration of an ongoing pattern of sectarian prejudice, while her sister simply consigned it to the past.
45 Passerini, *Memory and Totalitarianism*, p. 17.

CHAPTER THIRTEEN

1 Department of Health, *A Plan for Women's Health* (Dublin, 1997). Because women's experience is discussed alongside health policy, 'Ireland' for the purposes of this essay refers to the twenty-six counties of the Republic.
2 Sheila Kitzinger, *The Experience of Breastfeeding* (London, 1987), p. 189.
3 Personal experience: having breast-fed four babies since 1989.
4 In the past twenty years or so, breast-feeding has been in serious decline throughout the world as a whole and this has given rise to controversy. A. Chetley, *The Baby Killer Scandal: a War on Want investigation into the promotion and sale of powdered baby milks in the Third World* (London, 1979) is the authoritative account. See also the excellent book by Gabrielle Palmer, *The Politics of Breastfeeding* (London, 1988), particularly Chapters 2, 3 and 8.
5 Palmer, ibid., chapters 5 and 6, give breast-feeding advocacy's explanation of why breast-feeding went into decline; Kitzinger, *The Experience of Breastfeeding*, pp. 187–98 offers some additional insights. The brilliant book by Christina Hardyment, *Perfect Parents: Baby-care advice past and present* (Oxford, 1995; first published as *Dream Babies*, London,

1983) outlines rather more neutrally the cultural changes in parenting over the past few centuries. Strange to say there is no overall history of this huge subject, though V. Fildes, L. Marks and H. Marland (eds), *Women and Children First: international maternal and infant welfare 1870–1945* (London, 1992); Ellen Ross, *Love and Toil: motherhood in outcast London* (London, 1993); Valerie Fildes' own book, *Wet-Nursing* (London, 1989) and Jane Lewis, *The Politics of Motherhood: child and maternal welfare in England 1900– 1939* (London, 1980) all contribute somewhat to our knowledge of the conditions under which mothers could, or would, breast-feed and the attitudes of health professionals towards them.

6 Ruth Barrington, *Health, Medicine and Politics in Ireland 1900–1970* (Dublin, 1987), chapters 8, 9 and 10. The shift from home to hospital is discussed in C. Clear, *Women of the House: Women's House Work in Ireland, 1922–64* (Dublin, 2000), chapters 5 and 6.

7 Chris Curtin and Tony Varley, 'Children and Childhood in Rural Ireland: a consideration of the ethnographic literature' in C. Curtin, Mary Kelly and Liam O'Dowd (eds), *Culture and Ideology in Ireland* (Galway, 1984), pp. 30–45.

8 Nancy Scheper-Hughes, *Saints, Scholars and Schizophrenics: Mental Illness in Irish Culture* (unpubl. PhD thesis, University of California, Berkeley, 1976), passim, and p. 176.

9 John Charles Russell, *In the Shadows of Saints: Aspects of Family and Religion in a Rural Irish Gaeltacht* (unpubl. PhD thesis, University of California, San Diego, 1979), pp. 121–5.

10 Ibid.

11 *Department of Local Government and Public Health Report 1931–2*, pp. 55–8.

12 James Deeny, 'Infant Mortality in the city of Belfast 1940–1', *Journal of the Statistical and Social Inquiry Society of Ireland*, Vol. XVII (1943–4), pp. 220–39.

13 *Woman's Life: the Irish Home Weekly*, 1936–39, 'Happy Irish Babies' column.

14 Alexander J. Humphreys, *New Dubliners. Urbanization and the Irish Family* (London, 1966), p. 145.

15 For my research I solicited personal testimony by means of a letter in national and provincial newspapers in May 1995. I received thirty-seven letters in reply, then went on to interview, further correspondence, etc. Some of the contributors gave testimony which is pertinent to the subject under discussion, and personal details about these contributors are given in the appendix of this article. See C. Clear, *Women of the House*, pp. 216–19.

16 I refer to myself, born in 1960, in a large lower-middle class urban Catholic family with rural connections.

17 Pádraig O Héalaí, 'Pregnancy and Childbirth in Blasket Island Tradition', *Women's Studies Review*, Vol. 5 (Galway, 1997), pp. 1–16. 'Mise 'gus Máire', by Sean Eoghan O Súilleabháin from Cúil Aodha, Co. Cork, is sung by Jimmy Crowley on *Jimmy Mo Mhíle Stór* (Gael-linn, 1985). Linda May Ballard, 'Just Whatever They Had Handy', *Ulster Folklife*, Vol. 31 (1985), pp. 59–72, discusses this folklore in Northern Ireland.

18 Méiní, who became a very authoritative and respected figure in the island, had spent time in America; did this have anything to do with her infant feeding practices? Leslie Matson, *Méiní: the Blasket Nurse* (Cork, 1995), pp. 72–3.

19 Coimisiúin Béaloideasa Éireann (hereafter CBE)/Irish Folklore Commission, Iml. 42, p. 33. Charleville District, John McAuliffe (76), 1935. Mss in Folklore Department, UCD and on microfilm.

20 CBE, Iml. 259, p. 416, Co. Port Láirge (Waterford), Liam O Caoimh, pinsinéar, 1936.

21 William Downey (b. 1928, Co. Laois), 'A Memory of "the talkies"' in M. Ryan, K. Gilmour and S. Brown (eds), *No Shoes In Summer: Days to Remember* (Dublin, 1995), p. 264.

22 C. Arensberg and S. Kimball, *Family and Community in Ireland* (Boston, 1940), p. 197.

23 Michael Curtin, 'Failure to Breastfeed: a review of the feeding history of 1,007 infants', *Irish Journal of Medical Science* (1954), pp. 447–56.

24 Ibid.

25 Survey cited by Tony Farmar, *Holles St 1894–1994: the National Maternity Hospital: a centenary history* (Dublin, 1994), pp. 136–7.
26 Personal testimony from Professor Mary E. Daly, UCD, who was born in Lourdes hospital.
27 *Department of Local Government and Public Health Report*, 1931–2, pp. 55–9.
28 James Deeny, *To Cure and To Care: Memoirs of a Chief Medical Officer* (Dublin, 1989), pp. 120–3.
29 Ibid., p. 94; Alex Spain, 'Maternity Services in Eire', *Irish Journal of Medical Science*, No. 229 (January 1945), pp. 1–23.
30 Maire Mullarney, *What About Me?: a woman for whom one damn cause led to another* (Dublin, 1992), pp. 114–5.
31 M. Truby King, *Mothercraft* (London, 1938), pp. 18–19 and passim.
32 C.F.V. Coyle, MB, MAO (Tutor in Obstetrics, National Maternity Hospital), 'Breastfeeding and Some of its Difficulties', *Journal of the Medical Association of Eire*, Vol. 17 (July 1945), pp. 86–8.
33 Mullarney, *What About Me?*, p. 114.
34 Kitzinger, *The Experience of Breastfeeding*, passim; La Leche League, *The Womanly Art of Breast-feeding* (Illinois, 1963, London, 1975).
35 The existence of lucky women whose milk supply is so abundant and whose babies are such efficient feeders that the babies can thrive on a regular schedule and sleep seven or eight hour stretches from birth, could have convinced some authorities who made no allowances for diversity and different circumstances, that this was possible, with perseverance, for all women.
36 'Duties of the Health Visitor', *Irish Nurses' Union Gazette*, No. 32 (January 1930), p. 8.
37 Palmer, *Politics*.
38 Not all medical/midwifery personnel were blind followers of 'progress'. For example, James Deeny (*To Cure and To Care*) blended modern, almost coercive public health thinking with respect for ordinary people's experience. This respect is also evident in the works of two other doctors/obstetricians who qualified in the 1940s and 1950s, John O'Connell, *Doctor John: Crusading Doctor and Politician* (Dublin, 1989) and Michael Solomons, *Pro-life: the Irish Question* (Dublin, 1992). The term 'meddlesome midwifery' was in common use in the 1940s and 1950s in Ireland, to describe unnecessary intervention, see, for example, S.J. Boland, 'Radiology in Ante-natal Care', *Journal of the Irish Medical Association*, Vol. 36 (1955), pp. 20–1, and 'Discussion of the Dublin Maternity Reports', *Irish Journal of Medical Science*, No. 371 (November 1956), pp. 523–4 and passim.
39 In the personal testimonies I collected, women voiced strong objections to, and unhappy memories about, going in with a sister/sister-in-law; this is discussed in Clear, *Women of the House*, chapters 8, 9 and 10; Patrick McNabb, 'Social Structure' in J. Newman (ed.), *The Limerick Rural Survey 1958–64* (Tipperary, 1964), pp. 226–7, noticed the same phenomenon; see also a short story in *The Irish Countrywoman*, Vol. 9 (1963–4), Elizabeth Brennan, 'Fine China', pp. 23–7. Useful and readable surveys of the Irish family in the twentieth century are to be found in C. Curtin and P. Gibbon, 'The Stem Family in Ireland', *Comparative Studies in Society and History*, Vol. 20, No. 3 (July 1978), pp. 429–53; and Tony Fahey, 'Family and Household in Ireland', in Patrick Clancy (ed.), *Irish Society: Sociological Perspectives* (Dublin, 1995), pp. 206–33.
40 Michael Shiels, *The Quiet Revolution: the electrification of rural Ireland* (Dublin, 1984), chapter 17; Mary E. Daly, 'Turn On The Tap: the state, Irish Women and Running Water' in M. O'Dowd and M. Valiulis (eds), *Women and Irish History: Essays in Honour of Margaret MacCurtain* (Dublin, 1997), pp. 206–19.
41 Ann Kennedy, 'Diary of a Farmer's Wife', *Irish Times*, 14 November 1956.
42 Michael Curtin, 'Failure to Breastfeed'.

43 Ibid.
44 Kitzinger, *Experience of Breastfeeding*, p. 177.
45 Gerald Kelly, S.J., *Medico-Moral Problems* (Dublin, 1949), pp. 130–8.
46 Terence Brown, *Ireland: a social and cultural history* (London, 1985), p. 197.
47 Establishing a relationship with the contributor meant revealing something of my own life, which in turn might have determined contributors' reactions to some of the issues which I brought up. The problems and rewards of using personal testimony and oral evidence are discussed comprehensively in all of the contributions to R. Perks and A. Thomson (eds), *The Oral History Reader* (London, 1998), particularly in K. Anderson and D. Jack, 'Learning to Listen: Interview Techniques and Analyses' pp. 157–71; J. Bornat, 'Oral History as a social movement', pp. 189–2,205, and J. Sangster, 'Telling Our Stories: feminist debates and the use of oral history', pp. 87–99.
48 See, for example, Health Hints by 'Torcy', 'A Tip For Expectant Mothers', *Irish Messenger*, Vol. LX, (November 1947), p. 246.
49 Maura Laverty, *Lift Up Your Gates* (London, 1946), pp. 110–21.
50 Palmer, *Politics* (London, 1988, 1991), pp. 144–6.
51 Sheila Kitzinger, *Ourselves as Mothers* (London, 1992).
52 See the contributions to John A. O'Brien (ed.), *The Vanishing Irish* (London, 1954), and articles such as Kevin Devlin, 'Single and Selfish', *Christus Rex*, Vol. 6 (1952), pp. 223–31. *Report of the Commission on Emigration and Other Population Problems 1948–54* (1956) R. 84. pp. 98–101, and passim, and in Dr Lucey's Minority Report, passim.
53 Damian Hannan, 'Patterns of Spousal Accommodation and Conflict in Traditional Farm Families', *Economic and Social Review*, Vol. 10, No. 1 (1978), pp. 61–84, and 'Changes in Family Relationship Patterns' in *Social Studies: an Irish Journal of Sociology*, Vol. 2, No. 6 (December 1973), pp. 550–63. On hairdressers, see *Census of Ireland* 1926, 1936, 1946, 1961, Occupational tables in General Report; the number of female hairdressers rose from 170 in 1926 to 1,295 in 1936, 1,840 in 1946, to 3,409 in 1961. It should be remembered that the population was in decline over this period.
54 Cormac O Gráda, *Ireland: a New Economic History* (Oxford, 1994), pp. 218–35; See also Brendan Walsh, 'Some Irish Population Problems Considered', ESRI paper 42 (November 1968); Robert Kennedy Jr., *The Irish: Emigration, Marriage and Fertility* (California, 1973), pp. 173–205; for contemporary comments, see J.F. Knaggs, 'Natality in Dublin in the year 1955', *Statistical and Social Inquiry Society Journal*, Vol. XX (1957–8), pp. 37–55.
55 The long lying-in period was an ideal which even the women in the tenements in Dublin attempted to realise; see Kevin Kearns, *Dublin Tenement Life: an Oral History* (Dublin 1994), pp. 115–16. For more general information, see the works cited in note 5.
56 Mary Maher, *You and Your Baby* (Dublin, 1973), pp. 77–9.

AFTERWORD

1 Thomas O'Loughlin, 'Sister Act', interview with Margaret MacCurtain, *History Ireland*, Vol. 2, No. 1 (Spring 1994), p. 53.
2 Ibid., p. 54.
3 For the full text of this discussion, see the H-Women home page at www.h-net.msu. edu/~women/.
4 For example, see the CD-Rom created by the Women's History Project, *Directory of Sources for Women's History in Ireland*, Dublin, 1999.
5 Mrs Thomas (Helena) Concannon, *Daughters of Banba* (Dublin, 1922), p. ix.

Notes on Contributors

Noel Armour is a former graduate and postgraduate of the School of Modern History of the Queen's University of Belfast. He has a keen interest in early Unionist and Liberal politics and the essay published in this collection is a reflection of that interest.

Lisa M. Bitel is Professor of History and Gender Studies at the University of Southern California. Her books and articles have covered such topics as Irish saints, dreams, cursing rituals, sex and sexuality, women and gender ideologies. She is currently writing a book about Saints Brigit and Genovefa.

Gráinne M. Blair is a feminist historian with research interests in the development of the Salvation Army in Ireland. She has published a number of articles on the Salvation Army rescue network and is currently writing a multiography of Lola Montez.

Alison Buckley received degrees from Randolph-Macon Woman's College, the University of Delaware and Trinity College Dublin. She currently teaches in the United States and works in the private sector.

Caitríona Clear lectures in history at the National University of Ireland, Galway, and has published on the history of women in nineteenth- and twentieth-century Ireland. Her other research interests include the history of poverty and oral history.

Moira E. Egan is a doctoral student in history at the City University of New York. She is a member of the Doctoral Students' Council Steering Committee and has worked in shelters for homeless women.

Dianne Hall holds a PhD from the University of Melbourne, where she is currently a fellow. Her book *Women and the Church in Medieval Ireland c. 1140–1540* was published in 2003.

Alan Hayes is publisher of Arlen House, Ireland's oldest feminist press. He is the editor of *The Years Flew By: Recollections of Madame Sidney Gifford*

Czira (2000) and the co-editor of *The Irish Women's History Reader* (2001). He is currently working on a book entitled 'The Gifford Women: "John Brennan" and her Sisters'.

Sharon Lambert graduated from Lancaster University with a BA and a PhD in history. Her father was from Co. Sligo and she has had a lifelong interest in Irish culture. She is the author of *Irish Women in Lancashire 1922–1960: Their Story* (2001). Sharon lives in Lancaster, where she works as an oral historian and teaches community history.

Áine McCarthy is a writer and reviewer, who has contributed widely to the Irish and British national presses, including *The Irish Times*, *The Sunday Tribune* and the *Guardian*. She has published two non-fiction books and has just completed her first novel. She teaches Women's Literature to both BA and MA students at University College Dublin.

Mary Muldowney is working for a Ph.D. on the impact of the Second World War on women in Belfast and Dublin in the Department of Modern History, Trinity College Dublin. Her thesis is based on oral history inter-views with women from both cities, looking especially at their work inside and outside the home.

Rosemary Raughter has published a number of articles on female philanthropy and on women and religion in eighteenth-century Ireland, and has contributed to the *Field Day Anthology of Irish Writing*, volumes IV and V. She is currently researching a biography of Lady Arbella Denny.

Louise Ryan has a doctorate from University College Cork. She is a research fellow at University College London. Her books include *Irish Feminism and the Vote* (1996) and *Gender, Identity and the Irish Press, 1922–37: Embodying the Nation* (2002). Louise is currently co-editing a book on women and Nationalism.

Diane Urquhart is the Acting Director and a lecturer in modern Irish history at the Institute of Irish Studies of the University of Liverpool. She is a graduate of the Queen's University of Belfast. Her publications include *Women in Ulster Politics, 1890–1940* (2000) and she is currently working on a study of upper-class women's use of political patronage in the nineteenth and early twentieth centuries.

Index